A Pinch of Dry Mustard

By Barbara Roose Cramer

Edited by
Joanne James

Cover Illustration by
Steven Glenn Cramer

Order this book online at www.trafford.com
or email orders@trafford.com

Most Trafford titles are also available at major online book retailers.

Printed in Victoria, BC, Canada.

ISBN: 978-1-4269-1806-3 (soft)
ISBN: 978-1-4269-1807-0 (hard)

Library of Congress Control Number: 2009937697

*Our mission is to efficiently provide the world's finest, most comprehensive book publishing
service, enabling every author to experience success. To find out how to publish your book, your
way, and have it available worldwide, visit us online at www.trafford.com*

Trafford rev. 11/16/2009

 www.trafford.com

North America & international
toll-free: 1 888 232 4444 (USA & Canada)
phone: 250 383 6864 ♦ fax: 812 355 4082

For Kendall, our precious gift from God.

"Also by the author"

THE BARRELMAN

A Thirty-Five Year History of the Denver Broncos Football Club, 1992

Introduction

Her long blond hair, high-lighted by the late summer sun fra[r]
Sarah's lovely face. Her hand gently moved one of the yellow and [l]
flowered curtains to the far edge of the window. She peered out
window, touching the cold windowpane; the coldness matching her c
uncertain mood. She watched gently falling snow being swallowed
by the fierce thrashing sea while long-winged seagulls sailed gracef[u]
above, ignoring the gigantic waves crashing against the rocks bel[o]
As she looked out upon miles and miles of blue-black Ocean, she [v]
reminded that it had been only 2 days since Ben's fishing boat had b[e]
lost at sea. Frightful images of him slowly sinking to the bottom of [t]
deep, dark, ocean blocked out her memories of his face. She imagin
him surrounded in darkness as his boat sank deeper and deeper in
the vastness of the sea. Tears began to fall from her blue-green e[y]
staining her solemn, ashen face. She felt the baby move inside her a[n]
touched her belly with trembling hands. She imagined bubbles risi[n]
to the surface above the upper boundaries of the white-capped oce[a]
and pictured Ben gasping for his last, dying breath..........

* * * * * *

Tuesday

* * * * * *

CHAPTER ONE

The alarm went off at exactly 4:30 a.m. Tuesday morning. Ben reached over his sleeping wife, turned off the alarm, gently moved the quilt away and sat up on the edge of the antique four-poster bed. From experience, he knew the floor would be cold, so he quickly felt for and put on his soft, tan slippers, got up and walked into the kitchen before turning on a light. He punched the "on" button to start the coffee pot, pulled up one of the kitchen window blinds to see what the day might hold in store and proceeded into the bathroom for a shower. As he turned on the water, he grabbed a blue towel from off the shelf and took a peek around the corner of the door to check on Sarah.

"Sleep as long as you can, my love," he murmured. "I'll try not to disturb you."

With that, he turned and walked back into the bathroom and hung his towel on the silver hook on the back of the shower. He shed his pajama bottoms, turned the water on hot and stepped in. The hot water streamed down onto his face, browned by the summer sun. As he lathered himself up, he thought of what the future was about to bring. In just a matter of days, Sarah, his wife of a little over a year, would give birth to their first child. They had not planned this child, but when Sarah found out that she was pregnant, they were both elated, as were her parents and his father. It would be the first grandchild, and he knew that this baby would be both loved and spoiled.

He rinsed the soap out of his shoulder length blond hair, applied a small amount of conditioner, rinsed again, and then turned off the shower. He stepped out onto the round blue and yellow-checkered carpet, caught the scent of fresh coffee, dried himself off and walked quietly into the bedroom to dress. He had laid his clothes out on the old colonial, red and blue striped chair the night before: a pair of blue jeans, his old Boston Bruins t-shirt and a heavy brown wool sweater—the same type of clothes he wore every day. Since his clothing smelled strongly of fish and salt water every day, he seldom wore the same things two days in a row. Sarah saw to it that his work clothes were washed often so as not to smell up the laundry room. When she was first pregnant, the fish smell added to her severe morning sickness and nausea, but now that she was in her last trimester the smell didn't seem to bother her anymore.

Ben finished dressing and walked back into the bathroom. He shaved, brushed his teeth then walked into the kitchen to pour a steaming mug of coffee. He paused for a moment, tore a sticky note off the pad by the telephone and wrote, "I love you" on the note. He added some X's and O's, and stuck it on the coffee cup where Sarah's name was imprinted in blue, placing it next to the coffee pot. He poured coffee into his own cup and sat down at the kitchen table to put on his old work boots. He stood up, took his heavy black jacket and his Fish for Fun cap off the coat rack, put them on and headed out the door, coffee mug in hand.

Ben was greeted by a cold, brisk wind, and as he headed for the harbor he glanced at the sun just rising. Pinks, oranges and yellows streaked across the eastern horizon. Although there were a few clouds, Ben figured it would be a pretty mild day for the end of October. He walked the three short blocks to the dock, whistling as he walked, and stopped in at the Breakfast Hut.

He no longer made himself breakfast or expected Sarah to fix it for him. He got up so early every day, and she was getting so uncomfortable and was so tired now, it just seemed easier for him to stop in at the Breakfast Hut to eat. This also gave Sarah the extra rest she needed.

"Hey, Ben," a high-pitched voice said, coming from behind the counter as Ben walked through the door. "Any babies at your house yet?"

"Nope, not yet," Ben commented, as he took a seat at the empty counter and set down his empty mug. "Hopefully, in a day or two. I plan to work today yet and then stay at home with her. They plan to induce labor on Thursday. She's about a week overdue."

"Good." Putting a face to the high-pitched voice, Ben watched as Loren Goodwell came through the door to the left of the counter. She had a coffee pot in her left hand and biscuits and gravy in her right. As she filled Ben's mug with black coffee, she commented, "I hope she sails right through this delivery. I remember my first one, kind-of-tough beginning, but she turned out great, and that was twenty-two years ago."

Loren walked around the counter and set Ben's usual order in front of him. Reaching around him and over the counter, she set the coffee pot back on the double hot plate, then took a seat on the stool beside him and talked while he ate.

Loren was a good woman with a good heart but her track record with men was, to say the least, poor. Ben could never understand why. She was an attractive, slender woman, maybe forty-five, with a short bob haircut and a pleasant personality. She had been married three or four times, and she had always picked, from what Ben heard, the wrong guy. They pushed her around, used her as a punching bag a time or two, took her money and moved on. Only the second marriage to Bud Goodwell had lasted over five years—long enough to produce a child, and although the man was a "loser", as Loren would say, they had produced a wonderful daughter together.

"How is Jill?" Ben asked as he sipped on his third mug of coffee this morning. "Is she still in Portland?"

"Yup, and doing very well, I might add." Loren smiled as she told Ben how Jill, directly after graduating from college, had been hired as a hostess on a cruise ship and was in love with a 1st Lieutenant in the Coast Guard based out of Portland.

"I wish I could see her more often," Loren replied, "but she's on ten to fourteen day cruises and then spends her time off with her Lieutenant. I really do miss her and wish we could spend more time together, but I see her every six weeks or so."

Jill was Loren's only child, and Ben wasn't sure who was the more fond of whom. During all of the bad relationships, Loren had protected Jill, worked long and hard at several jobs to save enough money to give her a good life, including a college education. Jill was appreciative of everything her mother had sacrificed for her. She had grown up to be a very proper young lady with a promising future ahead of her.

Ben heard previously that Jill graduated from college and was doing well in Portland, but he didn't realize she was dating someone.

"Has this young man ever been to Booth Bay?" he asked. "What's his name, I just might know him."

"He came down here once with Jill." Loren smiled as she mentioned her daughter's name, "and he seems to be very nice. I was impressed with him. I just hope she doesn't rush into anything. I don't want her to have her mama's problems. His name is Tom Casey."

"Tom Casey! Wow, I know Tom," Ben said smiling. "We went to the same middle school; he's originally from this area. He's been up here a few times checking on pirating issues. He doesn't go out on the Aid Boats much, but he's a great asset to the Guard, and everyone here in the Harbor likes him. That's great, Tom and Jill, wow, wait until I tell Sarah."

Ben was excited for both Jill and Tom. She was a nice woman, real cute too. He had noticed her a time or two over the years, but had never been interested enough to ask her out on a date. He would have to talk to Tom soon and congratulate him. He smiled as he thought about the two of them together. They would make a great pair.

There were only two other men in the Hut this early in the morning. They were sitting in a booth finishing their breakfasts and drinking coffee. After Loren had refilled their coffee cups a second time, she sat down and chatted with Ben a while longer. They talked about Sarah, their old house that overlooked the bay, working on the nursery and a little more about Jill. It was time for Ben to go and Loren filled up his mug one more time. Ben laid $10.00 on the table, picked up the mug and headed for the door.

"Let me know when that little one comes," she yelled at Ben.

Ben waved back, took one last look at the two other men in the Hut, then crossed the deserted street and headed to where his boat was docked. He didn't notice the two men in the far corner booth watching him as he walked away. He didn't notice the large tall man standing at the corner under the dock streetlight either.

As Ben walked toward the boat, he hoped Jeremy was waiting for him. They could head out to sea right away. He tilted his head backward, looked up at the sky, saw that a few more clouds had gathered and wondered if he should call the weather station before heading out to pull in his pots.

"Hey, Ben," Jeremy yelled, as he saw Ben coming down along the wharf. "What do you think of the clouds this morning? Think we'll be having any weather problems out there?"

"Not sure," Ben answered, "Turn on the weather channel, check with the Coast Guard too, will you? I'm going to make sure everything is set up; all we got to do today is pull in traps and let's hope they're full! Let's get going right away, get the job done, and head back in, ok?"

"Sure thing, boss," came a cheery voice "I'll get to it right away. How's the little woman this morning?"

"Good," Ben replied.

Jeremy boarded the SARAH JEANNE, one of three-40-footers owned by the Kestwicks. He watched Ben head over to check in with Captain Ron at the Port Authority. He knew Ben would give him the chart times for departure and tell him they hoped to return before dusk. Then he'd walk back to the boat and they would leave. Jeremy knew the routine well.

Jeremy was above deck checking the radio, making sure the firearms were in the proper place, and making sure they had plenty of flares. There had been more pirating at sea in the last couple of months, thieves trying to steal pots, so Ben carried three small, licensed weapons below deck. Carrying weapons was a rule of the sea, approved by the authorities. It had been five days since they'd been out setting lobster pots, and if there was one thing Ben Kestwick was a stickler about, it was safety, and Jeremy knew it.

With charts filed, Ben returned, untied the boat from the dock, jumped on board and went above deck to join Jeremy. He started the engines, took the wheel and headed east, knowing that before long the boat would be moving at fifteen knots. With a bit of luck and good weather, they would be able too untie the lobster traps from the Kestwick green buoys, quickly load the cages on deck and be back at Booth Bay Harbor to unload and weigh in before dark. It was the law—no trapping after sunset. The crew had set out twenty traps five days earlier on two separate runs with the SARAH JEANNE. He was certain the traps would be full, most of the time they were.

Ben took one more look at the sky, which was now a beautiful blue. The clouds were increasing to the north, but he felt no uneasiness. He did think of Sarah one more time, however, wondering how her day would go and what Thursday would bring.

"The weather looks good, Ben," Jeremy told him as they headed out of the harbor, "The weather guy said partly cloudy, about fifty degrees, some wind, about ten knots, we should be ok".

"Let's hope they're right," Ben said, "We're about fourteen to fifteen miles out Jeremy; let's hope those traps are full up! We are about out of season, and I would rather trap in good seas than in all that snow and cold that's coming soon. With a new baby coming, I plan to be at home for the next few weeks being a daddy!"

"Sounds good to me big-daddy," Jeremy said, and chuckled to himself as he thought of big 6' 5" Ben holding a tiny baby in his arms.

*   *   *   *   *

Jeremy Brookings had been a licensed lobster harvester for at least twenty years. His daddy had taught him the trade when he was only twelve years old, and he had worked for many different lobster boat captains over the years. Ben's dad, Martin, had hired Jeremy over ten years ago. When Martin semi-retired and Ben took over the business, Ben had kept Jeremy on. Everyone in Booth Bay Harbor knew Jeremy Brookings, "the old sea dog", people called him. He was not very tall, maybe 5'7", and seemingly, not too big on brains, but when it came to lobster trapping, he was the hardest working and fastest trapper in Booth Bay Harbor. He also had a taste for good liquor and was known to frequent several of the bars along the harbor late at night after work. Some boat owners didn't approve of his type of lifestyle, but the Kestwicks had never had any problems with the accomplished fisherman. Jeremy had no wife or family, or at least not that anyone knew about, and no one was ever quite sure where he lived. They just knew he always showed up for work on time and seemed to be an honest man. He was one of the best lobster trappers around and the Kestwick family paid him well.

Jeremy hadn't figured on being a lobster trapper his entire life, as it was not the easiest job on the open seas. The work was hard, the weather could be unpredictable, and the sun beating down on him for hours at a time made him especially thirsty. As the years went by, he realized, however, how much money he could make for working several weeks throughout the spring and summer, so he stayed on and became very good at the trade.

For the ten years he had worked for the Kestwick family, he hauled in forty-to-fifty of the large steel cages (known as traps or pots), on their boats every week. After reaching their designated drop off spot, he would run the wenches and drop the traps in 120 feet of water, head back to port, and do the same routine all over again the next day. In five to seven days, he would head back out to sea to pull in the traps. Jeremy and the rest of the Kestwick crews spent from the end of March until the end of October trapping in the seas east of Booth Bay Harbor, and, as far as he was concerned, there was no better paying job anywhere.

As it was against the law to catch and sell juvenile lobster, Jeremy hoped as they headed out to sea that most of the juvenile had escaped through the pot's mesh entrances, and their traps would be full of only the right size of lobster. Only lobster measuring more than 11 1/2 inches could be sold; all others had to be thrown back.

"No sense wasting time separating those darn little ones from the traps," he thought to himself. Depending on the going rate, the bigger the lobster (other than the breeders), sold at port, the more money Jeremy could add to his bankroll.

The wind had picked up to about thirteen knots when Ben, standing at the wheel of the SARAH JEANNE, noticed a small craft off to the north. This was not so unusual since there were always small, privately owned boats, small fishing craft or cruise lines out this far, but most boats were familiar to him. Most of the trappers from Booth Bay Harbor were his competitors but also his friends, and he could recognize almost every boat by color, flag, insignia or number.

The craft did not seem to be in trouble, but as it came closer, Ben hollered at Jeremy, who was busy in the galley, to come up. Ben slowed the boat down and, as Jeremy came up the stairs, the small craft came closer and pulled abreast to the SARAH JEANNE. Ben brought his boat to a complete stop but did not cut the engines. He heard, "Ahoy, there" and walked out along the gangway as a tall man leaned over the rail of the smaller craft. He started to speak to Ben, words that Jeremy could not hear or understand. Not moving any further up the stairs and completely out of sight of the stranger on the other boat, Jeremy could see just enough of Ben to notice him pointing towards the north. Ben said a few more things, as the tall man seemed to say thanks, and then he motioned to the crewman at the wheel to turn the craft towards the north. There was no reason for Jeremy to be concerned, as other boaters came side by side once in awhile during trapping, but as the boat moved out of sight, an uneasy feeling came over him.

"What was that all about, boss?" Jeremy asked, as he walked over to where Ben was standing at the wheel. "Trouble?"

"I'm not sure," Ben said, a troubled look on his face. "The guy said he was out of Portland and was looking for the Blue Lady, but he's a long way from Portland. He could have easily stopped in at the harbor and found out where the Blue Lady's docked or if she's still out." Ben walked away from Jeremy, looked ahead and said, "Did you by chance get a look at his HIN?"

"I didn't, boss," Jeremy replied, "I was just kinda standin' at the top of the stairs, out of sight; how about you?" He didn't tell Ben that he had gotten a bad feeling about the tall man on the boat. It was probably nothing, but he subconsciously wondered how fast he or Ben could have gotten to the weapons stored below deck.

"I didn't want to look conspicuous," Ben said, "and the identification number was down lower on the hull, much lower than on our boats, so I couldn't tell. I should have asked for some identification. When I asked what he needed from the Blue Lady, the guy just said he was a friend down from Portland and didn't want to miss seeing Jack Currier. I think I might just call it in to Lieutenant Casey when we get back, never hurts to be cautious."

"Well, let's get moving," Ben said. "A few more miles and we're there."

Ben set the SARAH JEANNE on about twenty knots, steered the wheel to the northeast and wondered what the tall man really wanted. He also noticed the wind was picking up.

It turned out to be a good day. The SARAH JEANNE dropped anchor 14.8 miles out and they began to pull up the traps. They were thrilled as nineteen traps were loaded with lobster and only a few juveniles had found their way in. As the summer season came to a close and the weather began to change, some trappers found pretty lean trapping, but this would be a good catch, a good way to end the season. Ben smiled as he and Jeremy pulled in one full pot after another and the thought of the tall man in the unmarked boat was forgotten as they busied themselves with the haul.

Ben began trapping in the early part of March. Now it was already the end of October, the end of the summer lobster season. This season had been better than most. The price per pound had been excellent this year. Truck lines gave them decent prices on shipping, and there had been only a few minor repairs and mechanical problems with the three boats. All in all, Ben was pleased. He looked up to the heavens and gave a thumb's up. "Mom, you would be proud."

*   *   *   *   *

Martin and Jenny Kestwick had continued in the family lobster trapping business after they were married. They both loved the sea and, although Jenny's parents thought she should go off to college somewhere and start a career, she disagreed. "Here is where I belong," she would say, "This is home."

She and Martin were married in Booth Bay Harbor; Ben and his brother were born there, and the family business continued to flourish. When Ben and his brother got a little older, Jenny worked at the docks and kept the accounts on the business and an eye on lobster prices. She cooked a variety of lobster and fish dishes for her family, neighbors and friends, and, after much coaxing, even wrote and published a cookbook on the "Great Fish Recipes of Maine".

"Make sure you include the mustard recipe," they all encouraged, "That recipe alone will sell hundreds of cookbooks."

Everyone in Booth Bay Harbor's favorite recipe was a lobster noodle dish with just a pinch of dry mustard. Jenny had created the recipe herself, given it to everyone in town who asked for it, and assured everyone she would include it in the cookbook. When she sold over

500 copies of the book at the little bookstore in town, she donated all of the profits to charity. She was a great cook, provided a wonderful home life for the three men in her life, and now her men missed her desperately.

Jenny had died two years earlier of cancer. She and Martin had been married thirty-four years when she first received the diagnosis. She fought to beat the disease, but in the end the cancer won and Ben's dad had taken her death very hard. Nothing that Ben said or did helped his father overcome his grief. He knew it would just take time. Ben insisted that Martin go down to the docks everyday and tried to get him involved again with trapping, but nothing seemed to work. Martin wanted no part of the boat or the trapping business any longer. He sunk further and further into his grief, and Ben worried about him constantly, but hoped that a new grandchild would bring his father out of his depression. It also made him sad to know his mother had never gotten to meet Sarah and would never meet her new grandchild. He made a mental note to stop by the cemetery this week and take flowers to his mother's grave.

Ben and Jeremy took a short break after the final cage was pulled in and secured on deck for the trip back to Booth Bay Harbor. There, the lobsters would be weighed, dropped into buckets of salt water and seaweed, and prepped for the trip to market. Ben thought that they should finish up well before sunset. Ben went below, took two sodas from the small cooler, two bags of Frito Lays and an orange for each of them and took them up top.

"This should hold us until we get back," Ben said, handing the snacks to Jeremy. "I think Sarah and I will go out for dinner tonight. Might be the last night we have alone for the next twenty years."

Jeremy almost choked on his soda as he chuckled at Ben's remark, and Ben laughed too.

"You could be right, boss," he said still laughing. "I hear them babies can be a handful, and give parents no rest at all for at least eighteen years or so. Pretty expensive too, I think. You better hope it's a boy; a boy wouldn't be so pricey. Girls cost lots of money when they get older, I hear."

"Sarah wants a boy," Ben said, "But I think it's what she wants for me not for her. She thinks I should have a boy to train on the docks just like my father and me. She never had a brother either, and I think she would like to raise a boy first. Anyway, we should know in a few days. Thursday is the day, Jeremy."

With that, the two men finished their snacks, threw the trash in a black bag at the bottom of the steps, and went back to the business at hand. Jeremy headed over to the railing and was about to pull up anchor when he yelled down to Ben.

"There's a boat coming in fast," Jeremy shouted, somewhat alarmed, "I think it's that same boat from this morning!"

Ben headed towards the stairs, but before he started the climb, he picked up a weapon from the storage unit. He made sure it was loaded, tucked it in his belt and took a deep breath. His thoughts as he went up on deck were of Sarah.

CHAPTER TWO

Jonas Waverly took a quick glance at the sunflower-shaped yellow and white kitchen clock and picked up his old gray dented lunch bucket from the kitchen counter. He presumed it would hold the usual fare of turkey bologna on rye with just a touch of mustard, an apple, two homemade peanut butter cookies and a thermos of black coffee. Being a simple man, he didn't ask for much and Mary Anne, his wife of thirty-three years, knew he was not much for variety and would never complain. She almost always packed him the same daily lunch. At times, she'd change his sandwich from rye bread to wheat and the meat from turkey to beef, but Jonas didn't seem to mind one way or another, as long as he didn't have to buy his lunch at the Mill's cafeteria. He didn't care for the Chef's Choice of the Day nor did he want to get involved with his co-worker's chitchat regarding the Mill. He was quite contented to just read, relax, or reminisce about his family.

Jonas walked closer to the door, took his worn, but warm, denim jacket from the coat rack, threw it over his shoulder and was about to kiss Mary Anne goodbye when a truck appeared in his driveway. Joe Spencer, neighbor, friend and co-worker at the Mill was almost always on time, even early at times, which pleased Jonas. Joe had to be on the job forty-five minutes after Jonas' 6:30 a.m. shift began, and because they lived only two blocks apart, it worked out for them to share a ride. It took Joe almost thirty minutes longer to get to the logging camp so he would drop Jonas off at the Mill first, then continue on into the Whitecap Mountain forest area where Joe worked as a logger for the

Mill. The two men not only shared the ride and the gas expenses, but even more, they seemed to enjoy each other's company, and Joe didn't seem to mind doing all the driving.

"I can almost always count on Joe," he said more or less to himself, "to be punctual every day; I like that about Joe." Mary Anne nodded her head in approval as Jonas gently kissed her on the forehead and walked towards the kitchen door. He opened the door, stepped outside, put on his coat and took one look back, then gently closed the door behind him.

"Hey, Joe," Jonas said, smiling as he opened the door and stepped into the cab of the old battered, red and white 1989 Chevrolet pick-up. "Good to see you this morning, it's a bit chilly out here."

"Good to see you, too," Joe commented, although Jonas noticed his jovial early morning demeanor seemed to be lacking today. "When the sun finally comes out a bit more it should warm up a little," he said. Then, seemingly as an afterthought he added, "and how's Mary Anne?"

"Fine," Jonas commented, "She's off to see Sarah this week in Booth Bay Harbor, so she's packing a few things. She's going to stay with Sarah for a few days until the baby is born, which should be soon, and then stay on for a few more days after."

Joe turned to look at Jonas, noticing that there was no longer a smile on Jonas' face but more a look of concern, but Jonas continued on, saying, "Can you believe this, Joe? Jonas Waverly about to become a grand pappy for the very first time? Who would have ever thought?" The smile temporarily returned to Jonas's face, then once again faded away.

Joe looked over at Jonas, who was watching a hawk gliding over the telephone wires just to the north side of the old truck. His mind seemed to be somewhere else so Joe commented quietly, "Yes, what an important time in your lives, Jonas. I sure hope that Sarah has a healthy baby." He had his own thoughts on another place and time as well, a time when he too was wishing for a healthy baby to be born. "Does she know if it's a boy or a girl?" Joe asked.

"Don't know," was Jonas' only comment, as he kept staring out the window.

Watching the hawk, Jonas wondered, as he had done so many times before why Joe had never married or had children of his own. He had asked Joe years ago if he had ever been married, and Joe would always chuckle and admit that he had just never found the right woman. Jonas and Mary Anne had introduced him to a few single women or widows in the past few years, but after a few dinners at the Waverly home, playing cards or watching a movie together, Joe just always commented, that they were just not quite right for him. Jonas figured Joe was contented with his life style and never pushed him any further on the subject. Plus, it was really none of their business what Joe did or didn't do.

Looking at Jonas through the corner of his eye, Joe figured the Waverlys to be younger than him. He wasn't sure just how much younger and he never thought to ask Jonas his age, but the fact that the Waverlys had waited nine years to adopt Sarah, who just turned twenty-four this past spring, assured Joe that Jonas and Mary Anne had to be in their early fifty's maybe just a few years older than he was. They had been living in the southern suburb of Millinockett for several years before Joe moved into the area, and Sarah had been twelve when the three of them first met. He enjoyed their friendship. They were not what you would call "really tight" in the beginning, but friendly enough, and he loved their daughter, Sarah, almost like a father himself. For the past twelve years, he had watched Sarah Waverly grow into a smart, talented yet typical teenager and young adult. He had watched her take part in high school plays and musicals, watched her heart break when her first love dropped her for another, and even watched from the sidelines as Jonas taught her how to drive her first car. It was a painful and yet joyful experience for Joe Spencer to watch Sarah Waverly grow up. He felt as those he was a blessed man, but he longed for more.

* * * * *

Joe knew how much Jonas and Mary Anne Waverly loved their daughter. After almost nine years of trying to have a child of their own with no success, they adopted Sarah. She had been two years old when the Waverlys brought her to Millinocket from a foster home in Augusta. They fell in love with her from the first moment they saw her. She was a bubbly little two-year-old with blond curls, rosy cheeks and what would turn out to be a sweet nature. After receiving and signing off on the proper paperwork to get the adoption procedures started, they brought little Sarah home, first for just a day at a time, then two or three days and nights at a time, and then for good. They knew waiting the appropriate six months to finalize the adoption would be difficult but they felt positive that God had sent this child to them, and prepared for the day when she would be legally theirs. After she had been living with the Waverlys for three months, and when Mary Anne was home alone with her, Mary Anne received a telephone call from their lawyer. Sarah's biological mother had decided that she wanted her baby girl back. At first, Joe was told, the birth mother hired a lawyer, went to civil court and fought for the return of her child. With no success, she hired another lawyer and took the case to yet a higher court. However, after the judge and the Waverly's lawyer found out more about the birth mother's background and what kind of problems she had encountered in her life, including jail time and a botched suicide, her requests were denied. The Waverlys, of course, never knew the birth mother's name, nor did they wish to know. They only knew that while in her teens she had been sentenced for selling and using narcotic drugs. She had also, within a four-year period, gotten pregnant twice and given both babies up for adoption. There was also very little said about Sarah's biological father. The lawyers and social workers from the adoption agency in Augusta knew who he was but not where he was. They also knew that he had wanted to keep this baby, raise her on his own if need be, but he, too, had been in trouble with the law, spent time in prison, and there was no way that he would ever be found fit or financially be able to raise a child. They did know his blood type was B negative, that he was now clean, and what part of the country he was from, but, other than that, there was very little information available. The courts had agreed that there was no other way to handle this case but to allow little Sarah to be adopted. One year after the adoption procedure began, Jonas and Mary Anne Waverly had the family they had always wanted and they named their precious little girl Sarah Jeanne.

The three of them returned home from Augusta, final adoption papers in hand. There were parties and showers held in their honor and Sarah's life literally began anew. This little girl never knew what type of life she might have had, but she would definitely find out what a wonderful life lay ahead for her, including being a part of Joe Spencer's life.

The three of them became acquainted for the first time at a town meeting. Once a year newcomers were welcomed to the area with speeches given by the mayor, gifts handed out by the locals, and cake and punch served by the local ladies group, of which Mary Anne was a member. Later on when Joe bought a home in their same area of town, the neighbors, including the Waverlys, helped him move in. They became friends, and little Sarah Jeanne Waverly took to Joe from the very start. He brought her little presents from time to time, and Joe even babysat for Sarah when Jonas and Mary Anne took time for a short evening out. Shortly after, she started calling him Uncle Joe.

* * * * *

"Well, we're almost here, Jonas," Joe said, as he maneuvered his truck through the winding streets of Millinockett to the outskirts of town. "I hope you have a good day." He pulled the pick-up into a large parking area in front of a large gray-green building with a massive front door. On the door was painted bright green letters, "Pulp Manufacturing Plant, Employee Entrance on the South Side." Joe stopped the truck and Jonas stepped out. The sun was just beginning to peak out from under a cloud when Jonas, closing the door, looked at Joe and said, "You were right, the sun is going to shine brightly today. See you at 4:30 p.m." He turned and headed for the south side of the paper plant, lunch bucket in his right hand as he opened the door with his left. As Joe was pulling his truck out of the parking area and Jonas was placing his jacket and lunch pail in his locker, he thought to himself that Joe's eyes were seemingly darker blue and more mysterious looking than normal this morning. He wondered if there was something on Joe's mind. Perhaps he would ask him about it later.

* * * * *

The Great Northern Paper Mill where more than half of the townspeople of Millinocket were employed had been an opportunity for both full time and temporary employment for over seventy-five years. Jonas and Mary Anne had both been employed at the Mill right after graduation from high school, although Mary Anne had chosen to only work part time.

Jonas had worked at the Mill for almost twenty-five years. He had gone from working in logging up past the Baxter State Park area in the Allagash Wilderness into the chipper area and finally into paper production. He loved working out of doors, helping with the harvesting of trees, getting them down the waterway to the river and then to the lakes where the trees were loaded onto logging trucks and taken to the Mill. It was easier in the beginning. Mary Anne worked part time and there had been no children to care for so he worked 36–48 hour shifts at the logging camp. It had been an enjoyable way to make good money. When Sarah came into their lives, however, he wanted to be a good father, be at home evenings, go to her school activities and take her to her piano lessons and concerts. He helped her in any way he could to grow up into a fine young lady. He had asked for better hours and was transferred to the area of the Mill where the logs were either made into lumber or paper. To be honest, he really loved the logging job more, but now he was a manager and well liked by both his employees and supervisors. The position suited him, and it also supported his family well.

Joe, on the other hand, hadn't faired quite as well. He was a pleasant enough employee who most of the time worked hard to earn his pay, but supervisors had complained lately about his attitude and his work habits. There were many times when he had been either late for work or had not showed up at all. However, there was always a good excuse for his tardiness or absenteeism, and, although reprimanded on occasion, he had remained on as a logger for the Mill.

Located inland about one hundred and sixty miles from Booth Bay Harbor, the Waverlys had not only been born and raised in Millinocket, but Jonas's father had worked at the Mill, as well as his grandfather, Jacob, before him. Jonas also loved the fact that Millinocket was a small town with only 5000 people, give or take a few, and it was surrounded by several lakes and rivers. He could go fishing, one of the things he enjoyed more than anything, and on his days off from the Mill he almost always went up to Moosehead or Schoodic Lake to fish. Some of the fish would be cleaned and frozen for later use, but Mary Anne could make all types of fish taste like a delicacy, and so they ate fish often. On special occasions, they drove down to Booth Bay Harbor where they ate their favorite seafood—lobster. They would stop at the Aqua Bay Marina for lunch and Mary Anne would spend the day walking through town, shopping at the small boutiques and watching the pleasure crafts coming in and out of the bay. After Sarah came into their lives, she and Mary Anne would feed the ducks at the Marina or take off their shoes and socks and walk through the sandy beach areas. Jonas would speak with old friends who owned fishing boats or pleasure crafts for rental to the tourists, or once in awhile he and his ladies would take a pleasure craft out on their own for a few hours. Then at day's end they would make the beautiful drive back to their home in Millinocket, at 333 Rock Creek Drive.

*   *   *   *   *

"What a beautiful day this is going to be," Joe muttered to himself, as he turned on his right turn signal, slowed down just a little and made the turn onto the road leading to the highway. If anyone saw him at the Mill dropping Jonas off at the paper plant, they would presume he was headed for his shift farther up the road at Millinocket Lake. There were hundreds of logs backed up on the lake today, waiting to be loaded, and although he loved the logging job and it made him a good living, he needed to skip work today. He called in sick just two hours ago, claiming he must have a "bug" of sorts, and he needed rest and would see a doctor if he wasn't better within twenty-four hours. The receptionist at the Mill's Logging offices believed him, wished him well and put him down for a day of sick leave. No one would ever suspect that he was not down with a bug unless Jonas mentioned it to someone, which was very unlikely.

As he approached the outskirts of town, he noticed in his rearview mirror that a highway patrol car was coming up behind him. He slowed down to just below the 65mph speed limit and waved as the patrolman passed him on the left.

As he left the highway and turned onto the entrance of I-95, Joe thought of Jonas once more, this kind and gentle family-oriented man who had not only become a co-worker but a good friend and a big part of his life these past twelve years.

*   *   *   *   *

When Joe had re-located to this mid-western town not too far from the capital of Augusta, everything had gone according to his plans.

After being in prison for a short time, moving from town to town and doing odd jobs, Joe found himself in the city of Dover-Foxworth. He was only a few years out of high school, strong and healthy and a good worker but with a record. He was hired on and worked at several scab jobs, including a few months in forestry throughout Maine, but he only ever stayed three to six months in one place. His body and mind were restless and his heart was still broken. He regretted the trouble he had been in during his high school years, but the past was just that—the past. He couldn't change it, but he needed to put his soul to rest. If he was to make something of himself, he needed answers to the questions concerning his past. No matter how hard he tried to go forward and put the past behind him, he could not.

One night while watching an NBA game on television, he recalled his years in high school, the awards he won and later when he received a partial basketball scholarship to a local college. "Man, I blew that!" Joe thought, "What a fool I was back then."

As Joe continued down memory lane, he was reminded of a guy named Jonas. They had been basketball rivals in high school and had played each other during a state tournament. Jonas had left a real impression on Joe.

"What was that guy's name?" he asked himself, "Jonas, Jonas, Jonas something. I think it was a name like Waffler, or Wavering or something with a W. His family lived around here somewhere, and his family was big in the logging business. Gosh, I would love to see him again. He was a great–got-it-together kind of guy. Probably made it big time somewhere. I should try to find him, I think his family worked up north somewhere. Maybe I could get a job logging or something. I'm going to check it out."

Joe felt like he was being given a second chance. He checked Census Records on line, called telephone operators for numbers in towns up north, checking on the name Jonas, anything with a last name like Wavering. Finally, he located a Jonas Waverly in Millinockett. He was sure it was the same Jonas he had known from high school basketball games. He decided to begin looking seriously for him. What did he have to lose? Besides it would be fun looking up an old friend.

Joe gave up his apartment when the lease came due and found a job and re-located to the town of Medway. During the weeks that followed, he drove to Millinockett on the weekends or after work, pretending to look for a new position. But what he really was after was locating a man with the last name of Waverly. Everything worked out well after a few months. He found a Jonas Waverly working at the Mill and made a point to ask for him one day when he took an application into the personnel offices. When the application crossed Jonas' desk, he didn't recognize the name at first, but when he saw Joe in person, he knew right away it was Joe Spencer from Yarmouth.

"I don't believe this, Joe," he said, a surprised look on his face as he shook his hand.

"What in the world brings you this far north, and after all these years?" he asked. "What has it been, fourteen, fifteen years or more? Are you playing pro-ball?"

Joe had responded yes, it had been a long time, and no, he didn't get the basketball scholarship or a chance to play basketball after high school. He needed a job and could Jonas put in a good word for him at the personnel office.

"Of course Joe," Jonas said, smiling, "just let me ask you a few questions. Have you had experience logging or doing forestry work?" He looked over his application while asking him a few more questions and replied, "It does look like you've had some experience in forestry. I think we can work out something. Anything else I should know?"

"I've been working in logging now for a few months," he said, not quite telling the whole truth, and I need you to know that I spent a few months right after high school in a youth correctional center. I got mixed up in drugs, but I have been clean now for over twenty years."

"I'm sorry to hear that, Joe, but I think we can find something for you. Ill put in a good word for you, and I think we can find you a position here."

Joe breathed a sigh of relief when Jonas stood up and asked no further questions about his record. "Someone will call you, Joe, I know they have openings right now in the logging camp. Let's keep in touch, okay?"

In only a few weeks, Jonas had played an important part in getting Joe on at the Mill. Joe gave notice and quit his job in of Medway and readied himself for the move to Millinockett. Jonas had worked hand in hand with the local realtor to locate the perfect house for him, a "bachelors pad", as Mary Anne called it. He joined the local gym and worked out twice a week with Jonas. They played a little one-on-one basketball every now and again to stay in shape, and, most importantly, he had learned to love and adore their daughter Sarah. As the weeks and months flew by, the Waverlys invited him over for family dinners more frequently and they invited him on family outings with other friends and neighbors. They even began inviting him to Sarah's musical concerts. Joe Spencer became a big part of the Waverly family. It had taken a little longer than he had figured, but things were now falling into place, just as he had planned all along.

* * * * *

Joe took a quick peek at his watch, saw that it was already 10:15 a.m. and then looked into his rear view mirror before turning on his left turn signal.

"I'll have to move quickly," he muttered to himself, "If I'm going to make it back by 4:30 p.m. to pick up Jonas."

He took the Waterville and Winslow exit, turned left onto highway 202 and headed for the bay. He thought of Sarah, such a beautiful woman, such a talented musician, and how over the years he had learned to care for her. As he steered his truck onto highway 218 and headed towards Booth Bay Harbor, his thoughts turned to a new baby about to be born, and he sincerely hoped it would be healthy.

CHAPTER THREE

Sarah turned in bed and moved from her side to lie flat on her back. Her unborn child, somewhat unhappy with the move, stirred and kicked her hard.

"Oh, my, little one," she said, "That was a hard kick, I'm sorry if I upset you. It shouldn't be long now, just a couple more days and I will be holding you in my arms. I can hardly wait to meet you." She continued to rub her protruding stomach.

As she spoke to her unborn child, Sarah wondered about the sex of the baby. She was hoping for a boy and so was Ben, although he said it didn't matter. She didn't know exactly why, but she just felt in her heart that she was carrying a boy.

She looked at the clock on the bedside table, saw that it was 9:30 a.m. and sat up as quickly as her bulky body would allow. She swung her legs over the side of the bed and stood up.

"Oh my. Do I ever need to get to the bathroom," she said to her baby. She patted her stomach and prayed that she would make it to the bathroom in time. The pressure on her bladder was painful, and she couldn't believe she had slept this long without having to relieve herself.

"We slept late, little one," she said, "and we have to give a lesson at 11:00 a.m. We had better get moving. I hope all this pressure isn't hurting you."

Sarah walked as quickly as she dared into the bathroom. She was amazed that after getting up at 3:00 a.m. to use the bathroom, she had slept this long without having to get up a second time. She hadn't even heard Ben leave. She hoped he had made coffee and eaten breakfast before leaving the house. If not, she imagined he would go to Loren's before heading out too sea. He always kept snacks and sodas on the SARAH JEANNE but not always the most nutritious food. She knew he was capable of taking care of himself, but, still, she worried about the man she loved. She would make a point to call Loren a little later on and make sure Ben had stopped in for breakfast.

Sarah took a shower, brushed her teeth, and dried her long blond hair. She tied it back with a red and white ribbon and dressed in a red smock and blue maternity jeans. It was very difficult putting on her socks and blue tennis shoes, but, after struggling a little and groaning a whole lot, she managed to sit on a chair and bend over far enough to put them on. She was wearing shoes with no shoestrings because tying her shoes had become hopeless over two months before, as her ankles were so swollen. She had gained so much weight and was so large, she swore she was going to have twins. The doctor had assured her of only one baby, but it would be a good sized one. "If I wasn't giving piano lessons this morning, I would walk around bare footed," she said, looking at her feet, "but that wouldn't be too professional now would it little one?"

Sarah walked into the kitchen, opened the refrigerator and took out a container of yogurt, the pitcher of milk, and an orange. She set them down on the yellow lace covered table and walked over to the coffee pot. Immediately she noticed the note Ben had left for her.

"Oh, little one," she said with a big smile, "Your daddy is the sweetest man, just look at this note. It says I love you, and there are X's and O's. He loves us so much, and he'll make the best daddy in the whole wide world."

She held the note to her lips, kissed the piece of paper, and then poured coffee into her cup. She sat down at the kitchen table, opened the container of yogurt and realized she had forgotten a spoon. As she stood up, a sharp pain burst through her back, almost taking her breath away. She sat back down at the table, took some deep breaths and wondered if this would be the day her baby came. She had not had any contractions until now, and she wondered if she should wait a few minutes to eat her breakfast. She also wondered if she should call her students and cancel their piano lessons. She decided to sit quietly at the table for a few minutes, perhaps give her obstetrician a call and also call her mother. This contraction business was all new to her, and since her mother had never given birth she probably couldn't help her with questions either, but still she wanted her mother. She read every book Doctor Foxton gave her on childbirth, and she and Ben had been to pregnancy and birthing classes. Right now she was not sure if this pain was a contraction or not. She wished she could call Ben, but she knew that was impossible, as he was at least fifteen miles out at sea today. In order to contact him, she would have to go to the Port Authority offices to call him on their land to sea radio as his cellular phone got horrible or no reception that far out at sea.

"I'll be okay," she said once again to the baby. "I'll just wait for a few minutes and then make the decision on whom to call."

She waited about ten minutes and experienced no other contractions. She ate her yogurt and orange, poured a glass of milk and drank it, and decided she could handle giving the two lessons she had scheduled for today. She loved her students and most of them were very good at practicing and showed up promptly at their scheduled weekly appointments. She told all of them and their parents at the end of last week's sessions that she would be taking two to three weeks off after the baby came. She hoped they would all practice regularly until their lessons started up again, and how proud she was of all of them. They all seemed to be okay with the vacation break and promised to be back the middle of November to resume their lessons.

Sarah got up from the table, put her glass and spoon in the sink, put away the milk, and poured one last cup of coffee. She carried her coffee cup into the living room, took a sip, and sat the cup and herself down at the piano. She played a few bars of "I Knew I Loved You" by John Tesh, Ben's favorite piece, and her mind went back to the time she had performed her first piano recital. Her mother had purchased a beautiful green lace dress for her to wear with matching shoes and anklets. "To match your eyes," she had said, and added, "and because you are such a beautiful and precious daughter. We are so proud of you."

The recital was held at the Millinockett Elementary School where she was in the fifth grade. There were thirteen, third, fourth and fifth graders participating in the recital, four boys and nine girls. They all took weekly lessons from either Mrs. Farthey or Ms. Barhor. Sarah started taking lessons from Mrs. Farthey when she had been six years old. Sarah not only loved her, but it was evident that her teacher loved her too. Her teacher recognized her musical talent and worked with her extra hard and extra long. In the end, her hard work had paid off. Sarah played beautifully. She often played for junior and high school choirs and drama and theatre groups, and she had won a partial music scholarship to Chelsea College where she studied music during the day and gave lessons in the evenings. She even dreamed of one day having a music studio of her own.

She remembered how her parents first rented a piano for her to practice on. They weren't financially able to purchase a piano outright, and they were also concerned that the piano might not be the instrument Sarah actually wanted to play. They should have never doubted Sarah, as she practiced diligently. She loved playing the piano from the first time she sat down to practice. Reading music came easily to her; she loved playing for others and her parents never had to ask her to practice. Most times, she practiced much longer than Mrs. Farthey required.

As she continued to play and remember her past, she was brought back to reality by a knock on the door. She took a glance at her watch, carefully stood up from the piano and walked to the front door. Jacqueline and her mother were right on schedule. Sarah opened the door, said hello, and invited them in.

"Hello, Jacqueline," Sarah said, embracing the child. "I'm so glad to see you again, and you, too, Mrs. Andrews."

Jacqueline seemed to enjoy the embrace, but Sarah saw a troubled and uncomfortable look in her mother's eyes. Sarah dropped her arms from around her student and asked, "Will you be staying with Jacqueline today during her lesson, Mrs. Andrews?"

"Yes, I will," Mrs. Andrews sternly replied. She took off her lovely yellow suit jacket and told Jacqueline to take her jacket off as well. She laid them down on the couch before Sarah could offer to hang them up. She took a seat in an old fashioned rocking chair close to the piano and asked Sarah to begin.

Sarah was used to Mrs. Andrews' sharp tone and attitude and she took a seat at the piano to the left of her student. She asked Jacqueline to practice her scales and then to play the piece she had been practicing during the week. Sarah listened as Jacqueline practiced and thought of how she had come to enjoy teaching this strange, shy child. She was a very smart eight-year old who learned quickly, but in the two months since Jacqueline began taking lessons, her mother had always stayed close each time. Sarah didn't mind having a parent wait for an hour during lessons, but they usually waited in the car or sat on the front porch. Sarah thought it was difficult for the child to perform well when a parent was waiting and watching in the same room. She had suggested that same thing to Mrs. Andrews in the beginning, but the mother always insisted on staying close to Jacqueline.

Sarah had met Mrs. Andrews at a charity event during the late summer. Several musicians living in the area, including Sarah, volunteered to play at a fundraising event for a local children's charity. After the event ended, Mrs. Andrews approached Sarah. She did not compliment her on her playing or seem excited to be at the event. Instead, she asked Sarah about lessons for her daughter. "I believe my daughter has musical talent," she had shared, and would Sarah be willing to teach her the piano?

Sarah and Mrs. Andrews agreed on the lessons, the day of the week that worked out the best for her and the fees. Jacqueline and Mrs. Andrews came to Sarah's home the next Tuesday for her first lesson. Sarah enjoyed teaching her, and her mother had been right about Jacqueline's potential. When Sarah tried to get close to her, however, or ask her any questions about hobbies, school, or her friends, Mrs. Andrews would always interrupt and ask Sarah to please just teach her piano. "Our family does not share anything about our personal lives with strangers," Mrs. Andrews had politely said.

Sarah didn't consider herself a stranger but went along with the request. She wondered where Jacqueline's father was? Why did Mrs. Andrews want her daughter to play the piano so badly, and, most of all, why was she so protective of her daughter? She always seemed to be smothering Jacqueline. Sarah, however, did agree with Mrs. Andrews. She was just the music teacher, and she should do just that, teach. Still, she was concerned as she felt Jacqueline was a very unhappy little girl.

After an hour's lesson, Mrs. Andrews thanked Sarah, paid her, picked up her yellow coat and helped Jacqueline with hers. She then asked Sarah if the baby was expected this week, and Sarah told her just a little about a possible blood problem and hoped she would be able to deliver on Thursday. "The baby and I both have a possible blood issue," she said, "and the doctor wants to make sure we are both okay prior to delivery. He plans to induce labor on Thursday after I first have more blood tests, assuring us that everything will be fine during and after delivery."

Sarah thought Mrs. Andrews looked a little puzzled after her remarks about the blood tests. She continued, however, to speak with Sarah, wishing her the best and asking if Sarah knew what sex the baby was.

"My husband, Ben, and I chose not to find out," she said sweetly, patting her belly. "We want it to be a surprise, but I'm kind of hoping for a boy. Ben doesn't care either way, or so he says, but I am an only child, and I would love to have a little boy first."

Sarah continued, "Maybe if we have another child later, it would be a girl."

"I hope all goes well for you," Mrs. Andrews said again as she walked to the door. "I love my little girl," she said smiling at Jacqueline. "Oh, by the way, where are you having your baby?"

"In Portland," Sarah replied, wondering why Mrs. Andrews would ask that question. "I hope I make it that far," she commented, chuckling. "I've had a few contractions, but, hopefully, this little one will wait until Thursday."

Sarah thanked her, said goodbye to Jacqueline, and then reminded them there would be no lessons for at least three weeks.

"I will call you to remind you, Jacqueline" Sarah said, touching her slightly on the shoulder. "Make sure you practice your lessons every day."

Jacqueline nodded her head yes and said a soft goodbye as she went out the door with her mother. Sarah stood on the front step, watched them leave and looked up at the sky. She noticed that, although the sky was blue overhead, storm clouds seemed to be gathering from the north. She hoped Ben would make it back to the bay before it rained.

Sarah looked at her watch, noted the time. It was 12:15 p.m. "I should lie down and rest for a while before my next student comes at 3:00 p.m." she thought. "I won't sleep, just rest."

She first re-visited the bathroom. When she passed the open door to the nursery she stopped and took a peek.

"I can't wait to bring you home and show you your new room, little one," she said, "You're going to love your room and your mommy and daddy and your grandparents, and we all are going to love you. I'm getting so anxious for you to come. Just look at what we have ready for you."

Sarah walked through the door into the bright, cheery nursery, smiling as she looked about the room. She and Ben had worked every weekend and every evening for the past few months and it was now ready for the newest Kestwick. Since she always loved nursery rhymes, the new baby would also be entertained with them. The wallpaper was filled with pictures and poems of possibly every nursery rhyme ever written. It took Ben and her two weeks to put up the wallpaper and paint two walls, a sunshine yellow with white trim. The wallpaper covered the two opposite walls with pictures of Little Bo Peep, Humpty Dumpty, Yankee Doodle and the Itsy Bitsy Spider. There was One, Two, Buckle My Shoe, Mary Had A Little Lamb, The Old Woman Who Lived in a Shoe, Mary, Mary Quite Contrary, Peter Piper and more. The nursery included an antique cradle they had stripped diligently and painted white. The nursery also had a hand-me-down dresser in excellent condition from a yard sale, and Sarah's favorite, a white rocking chair. Sarah's mother had offered to make cushions for the chair in material that matched the yellow curtains with imprints of nursery rhyme figures, and she silently hoped her mother would bring the cushions along tomorrow.

Sarah walked up to a green and yellow baby stroller given to her by college friends, gently touched the white fringe and smiled. In the corner of the room sat a beautiful white antique crib. Sarah walked toward the crib and gently touched the lovable, ragged teddy bear and picked up the priceless Princess doll sitting elegantly inside the crib, the toys given to her by her Uncle Joe.

"I love this room," she said, picking up and hugging the doll, "and I can't wait to become a mother. I have a husband who loves me more than anything or anybody in the entire world, and I'm such a lucky woman." As she patted her tummy, she said to the child, "and so are you little one."

She walked from the nursery into the living room and picked up an embroidered pillow and a book on baby names. She sat down, looked at a few names…Sandra, Sienna, Sonja, Steven, Shawn, Seth, but the name Samantha kept popping up.

"Yes, Samantha is the perfect name for a little girl," she said "and Seth is a good name for a boy." She closed the book and laid it down. She covered herself with a blanket, closed her eyes and thought of her own childhood. "I hope I can be half the mother my own mother was," she thought, and, just for a moment, she thought of her birth mother, something she hadn't done in a very long time. She wondered what she looked like, was she happy, did she ever marry and have more children? She wondered if her birth mother had ever tried to locate her. Did she miss her, or had she forgotten completely about Sarah? She remembered that her birth name was Annie and her parents had chosen not to keep that name when they adopted her. Plus, she thought to herself, I love my name. I love the name Sarah Jeanne—Sarah Jeanne Waverly Kestwick.

Sarah had never tried to find her birth parents. She was so happy with her adoptive parents, and, although she thought of her birth parents once in awhile, she never pursued her past. She knew very little about her mother and even less about her father. She knew she had a half-brother somewhere, but he, too, seldom crossed her mind. "It would be nice to have had siblings," she thought, "but it just wasn't meant to be." With that, she closed her eyes, held tightly to the embroidered pillow and fell asleep. She dreamt of a baby crying while a mother sang a lullaby, sitting in a white rocking chair in a beautiful house overlooking the sea.

CHAPTER FOUR

Joe Spencer looked at his watch. It was 10:30 a.m. "I made very good time getting to Booth Bay Harbor," he said, grinning. "Not bad at all."

Once he was in town, he turned off Main Street immediately onto Lake Boulevard. He looked for a parking space in front of the Booth Bay Harbor National Bank building, but finding none, he drove around the corner. A half block down he saw one space. He did a quick u-turn to the right side of the street and pulled in, turning off the ignition, and put the keys into the left pocket of his green parka. He zipped up the comfortable old coat and opened the truck door. As he stepped out of his truck, he noticed several refrigerated trucks being loaded with boxes of fish, lobster and crab; all imprinted with different company logos. He looked around and marveled at the goings on of this small fishing village. He only came into Booth Bay once a month and he guessed it wasn't all that unusual for the town to be this busy on a Tuesday morning. It was just so different from Millinockett. There, people kept busy by working at the Mill or at a few local businesses in town. Shops closed down by 5:00 p.m. suppers would be prepared and eaten, and folks were in bed by 9:30 p.m. It was a working town, but not like Booth Bay Harbor. Here, by the sea, the people were at work or at the coffee shops by 5:00 a.m. and worked until sunset or beyond. Tourists either came for several days and stayed in the local motels and bed and breakfasts, or just came down for the day to shop, eat or take a pleasure cruise around the bay. The quaint little shops, restaurants and coffee shops did a booming business and during the summer time, day in and day out, boats went out on pleasure cruises or fishing trips every hour until after sunset.

As Joe walked across the street to the bank, he noticed the sign advertising the Kestwick Fishing Company hanging on a brown building with white trim on the windows and doors. As he looked further, he wondered if Ben Kestwick had gone out to sea this morning. There were several lobster boats tied up at the harbor, but he didn't see any of theirs in the harbor, but then that didn't mean much as the boats all had HIN numbers, numbers he did not recognize. He admitted that he wouldn't know one lobster boat from another. He did know, however, that one boat was named the SARAH JEANNE, because Sarah had called him to tell him all about it. "I might have to walk down to the docks later on and check it out," he said to himself.

Joe recalled that a few months after Sarah and Ben had married, she called Joe to tell him about Ben's big surprise. One evening she and Ben had gone down to the docks. He had suggested a sunset dinner cruise, and when they arrived at the docks, he had first taken her to where the Kestwick boats were docked. He told her he had a surprise for her, had blindfolded her, taken her hand and carefully walked her down to one of their boats. She immediately smelled fresh paint. When Ben took off the blindfold and she saw her name emblazoned in blue on the hull of the boat, she held both hands up to her mouth, and gasped while walking closer. The boat itself had a fresh coat of white paint, and her name was painted in her favorite color, blue. Ben carried her on board, set her down and then held her in his arms, all the while telling her how much she meant to him. They stayed for just a few minutes before leaving on the scheduled dinner cruise. For two hours, they pigged out (as Sarah recalled) on wonderful crab and lobster dishes and drank entirely too much champagne. They returned to their apartment, went to bed and made love throughout the night. Sarah was sure this was the night their child was conceived, and she shared with Ben that she had never known such happiness.

Sarah had told her Uncle Joe that, for Ben, naming a boat after someone he loved was something he had always dreamed of. His grandfather, Jacob, had called one of the first Kestwick boats Rebecca after his grandmother, and after they had both passed on, the names were painted over and only HIN numbers placed on the bows. After his mother and father were married, Martin had named one of their boats the JENNY MARIE, after Ben's mother and, until now, the other two boats had remained nameless. Now, along with his mother's name on one boat and Sarah's name on another, there was only one boat left to name. He hoped that some day he would have a daughter to carry on the tradition and then all three boats would be named after a Kestwick.

As Joe approached the bank, a woman with a child got to the door just in front of him. He opened the door for them both and walked in behind them. He noticed that the woman was holding onto the child's hand very tightly, and then motioned for her to sit on one of the chairs facing the teller windows, telling her to remain seated until she returned.

"Do not move from this chair, Jacqueline," Joe heard the woman say, "I'm only going up to the window. Make sure you sit still, and speak to no one, do you understand?"

"Yes, ma'am," the little girl said timidly. She leaned back into the deep cushioned chair and folded her hands in her lap. Joe thought, "That little girl is either very obedient or knows the routine well."

Joe took his checkbook and wallet out of his hip pocket, stepped up to the teller's window where he stood in line behind the little girl's mother. She was nicely dressed in a yellow pantsuit and matching jacket. Her beautiful, long blond hair flowed out from under a large round, brown, tan and yellow hat. He felt an uneasiness standing behind her and felt there was something very familiar about her. He watched her intently but couldn't quite put a finger on it. Had he seen her somewhere before? That was doubtful. He knew very few people in Booth Bay Harbor. But when she finished her bank transaction and turned to leave, he found himself following her with his eyes as she coached the child to get out of the chair, then took her by the hand and quickly exited the bank.

Joe turned back and stepped up to the teller's window, and, as the brown-eyed teller greeted him with a cheery hello, he laid his checkbook on the counter and filled out a deposit slip with the pen she handed him. He took ten one hundred dollar bills out of his billfold and placed them with the deposit slip. He asked for the balance in his account, and, the young woman shortly gave him both a receipt and his bank balance. She thanked him by name for coming in. He placed the papers in his wallet, picked up his checkbook and started to turn away.

"Excuse me," he said to the teller. "Can you tell me who the woman was in front of me just now?"

"I'm sorry, Mr. Spencer," she said. "I am not allowed to give out that information but if you wish to speak with a bank officer," she said pointing to the left, "Mr. Campbell could possibly assist you."

"Thanks, anyway," he said, as he turned and headed for the door.

Once outside and standing on the sidewalk in front of the bank, he looked both directions to locate the woman and her child but they were nowhere in sight. "Oh, well," Joe, said, "I probably don't know her anyway." But Joe could not get the woman and her child out of his mind as he headed towards the docks.

Joe had hoped to get in and out of the bank quickly, have something to eat, stop in at the real estate offices, and get back to the Mill in time to pick up Jonas. So far, the bank had not been very busy, the teller had been very efficient, and, except for the lingering picture of the woman and the child in his memory, things, were going well. He was right on schedule.

He walked the opposite direction from his truck, took out his wallet and then the piece of paper with his bank balance written on it. $134,017.99 was the amount written in blue ink. He smiled and placed the paper back in his wallet.

When Joe got closer to the docks, he looked around for a place to get a bite to eat. Seeing a restaurant a block or so down, he decided first to take a closer look at where the Kestwick boats might be tied up and walked in that direction. He saw several boats, but none with the name SARAH JEANNE on the hull, so he presumed that Ben was out to sea setting or bringing in traps. He turned around to head back to the little coffee shop he had seen earlier at the end of the block. He was surprised to see the woman and child from the bank walking towards him.

"Now that's a coincidence," he muttered to himself, "I wonder what she's doing down here?"

As the woman came closer to him, he noticed she pulled her hat down a little farther over her forehead. She picked up her step just a little, and, as Joe said a friendly hello to the both of them, they passed him on the inside of the walkway. She never returned the greeting. The child looked up at him just slightly before the mother tugged at her hand and suggested she keep moving.

"Now, that was strange," Joe thought to himself. Normally, people in Booth Bay Harbor were very friendly, always saying hello when they met one another on the docks. Locals were especially friendly to tourists. He wondered if she lived here or if she was a visitor, and he also wondered why she was in such a hurry. A visitor would take time walking the docks and seeing the bay and the ocean. "I don't think she is a visitor," he said to himself, and once more this strange woman aroused his curiosity. He watched the woman and child as they passed the Kestwick Boat Company. The woman seemed to pause for a moment, look out over the bay, and then continue to walk briskly away. He continued to watch them until they were out of sight.

"Normally, out of sight, out of mind," Joe thought to himself. "Not this time. There is something about that woman, something very unsettling. I must know her from Millinockett or the Mill or from somewhere in my past, but if so, why wouldn't she have spoken to me?"

He turned back and headed for the restaurant, his curiosity going wild. This strange woman in yellow, for some reason, did not want him to see her face or be recognized. "Perhaps it's nothing," he thought to himself, but he didn't believe it.

Joe walked into the Breakfast Hut to find it filled with customers but immediately took an empty seat at the counter. He ordered coffee, asked if they were still serving breakfast at 11:00 a.m. and when the waitress said they were, he ordered a three-egg breakfast with hash browns, toast and a side of pancakes. He didn't eat meals out very often, but when he did, he loved breakfast any time of the day or night. He took a look around the restaurant but recognized no one. As he sipped on the steaming coffee, he noticed several older couples sitting in booths or at tables. Vacationing retired people he presumed. There was a police officer at the far end of the counter, sitting with another man in uniform, but he did not recognize the insignia on his sleeve, and several other men were just talking over coffee. Dockworkers he supposed. The waitress, June, who had introduced herself earlier, brought his breakfast. He asked for catsup, smothered his eggs with it, and ate what was one of the better breakfasts he had ever tasted. Thirty minutes later, June brought him his bill and he left her a generous tip, paid the bill, and headed for the door.

Watching him leave the Hut, Loren asked June if she knew his name, and whether he had ever been in the Hut before. June said she didn't catch his name, and that she had never seen him before.

Joe got to his truck, unlocked the door and got in. He turned the key in the ignition and backed out of the parking space. He headed back to Main Street and made a right hand turn. Three blocks ahead he parked in front of the Jensen-Ferguson Real Estate Offices. He took one look at himself in the mirror and opened the truck's door. He walked the few yards to the offices, opened the door and went in. There were several photos of houses and two-story buildings, as well as real estate certificates and awards, covering the walls. Joe smiled at an older gray-haired woman in a beige sweater and slacks sitting at the front desk. A secretary, he supposed. Two men were involved in a conversation at a back desk. A younger man was on the telephone and, before Joe could look around any further, the older woman cordially asked if she could help him.

"I have an appointment with Jerry Ferguson," he said.

Upon hearing his name, a young man, possibly in his early thirties, ended his conversation and hung up the telephone. He stood up from behind his desk and walked over to Joe.

"You must be Joe Spencer," he said, as he held out and shook Joe's hand. Joe said, that yes, he was and Joe followed the young man to his desk.

"Thanks for seeing me," Joe said in earnest, and took a seat.

"Would you like coffee, Joe, is it okay if I call you Joe?" he asked. "I'm going to get myself a cup."

"No thanks on the coffee offer," Joe, said, "I just had one at the restaurant. If it's okay, I would like to get down to business, as I have to get back soon, and, yes, you may call me Joe."

The young man assured Joe that he would be right back, and promised they could get down to business directly. He left just for a moment, returned with coffee cup in hand, set it down on his desk, and introduced himself as a partner in the firm. Before he took a sip of his coffee, he opened the file of papers and photographs lying on his desk and turned on his computer.

"I've got a few photos for you to look at," he said to Joe, "And also some more photos on the computer. I hope you'll be interested in a few of these, and we can go out and take a look at them. I think there will be at least one or two buildings that will catch your eye."

He laid out the photos on his desk in front of Joe and gave him further information on each one. He then turned to a website where there were several more photos of properties for Joe to look over. Joe picked out a few photos from the computer and Jerry made two copies of each. Joe asked Jerry a few more questions, and, after a few more minutes, they both stood up.

"I'll go and get my car," Jerry said, "and meet you out front. These three buildings are very close by, it won't take us long to get there. I know you have just a limited amount of time today." Joe thanked him and headed for the front door as Jerry went out the back.

Jerry was correct. It only took a few minutes to get to the properties. Joe wasn't impressed with the first property; it needed a lot of work, did not have a front entrance, and was too small. The next one was also a small building, with two rooms and one bathroom, but it had a front entrance and was only a few blocks from the harbor. It had a lot of potential for his needs, didn't need too much repair or change and Joe imagined a finished project. It was located in a mini mall, the price was about right, and Joe liked what he saw. Jerry insisted he take a look at the other properties, but Joe said, no. This one was the right one for his needs. Joe asked Jerry if they could go back to the office and work on some figures, and Jerry agreed.

The two men returned to the real estate office and after a brief discussion, agreed on a price. Joe, chuckling, assured Jerry that he wasn't going to purchase the property for anything illegal and they could go forward with the paperwork. Joe wrote a sizeable check for a security deposit, and asked Jerry to hold the property for the usual three days in case he changed his mind.

"I need to think about it a few more days before I sign the final paperwork," Joe said. He told Jerry he would be back on the weekend if the offices were open. Saturday was the best day since he had to work the rest of the week. Jerry assured him that he would be at the offices until 5:00 p.m. on Saturday, and made arrangements to see him and finalize the sale at 3:00 p.m.

Joe left the real estate offices after a little more than an hour. As he climbed into his truck, he thought the day had gone well. He would have plenty of time to get back to Millinockett to pick up Jonas. As he pulled onto the interstate, the woman in the yellow suit crept back into his mind. Just where had he seen her before, or had he? Just what was it about her that stuck in his craw? What was it about the little girl that made him feel so uncomfortable? He didn't know what it was, but he knew there was something about this woman, something more he needed to find out about her, and he intended to do that exact thing soon.

An hour later as he turned off the interstate and headed for the Mill, his thoughts returned to Sarah and the building he had just purchased. It was an investment for her future. He smiled to himself as he thought of how excited she would be when he told her the news, or would she? He had planned this for so long, things just had to work out. Finally, he would be able to do something right for his precious Sarah.

CHAPTER FIVE

Joe Spencer drove about twenty-five miles in a hard rain. It began to sprinkle just a few miles out of Booth Bay Harbor, but by the time he got to the Mill to pick up Jonas it was raining harder. He arrived in Millinocket in plenty of time to pick up Jonas, then drove him into town, dropped him off at home and told him he would see him in the morning.

Mary Anne was preparing dinner when Jonas walked in the door. It smelled heavenly in their homey kitchen, and he kissed his wife on the cheek and gave her a small love tap on her shoulder. He commented on the rain and asked if she had heard from Sarah?

"No, I haven't, Jonas," she said calmly, "I plan to call her after dinner. Tomorrow, in late morning or early afternoon, I'll drive down to stay with her. I'm already packed. I just need to put gas in the car in the morning and then I will be on my way."

"It's raining real hard right now," he said, "I hope it clears up by morning, don't want you driving by yourself in a hard rain." He told her the wind was blowing hard and it was coming in from the north.

Mary Anne shrugged and told him not to worry. A little rain never bothered her before, and she moved toward the stove.

"What are you cooking?" he asked, as she lifted the lid off a steaming pot. "It sure smells delicious."

"What you smell is bread baking," she said, chuckling as she stirred the contents of the pot. "I think you're losing your sense of smell in your older age. I have already made some apple cinnamon muffins and a batch of oatmeal cookies too."

"Not me," Jonas said, putting his arms around his wife's tiny waist. "I can smell lobster and noodles anywhere. It's Elegante isn't it?"

Mary Anne agreed, showed a big grin and opened the oven door to check on her bread. It was almost done so she sat down at the kitchen table for just a minute. She had not made Elegante in a while, nor had she made homemade bread of late. She wanted to take bread and cookies to Sarah tomorrow, and she wanted Jonas to have a good meal before she left him for a few days. "Men," she thought to herself, "don't know how to cook a decent meal when their wives are gone."

"I made enough to take some to Sarah and Ben too. That way Ben can just heat it up while Sarah is in the hospital," she said smiling, and stood up once again to check the bread.

"I sure hope everything goes well for Sarah," her father said, a concerned look on his face. "I understand first babies can sometimes be difficult deliveries."

"Her doctor has been watching her very closely," Mary Anne commented. "She has felt fine all along, and, except for the concern over her blood, I honestly think she'll do very well. I'll call you from Portland and let you know exactly what is happening every minute of the day!" She chuckled as she stood close to Jonas, gave him a big hug and called him grand pappy.

Mary Anne told Jonas there was time for him to clean up before dinner and asked him to relax for a few minutes. She said she would call him when the food was ready. Jonas took her suggestion, and after he had refreshed himself from a hard day's work, sat down in his easy chair. He turned on the television to watch the remainder of the evening news. There was very little news that interested him, but when the news ended and the weather report came on, he watched and listened more intently. There was a storm coming in from the north. There were severe winds and hard rain in the forecast and the possibility of snow. It was a fast moving storm, and it would likely end later in the evening. The meteorologist suggested that no boats go out this evening. It would also be a smart move to recheck all boats tied in the harbor, as the wind would be increasing throughout the evening hours. She did predict that the weather would improve by late morning.

Jonas turned off the television, walked into the kitchen and shared with Mary Anne what he heard concerning the weather.

"I hope Ben got in early tonight," he said. "The weather looks pretty bad, especially the winds. I think we should call Sarah and see if Ben made it home already."

"Why not wait a little longer, Jonas," his wife suggested. "Dinner is ready, and Ben usually is out trapping until dusk, and by the time he weighs in and finishes up, it's always around 7:00 p.m. when he gets home. He's a very cautious man, Jonas, he'll be fine."

With those comments said, Jonas and Mary Anne sat down to their dinner. Jonas said a prayer thanking God for their family and for the food and Mary Anne began to dish up their meal. As always, the Lobster Elegante was delicious. The succulent lobster was fresh and Mary Anne prided herself in her homemade noodles. Along with a salad and the muffins she had made earlier, it was an enjoyable and delectable meal. Later on, Mary Anne poured them both coffee, and for the next thirty minutes they talked about the Mill, the new baby, and how long Mary Anne thought she would be away.

"I hope to be home by Sunday, dear," she said to Jonas. "If Sarah has the baby on Thursday, she will most likely be home by Saturday. I will stay the first two nights with her, and then come back home. I think Ben can help Sarah out with the baby, and he is taking two weeks off work I believe. I really think the three of them should be together with no one bothering them the first week. I will go back later on if Sarah asks me to come."

"I want to come down, too," Jonas replied, "but I can't take off work this week. Driving back and forth to Portland is too long a trip at night, so, depending on how things go I'll wait until she's back home with the baby and try to come down on Sunday. Do you think that will be okay?"

They both agreed that Sunday would be the best day, and Ben could handle his new family from that point on. Jonas looked at his wife and chuckled. His wife would be taking a lot of trips to Booth Bay Harbor in the coming months. He remembered how excited she was when Sarah told them she was pregnant. Mary Anne missed out on being pregnant and taking care of a newborn and he knew being a grandmother would be very rewarding for her. He was happy for her, and for himself.

Mary Anne cleared the table and washed the dishes, letting them drip-dry while she prepared a to-go dish for Ben and Sarah. She placed it in the refrigerator, wrapped up a loaf of bread, muffins and a dozen cookies in aluminum foil and placed them all in a plastic bag, laying them with her purse and a few books on the kitchen counter. This way she hoped she would not forget anything in the morning.

Later, she joined Jonas in the living room, picked up a book and sat down next to him on the couch. This had become a nightly ritual, she reading a book, and Jonas doing crossword puzzles and dozing in and out of sleep. They would talk about their day or share some gossip from town, but at 9:30 p.m. they would retire for the night. Some nights they would stay up later to watch a favorite television program or have friends over to play cards or dominos, but that was always on the weekends.

Mary Anne looked at her watch and stood up to walk into the kitchen to get the telephone.

"Okay, let's call Sarah," she said, "and make sure Ben is home, and see if she is ready for me to come in the morning. As she started to pick the phone up from it's cradle, it rang, startling her.

"Hello," Mary Anne said cheerfully.

"Hi, Mary Anne, it's Martin Kestwick, how are you?"

"Well, I am just fine Martin," she said, "What a nice surprise. We haven't talked to you or seen you in awhile, how are you doing these days?"

"I'm doing pretty well," he said somewhat disheartened. "I wish I could say this was a social call, but I need to let you know that Ron from the Port Authority called. Ben has not returned to port as of an hour ago. He wants me to go over to Sarah's and let her know. We're going to call in the Coast Guard and start looking for him. That's better than telling her by telephone, don't you think, Mary Anne?"

Martin didn't allow her to answer him, but continued. He told her how bad the weather was there, how hard it was raining and how severe the winds were.

"Not sure they can put a chopper in the air until morning, but they are going to try to send out at least two boats right now," he continued, "and the Guard will send out another two boats in the morning to start looking for him and Jeremy at first light."

Mary Anne walked unsteadily into the living room. She sat down once again next to her husband, shook him from sleep and handed him the telephone. One look at his wife's face told him something was very wrong.

"Is it Sarah?" he mouthed. "Mary Anne is it Sarah?"

Mary Anne handed him the telephone and began to weep. Again, Martin Kestwick shared the news about Ben and Jeremy and told Jonas that he was headed to Sarah and Ben's home in the next few minutes. He told Jonas that Ron from the Port Authority had contacted Sarah a few hours earlier, and she had not seemed too concerned at that time. Now Ron was getting worried and had contacted the Coast Guard in Portland.

"I want to be the one who tells her," Martin said calmly, hoping to keep the Waverlys calm as well. However, he could hear Mary Anne crying in the background.

I'll go to Sarah's now and call you when I get there," Martin assured Jonas. "I hope she won't go into labor over this, Jonas. I'm not sure how I would be able to handle that, and it's a long drive to Portland in this weather. I'll try to talk with her as calmly as possible so as not to upset her. Sarah is a strong woman, I think she will be okay."

The two men talked for a few more minutes. Martin assured Jonas that Ben was a good captain, handled his boat in storms much worse than this one, and he was sure they would be coming into port soon.

"Just stay by the telephone, Jonas," Martin repeated, "and I will call when I get to Sarah's. If she needs or wants you to come down here, I'm sure she will tell you."

"Fine, Martin," Jonas said solemnly, "thanks so much for calling us. We will be in touch."

Jonas turned off the telephone and laid it beside him on the couch. He took Mary Ann in his arms and tried to console her. After a few minutes, she stopped crying and they discussed the situation. They agreed to wait until Martin called back. They could then make their decision about whether to drive to Booth Bay Harbor to be with their daughter or wait until there was more news from the Coast Guard.

As they waited and watched the clock, they held hands, bowed their heads and said a short prayer for their son-in-law, his friend and their daughter. They also prayed for their unborn grandchild, hoping that he or she would wait a little longer to be born, at least until Ben was located and safe.

CHAPTER SIX

The telephone's shrill ring startled Sarah from a deep sleep. "I cannot believe how easily I can fall asleep these days," she said out loud. She reached for the telephone, and the book entitled 1000 Baby Names fell off of what little lap she still had.

"Hello," she said sleepily, "this is the Kestwick residence."

"Sarah?" a voice asked anxiously.

"Yes?" she replied, "this is Sarah."

"It's Ron at the Port Authority," he said. "I don't want to worry you, but I wondered if you knew what time Ben was planning to return to port today? He told us this morning that he would be back by 7:00 p.m. and it's now almost 9:00 p.m. Have you heard from him?"

Sarah glanced at the clock on the wall, and realized that she had been asleep most of the evening. She had laid down after her last lesson, fallen asleep and evidently stayed asleep.

"I'm not sure, Ron," she said, a note of concern in her voice. "He usually doesn't stay out past dark; he knows the rules. I didn't realize how late it was. Do you think he's had trouble with the boat?"

"I'm not sure, and I don't want you to worry, Sarah," he said, "But if his boat isn't back in an hour or so, I think we should contact the authorities. The weather is bad, and almost everyone who went out today is back, except for the SARAH JEANNE."

"OK," Sarah replied, "please let me know as soon as possible if you hear from him or when he comes into port. Please have him call me right away." And then as an after thought, she asked, "Have you tried calling him, Ron?"

"Yes," came a quick reply, "there was no answer, which is rather strange. They weren't going out that far. His radio should be working fine." Then as an added gesture, he said, "Sarah, are you feeling ok, do you need me to send someone over to stay with you, or can I call someone for you?"

"Thank you, but no," she said calmly. "If I need anything, I know whom to call, just please keep me informed."

Sarah hung up the telephone, bent over as well as she could and picked the book up from the floor and laid it on the coffee table. She thought how earlier in the week she and Ben had picked out the name Samantha for a girl, and agreed that they both liked the name Seth if it was a boy. It was a middle name that they could not agree on. Should they name their child after the grandparents, or give the child it's own middle name or initial? As of last night they had not made a decision.

She carefully walked into the kitchen. She felt large and bulky and thought how nice it would be when she was slim again. She took a glass from the cupboard and set it on the counter. Opening the refrigerator door, she took out a pitcher and filled the glass half way with milk. She took out the container of yogurt, some cheese and cold meat, and as she placed the food on the table, she suddenly felt dizzy. She carefully sat herself down on a chair at the table, wondering if it was hunger or the phone call that brought on the dizziness. She felt the baby stir inside her, and it kicked her hard on her left side.

"Just a little bit longer, little one," she said as she patted her stomach. The unborn child seemed to recognize its mother's gentle stroke and calm voice and stopped stirring.

As Sarah took the glass in her hand, she looked towards the window into the total blackness and noticed that rain was gently hitting the pane. She wondered when it had begun.

She ate a few pieces of cheese and ham, drank the milk, but left the yogurt untouched. She stood up and began to walk into the living room when she felt another contraction.

"Oh my goodness," she said aloud, "Are you trying to tell me something, little one? I'm not sure this is very good timing, your daddy isn't home from work yet."

She knew that her due date was already past, but due to some possible problems with the baby's blood, the doctors now wanted to induce Sarah's labor. They wanted her in the hospital when she went into labor to be prepared for any unusual events that might occur during and immediately after she delivered.

Dr. Foxton had monitored Sarah closely after blood tests showed her to be Rh-negative. He wanted to make sure her baby would not be born Rh-positive and be a risk for hemolytic disease, scheduling her to be admitted on Thursday to Maine Medical. She and Ben were to be at the hospital by 8 o'clock in the morning. She hoped and prayed there would be no complications and that by early afternoon they would have their baby girl or boy.

Once in the living room, Sarah sat down on the couch, pushed the power button on the television remote and waited for another contraction. She flipped channels, trying to find a news or weather report. She finally realized that it was only 8:45 p.m. and the news would not be on for another fifteen minutes. She pushed the MUTE button, laid her head against the back of the couch, covered herself with a blanket and waited for another contraction. Nothing. Maybe this was another false alarm she thought to herself. She hoped upon all that was holy that it was. She did not need to go into labor until Ben got home, and she knew he would be calling her any minute to say he was on his way.

She heaved a big sigh, patted her stomach as to say, "Everything is okay little one," closed her eyes and remembered the note Ben left her this morning on her coffee cup. He loved her so very much, was such a thoughtful and caring man, and she remembered when they first met.

* * * * *

Sarah was a city girl but she loved the water. As far back as she could remember, she and her parents had spent part of every summer vacationing in Booth Bay Harbor. She wasn't sure what she loved most about the Bay. Was it the large vessels gracefully sailing into the harbor, the friendliness of the locals, the soft-sandy beaches, the jagged cliffs, the intimate coves or the salty air? This small town seemed to bring her refuge and comfort, from what she did not know. It just did. She knew that the harbor was where she belonged. After high school graduation, she came to Booth Bay for one summer, then came every summer afterward until she graduated from Chelsea College. She shared a small apartment overlooking the bay with Jeannelle, a college friend. They rented furniture, including a piano for Sarah, and she taught weekly lessons to eight advanced music students in the area. She worked part time on the marina as a waitress during the evenings, and during the little free time she had, she spent hiking, on the water or at the docks. Sarah loved her life, her music, her friends, the food and, most of all, the sea.

Sarah enjoyed living in Booth Bay Harbor, but she missed the closeness she had with her parents. She spoke with her mother often, and one late night she called her mom and told her, "Mom, there is only one thing missing in my life, I would love to marry and have a family. I want to be happy like you and daddy. Do you think I will ever find the right guy, mom? A guy like daddy maybe?"

Mary Anne Waverly assured her daughter that the right man would come along, and when he did, the time would be right for her too. "You have your music," her mother said. 'Don't give up on your career just yet. You have always wanted to teach, and you have plenty of time to marry and have babies."

Sarah agreed. She did love her music, and teaching had always been her dream. She learned to play the piano when she was very young, worked hard at playing, and learning came easily for her. When she received a scholarship to Chelsea College in Boston she and her parents drove to Boston together to enroll her. She took a full class load, studied hard and carried a 3.8 grade average her first two years. She was invited to and found time to sing in the Boston Chorale. She played piano and organ for several church functions during the school year, taught piano lessons two nights a week, and found time to date and hang out with her friends. She longed to find just the right man with whom she could spend the rest of her life. She dreamed of a man who would hold her in his arms and tell her he loved her. She wanted romantic candlelight dinners. She wanted a man who would make passionate love with her in her apartment overlooking the bay. She wanted a man who wanted to marry and have lots of babies.

"Oh, what a dreamer you are," she would say to herself, "You have plenty of time, and you have plenty of dates, just enjoy yourself for awhile. After all, you are only twenty-one years old!"

It was during the summer between her second and third year of college that she met Ben. She had been working two summers at the Aqua Bay Marina Restaurant when she had written in to the manager and requested a later start time. She invited three of her best friends to come with her for two weeks right after classes ended. After the two weeks of vacation, the friends would go their separate ways, and Sarah would continue her summer jobs in Booth Bay Harbor. She had mentioned to her friends more than once about this beautiful, small town by the sea with its salty air, quaint little shops, ice cream parlors and marvelous fish and chips. She had previously told them stories about the times she had spent summers there. She also promised to show them how to fish and how to look for the perfect seashell. She couldn't wait for them to take part in the nightlife at the Tugboat Bar and Grill, and told them how many suntanned, muscular, sexy men they could meet. After making reservations for them to stay at the Aqua Bay Marina Hotel, she booked a day on a pleasure craft from the Ocean Front Rental Agency. She also promised they would eat the best lobster in all of Maine, probably more than once, and it would be the most perfect summer break ever! Not only did her friends have the perfect summer of their lives, but it turned out to be perfect for Sarah as well. She had met and fallen in love with Ben Kestwick.

After a day on the water, the four college friends went into the Watering Hole Restaurant on their third night in town. The restaurant was only a few blocks down from their hotel and from Sarah's apartment. Together, they walked along the pier, laughing and talking the entire way. They enjoyed the evening breeze whipping through their hair, the gorgeous pinks, oranges and blues of the setting sun sparkling on the deep blue water, and most of all, they enjoyed each other's company. These were the times they would remember forever.

The restaurant was crowded when they arrived. Jenna, the hostess, told them there would be about a thirty-minute wait if they wanted a table looking out over the bay.

"That's great, Jenna," Sarah said, a twinkle in her eye. "Call us when you have a table."

"Sure thing, Sarah," Jenna replied, "How is it you're not working this summer?"

"Oh, I will be soon," she said, "It's just that I have friends in town for a little while, and I'm showing them the sights. I'll be back to work soon enough."

The young women assured Jenna that they didn't mind waiting. They ordered colorful, fruity drinks in fancy plastic glasses from the bar and walked back outside to wait. Together, they stood against the rail and watched sailboats coming in and going out of the harbor. They watched seagulls diving for unaware fish and were intrigued by the sounds and smells of the harbor.

"This place is noted for Lobster Elegante," Sarah told the others. "It's a lobster and noodles dish. They use lobsters caught right here in the bay, and the noodles are homemade. It's a little spicy, but not bad. It's made with just a pinch of dry mustard. I understand a local woman made this dish popular. My mom makes it often, and it's a lobster dish you just have to have when you come to Booth Bay. I can't wait for you all to try it."

They all agreed to order the Elegante and sipped their drinks, continuing their "girl talk" and before the thirty minutes was up, their names were called.

A pleasant waiter directed them to a table by the window and laid a menu in front of each of them. He freshened up their drinks throughout the evening, and more than once returned to their table and asked how they were doing. They assured him that it was the best lobster and noodles they had ever eaten.

They spent over two hours eating, drinking and chatting about college, their families, their music classes, and how great it was to be on break. When they were about to ask for a dessert menu, Sarah noticed a tall, nice looking young man walk into the restaurant. He sat down at the bar, ordered, and from the sound of the laughter, she figured he must know the bartender quite well. Anne Marie was in her late twenties, very attractive with the cutest dark curly hair. She was very friendly and made great drinks. Sarah had become acquainted with her early on and got to know her quite well in the past two years. As she turned her eyes away from Anne Marie, she looked the cute guy's way the second time and he caught her eyeing him. He smiled and winked at her. Sarah turned back to her friends, slightly embarrassed, and continued their conversation.

"What's up, Sarah?" her friends asked. "You look a little flushed, too many Tooty Fruitys?"

The four of them chuckled as Sarah mentioned the good-looking guy at the bar watching them. They all turned to look at him at the same time.

"Don't look! You guys are making it worse," she pleaded. But it was too late. The tall, blond, good looking guy was on his way over to their table."

"Hello, ladies," he said. "My sources tell me you four are down here for some fun in the sun. Can I buy you all a drink?"

"No, thank you!" Sarah said quite unconvincingly, but the other three did not agree. "Sure, join us," they said, "We can always use some more company."

So, the love story began. The girls all introduced themselves to Ben and he to them. They told him where they all lived, why they were in Booth Bay Harbor, that Sarah lived here during the summers and worked part time at the restaurant. By the time the evening was over thanks to her friends, Ben Kestwick knew just about everything there was to know about her. He knew she was from Millinocket and her daddy worked at the Mill. He knew she studied music, played the piano very well, and that she was beautiful! He knew she taught piano lessons, worked here at the Marina a couple nights a week, and that she was beautiful! He knew he wanted to see her again and not just because she was beautiful!

* * * * *

At 9:00 p.m. Sarah turned off the MUTE, and changed the television channel to the 9:00 p.m. news. The news came into Booth Bay Harbor via satellite from either Augusta or Portland, and she punched in the Portland station. The television anchorwoman talked politics and about a local murder. She told about another lost child, or perhaps it was a kidnapping, and local happenings in the Portland area.

When the meteorologist came on with the local weather, Sarah was glad that the news was over. "Isn't there ever any good news any more?" she wondered. She adjusted her clumsy body to a more comfortable sitting position at the edge of the couch and the baby stirred. "I want to pay close attention to the weather forecast," she told her child. She turned her head towards the living room window, and although there was only blackness, she noticed streams of water pouring down the outside windowpane. It looked like it was raining much harder than before. She listened as the brunette with entirely too much makeup told of a serious gale blowing in from the northwest. She reported that the storm had come on very suddenly, and rain would continue throughout the night and possibly turn to snow. She said that, by morning, it would be through the Portland and surrounding areas, and the temperature would be only in the high 40's by noon.

Sarah turned the sound down on the television, looked toward the window as she pulled herself up to a standing position. As she walked to the kitchen to make herself a cup of tea, she heard a knock at the door. Her heart skipped a beat and the baby inside of her moved suddenly. As she walked to the front door, her heart seemed to be beating normally again, and she opened the door. Her father-in-law, Martin Kestwick, was waiting on her doorstep. He said hello and asked if he could come in.

CHAPTER SEVEN

Natalie Pickford Andrews pulled into her driveway in Brunswick thirty minutes after Jacqueline finished her piano lesson. It was starting to rain slightly, and she encouraged Jacqueline to run to the house quickly so as not to get wet. Natalie picked up her purse from the front seat of her '99 silver-gray Chrysler, closed and locked the doors, and walked swiftly to the house herself. Once the front door was unlocked and they were inside, she took off her coat, asked Jacqueline to do the same, and asked her to hang them both up in the hall closet. Jacqueline did as she was told.

Natalie made sure the door was locked and the dead bolt secured. She walked into the kitchen and asked the eight-year old to follow her. Natalie opened the refrigerator, took out two apples, washed them at the kitchen sink, and they both sat down at the table. She handed an apple to Jacqueline and took a bite of her own.

"You did very well today, Jacqueline," Natalie said. "I was very proud of you. Your music is coming along very nicely, and Sarah seemed to be proud of you, too. Just remember, as long as you continue to practice two hours every day, do your chores, and do as you are told, you will be allowed to watch a little more television every day. And you will not have to be in your room so much. Are we clear about all of this?"

"Yes m-m-a-a-m," the child said timidly, stuttering.

Jacqueline took a small bite of her apple, chewed it thoroughly as she was told, swallowed, and then asked if she could have a glass of milk.

"After you have eaten the entire apple," Natalie coolly assured her. "Then you can have something to drink. Jacqueline, you also did well today by not getting into a conversation with Sarah. You know what I told you, only talk about your lessons when you are with her, and remember we do not want to be overly friendly with anyone we don't know well."

Jacqueline nodded her head in agreement. She wanted so badly to tell Natalie that Sarah was someone she liked very much and not just as a teacher. She knew better and kept those thoughts to herself.

Jacqueline ate the entire apple and then wrapped the core in a napkin before throwing it into the trashcan under the sink. She reached for the black handle on the cupboard door, opened it and took out a glass. She handed it to Natalie, who retrieved the carton of milk from the refrigerator. She poured a small amount into the glass and handed it to Jacqueline, who drank all of it, wishing she could have more. She rinsed and set the glass in the rack in the sink and went to stand at the table.

Natalie asked her to use the bathroom, wash and dry her hands, and then to begin to practice the piano. As if in a robotic state Jacqueline once again, did as she was told.

Natalie saw to it that Jacqueline was seated at the piano before going into her bedroom. The room was cold and dark, but she did not turn on the overhead light. Dark blue drapes hung over the windows, covering closed venetian blinds. A dark blue and gray comforter covered the standard size bed where two old fashioned pillows were the only accent. In the corner of the room stood an old mahogany desk and chair, and on top of the desk sat a milk glass lamp, a computer and printer. Hanging on the west wall of the room were three photos: one, a young man and woman perhaps in their mid-twenties, and two other photos of babies, each maybe two or three days old—birth photos. Natalie walked up to the photos and gently touched each one. She pulled out the chair from the desk and sat down, turning on the lamp and taking a large manila envelope from the drawer. The left hand corner of the envelope was stamped with a return address from Portland County Courts. She laid it on the desk and folded her hands over the envelope, closing her eyes as if in a meditative prayerful state. After a few minutes, she opened her eyes and the file and took out several different documents. They included birth certificates, court documents, prison release papers, personal letters and more. She picked up one of the official looking documents, leaned back in her chair and began to read.

She read the title of the document, "Final Decree of Adoption, State of Maine," something she had done hundreds of times before, and laid the paper aside. She picked out another document that read "Certificate of Live Birth, State of Maine". As she read the certificate over and over and leaned back in her chair, she heard the sounds of piano scales. She heard the musical scales being played, over and over.

"Jacqueline is practicing just like I told her," she mumbled, "She really is a good little girl, but she's not my Melanie Anne, but in time I will teach her to be."

Natalie read the name on the birth certificate again. Sean Michael Pickford, born February 15, 1986. Mother, Natalie Anne Pickford, father, unknown. It stated the hospital, Maine Medical Center, and the piece of paper was a legal, signed and sealed document. Natalie remembered the date like it was yesterday.

It was her sixteenth birthday. Her mother insisted that she see the family doctor. Natalie already knew her nausea and stomach problems were more than just the flu or bad food, and she was sure her mother knew it too. They were both correct. Natalie was two months pregnant.

"Who is the father?" her mother and father asked.

"I don't know," she insisted. "A man forced me into his car after a school party. He took me to his apartment, made me swallow pills and he raped me!"

Her parents were certain that at least part of her story was true. She had taken drugs. Her mother had found drugs in her bedroom dresser drawers on more than one occasion. When she approached Natalie about them, Natalie denied knowing anything about any drugs. When boys came to pick her up for dates, her parents were certain all types of things were going on: drugs, alcohol, sex. They did not believe that this pregnancy was due to rape, but Natalie would give up no boy's name, no matter how long and hard they drilled her.

The Pickfords were not the best parents, but they knew their only daughter was getting into trouble both in and out of school and knew she was getting a bad reputation. They heard rumors in town and at school events about Natalie and her drug and sexual habits. Their friends talked about Natalie behind her parents' backs. Her eleventh grade teachers called at least once a week to ask where Natalie was. Why isn't she in class? She is missing tests, she will not graduate if she doesn't improve. Her father caught her stealing money out of her own mother's purse and disciplined her. Her math teacher caught her stealing money from students' lockers, and the principal expelled her for three days. The Pickfords knew they were losing all control over their teenage daughter, but nothing they did helped her. As they were older, in their late fifties when Natalie was a teenager, they were not certain how to help her.

The Pickfords did ask for help from a school and a church counselor, and they both suggested an appointment at the county's mental health center. However, none of the counseling helped and Natalie made no attempt to change. She stayed out late at night so her parents grounded her. They kept her from sporting and school events, took her driver's license and car keys away, and she still got away from the house and into more trouble.

Natalie was asked to leave school when she learned she was pregnant. Six months later, she gave birth to a beautiful blond-haired baby boy. She named him Sean Michael Pickford, but she never planned to keep him. Three days after his birth and with approval and signed permission from her parents, Natalie watched as Sean Michael was taken away and placed in a foster home. With permission from the hospital administration, the Pickfords received one photo of their grandson. Natalie never shed one tear for her son. Four days later, Sean Michael was returned to the children's hospital in Portland, suffering from severe symptoms of drug and alcohol syndrome. After several weeks in intensive care and over a year of hospital care, therapy and foster homes, a loving family adopted Sean Michael. Natalie or her parents never heard of him again, and, as far as Natalie was concerned, it was a part of her life that never happened. She kept the photo of her child on the wall as a painful reminder of giving him up. She honestly had no idea who Sean's father was.

* * * * *

Natalie snapped out of her trance, stood up and went to check on Jacqueline. She was sitting at the piano, but she was not practicing. As Natalie approached, she could see Jacqueline was crying. She sat down next to her, took a tissue from the box on the piano and gently wiped her tears.

"What is it, Jacqueline?" she asked. "Why are you crying? Are you sick?"

"I want my mother," the timid child responded. "I want to go home."

This is your home!" Natalie said harshly, grabbing Jacqueline's shoulders and turning her face towards her own. "I have told you this before: I am your mama, and this is your home! Have you forgotten?"

"No, I just want to go home," she cried, "I just want to go home."

Natalie took a deep breath, calming herself down before speaking to the child again.

"You remember, Jacqueline," she said in a calmer tone. "Your parents could not keep you any longer, and they asked me to take care of you. You are my little girl now. Remember at school when I saw you on the playground, you said we could be friends. You said you wanted a new dolly and I got it for you. You said you liked to play the piano, and I got you a piano and lessons. I buy you the food you like and dress you in pretty clothes."

Natalie's tone of voice began to sharpen once again when she said, "Remember, Jacqueline. Remember, if you do not say I am your mama and do as you are told, you will be locked up in your room all day long. Do you remember? You will not get to watch television or go out to play. You will be locked up! Do you remember? I am your mother now, and you listen to me and do as you are told! Do you remember?"

Jacqueline cried harder. The more Natalie raised her voice, the more Jacqueline cried. She started to stand up, and Natalie sat her down hard on the piano bench. She continued to sob uncontrollably. Natalie was now out of control. She took the child by the arm, dragged her into the extra bedroom, threw her down on the bed and walked out. She locked the door behind her.

"There will be no supper nor any television or books for you tonight," she screamed. "You will learn to obey me, Jacqueline, you will learn to obey me!"

She returned to the kitchen, mumbling. "I must teach this child to love and obey me," she said more calmly now. "She is my child, my child, I have always deserved to have a child, and my babies were always taken away from me, so I deserve Jacqueline. She is mine, and I will teach her, teach her to love me. She will learn sooner or later to love me."

Natalie got a glass of water from the kitchen faucet, drank it down without a breath and returned to her bedroom. As she passed Jacqueline's room, she could still her crying, but she ignored the sounds. "She will learn," Natalie said to herself, "She will learn."

Back in her room she first opened the drapes, pulled up the venetian blinds and looked outside. It was dusk, and the rain was coming down hard. She noticed that her neighbor's lights were on. Most of them, she presumed, were getting ready to sit down to supper. "There will be no supper for you tonight, Jacqueline," she muttered to herself. "I will show you who's in charge here. No supper for you!" As Natalie looked up and down her street, she didn't notice her new neighbor standing on her front porch, taking the mail from her mail box, the neighbor who watched Natalie on a daily basis from directly across the street.

She closed the blinds and the drapes and sat down at the desk. She looked at Sean's birth certificate once again and put it back into the large manila envelope. She smiled as she pulled another legal document out of the packet. It also read, "Certificate of Live Birth, State of Maine". This time she read, Melanie Anne Pickford, born January 25, 1987, Maine Medical Center mother, Natalie Anne Pickford, father, Joseph Spencer. She held the document close to her chest, got up from her chair and walked to where the baby photos hung on the wall. She took one of the photos down, looked at it for a moment, and after a few moments gently put it back.

"Oh, Melanie Anne," she cried, "Why did I ever let them take you from me? You were mine, no one else's."

Suddenly, as before with Jacqueline, she changed from a gentle and kind mother to a mysterious and evil woman. Her body stiffened, her eyes darkened and her mouth tightened. She took quick and shallow breaths and, with an evil voice, she addressed the photos on the wall.

"I will get even. I will get my baby back! I will, and it will be soon! Jacqueline must have a sister. I will get my baby back, and no one can stop me this time."

Her evil eyes slowly returned to their natural dark green as she turned off the lamp and walked into the living room. She listened for a moment at the door, but there were no sounds coming from the extra bedroom. She sat down on the couch, picked up a magazine and began to read. As she read, she seemed to calm down. Her breathing became normal, and she let out a big sigh. Her thoughts went back to yesterday in Booth Bay Harbor.

She recalled the man who opened the door for her and Jacqueline at the bank. She was sure it was Joe Spencer. When she saw him again later on the docks, she was positive it was Joe, the young man she had loved more than anyone else in the world. The man who promised to love her, protect her, spend his life with her and who was Melanie Anne's daddy. It was Joe Spencer, the man she had not seen since she was released from prison nearly twenty years ago. It had been like seeing a ghost.

She didn't plan to go to the bank today, but she needed a couple of money orders. She had her car repaired last week, and now it needed new tires and everything was more costly than she planned. She also needed money to pay for Jacqueline's piano lessons and to get her hair dyed again.

More than anything, she needed always to have money available in case she needed to move from the area quickly. Her contact was late paying her this week, and, although she sold her quota of drugs this month, he was late coming through with her share. She kept some cash in her house, well hidden, for emergencies, but she couldn't take a chance on using that money. She always had to be prepared for emergencies. She never used checks for any financial transactions, only money orders or cash. She couldn't take a chance on anyone locating her or coming after her from information printed on bank checks. She chose to bank in Booth Bay Harbor rather than in Brunswick. That way there was never an easy way to trace her. If anyone did try to track her down, she would be gone in a minute. She was used to moving, and moving quickly.

It was ironic she had run into Joe, if indeed it really was him. She wondered what he was doing in Booth Bay Harbor. Last she heard, he was living in or around Boston.

"I will have to look into this," she thought, "I can't have anyone messing up my plan or finding out about Jacqueline."

She wondered, however, how he was. Was he happy? Was he married? Did he ever think of her and their baby? Her stomach knotted up and her heart ached just thinking of Joe Spencer. She also smiled at the thought of him, as she thought of those years long ago.

*   *   *   *   *

Joe Spencer was a sophomore in high school when his parents moved the family to the Portland area. Natalie was a junior in the same school, Portland Senior High. The word at school was that Joe Spencer had been in trouble with the cops. He spent time in a juvenile delinquency school on drug charges, but now his life was completely back on track. His parents felt the only way to keep him off drugs was to take him away from the troublesome area they lived in and move the family to a different city. They chose Portland.

Even before the move to Portland, Joe was a popular student. He studied hard, made good grades, played sports and was in the top of his class. Keeping up good grades and the constant peer pressure was hard.

One night after a basketball game, a friend took him aside and offered him drugs. He smoked a joint. He liked it. It seemed to take the pressure off, and, before he knew it, he was smoking more and needing it more. A few weeks later while out trying to score, he and two other students were caught by two undercover police detectives posing as dealers. The judge let Joe and his friends off on probation the first time, but the second time Joe was caught the judge sentenced him to the juvenile correctional school for ten months.

"To prove a point," the judge said, "Maybe this time you will straighten up, get clean, and your drug buddies will see what happens when you get caught."

He warned Joe and his parents that there would be no next time. If he bought drugs again and was caught, he would be sent to the Maine Correctional Facility in Windham, and that was no place for a sixteen-year-old kid.

Joe learned a lot being locked up. He fought hard to get clean and did everything his teachers and counselors asked him. He took all the classes needed to pass his sophomore year requirements, and due to good behavior, was released back to his parents in less than the allotted time. Joe was sincerely sorry for what he had done and told his parents so. He asked for their forgiveness and promised to make up for his mistakes. Had his parents known what lay ahead by moving from the small town of Rumford to the big city of Portland, they may not have been quite so anxious to go.

Joe immediately settled in at Portland High School. He made the basketball team, studied hard, and was as popular as he had been at his previous school, stayed clean and met Natalie Pickford.

Natalie was a beautiful, high-spirited girl, a grade ahead of Joe. She flirted with him while passing his locker, sat next to him at lunchtime in the cafeteria, and wrote and passed him notes in study hall, the only class they shared. Several students told him that she was on drugs at one time, had been pregnant and dropped out of school for a while, but now she was clean, just like Joe. What Joe or any of his friends didn't know was that Natalie was now dealing drugs instead of using them. Joe had no idea she was about to pull him into her web of desire and distribution of drugs.

One night after a basketball game, Joe met up with Natalie and some of her friends. They went out for burgers, rode around town for an hour or so, and then they dropped him off early.

A week later she asked him out. "There's a party on Friday night," she told him, "Would you like to come with me?"

He agreed and said he would pick her up at 7:30 p.m. but he had a game on Saturday, and he couldn't be out too late.

She assured him that it would be fun, that they could leave at any time, and he asked her to come with him to the game the next night.

Several of Joe's friends, as well as kids he had never seen before, were at the party. The word at school was that these kinds of parties were held often when parents were out of town. The beer flowed freely, guys and gals smoked pot and made out on couches, on beds and on the carpeted floors. Joe turned down all offers of alcohol and drugs but he stayed out past his basketball coach's curfew. He and Natalie found they could talk for hours. They talked about their earlier teenage years, both of their past drug problems, her pregnancy, and, before they knew it, it was 3:00 a.m. Joe knew he was in trouble.

He was right. His coach benched him for the Saturday night game and although Portland High School won, Joe was suspended for two more games. His parents grounded him for two weeks, and during that time he only saw Natalie in study hall.

Throughout the school year, Natalie and Joe's relationship blossomed. They spent as much time together as possible. Joe didn't question the nights she told him she was busy and couldn't see him.

"There are just some nights I have things to do," she would tell Joe, "Girl things." Joe had no idea that she was dealing drugs.

With Joe's help, Natalie improved her grades and graduation actually looked like a possibility. The two of them were inseparable, and Joe was sure he was in love. He was only a junior and was being considered for a full basketball scholarship, but he couldn't see anything except his relationship and future with Natalie.

One night after a basketball game, Joe asked Natalie out to a movie. It was a memorable movie and a beautiful night, and he had given her a Promise Ring. They talked until the early hours of the morning. Joe shared with her his dreams of college and basketball and Natalie shared with him how much she loved children and how she wished she had kept her baby. She and Joe had gone to her parents' home, sneaked quietly into the house and into her bedroom. There, they made love for the first time in her old-fashioned four-poster bed. Joe knew she wasn't a virgin, and he knew he should use a condom, but they were so filled with passion, so much in love, and so ready for lovemaking, they used nothing. That night their love child, Melanie Anne, was conceived.

* * * * *

Thinking of Joe calmed Natalie down temporarily, and instead of the hateful mother she had been an hour or so earlier, she had a change of heart about giving Jacqueline supper. Going to her room to let her out, she unlocked the door with a key held by a gold chain around her neck, opened the door and went in. Jacqueline was asleep, holding tightly to her doll. Her face was flushed and tear stained. Natalie gently touched her face, thinking how beautiful she was, and how much she wanted her to accept her as her real mama. Jacqueline stirred, opened her eyes, reached up and gave Natalie a big hug.

"I will not be a bad girl anymore, mama," she said quietly. "I will be a good girl for you. Can I come out now?"

"Yes, sweetheart," Natalie said sincerely, "You may. Let's you and I fix some macaroni and cheese together, play a game, have some ice cream and maybe watch a little television until bedtime. We can skip your school lessons tonight, but we'll have to study hard tomorrow to catch up, won't we?"

"Yes," the child said cautiously, "I will study hard tomorrow and do as you asked me, and practice my piano lesson too. I have my scales down real good, did you hear me playing them?"

"I certainly did," Natalie said, giving her a big hug. "I certainly did."

For the time being, Natalie was a sweet mother again. She took Jacqueline's hand as they walked into the kitchen. She took down a box of macaroni and cheese from the cupboard and put a pot of water on to boil. All thoughts of Joe Spencer or a baby named Melanie Anne left her mind. She was happy at this moment, making supper with her child Jacqueline, the child she truly believed to be her own.

"I am her mother," Natalie said smiling to herself, "I am Jacqueline's mother.

CHAPTER EIGHT

Sarah was only a little surprised when she saw Martin standing on her front stoop. "Come in. Come in. What a surprise," she said to Martin. "What brings you out here in a rain storm?" She raised her hands up to the sky as if in defiance of the rain gods and she thought, "There is no way Martin would come and see me this late at night if everything was okay with Ben. The SARAH JEANNE must have not made it into port."

"Come in, come in, Martin," she repeated. "You will catch your death out here. Isn't this rain something? I wonder if it will turn to snow yet tonight?"

She tried to cover up her anxiety with small talk and swallowed hard to keep her composure. Martin walked through the door into her living room, turned to her, and, as she looked into his eyes, she asked him softly, "It's Ben, isn't it?"

Martin said yes, shed his wet raincoat, and asked her to sit down on the couch with him. He first asked if she was feeling okay. When she said yes, she was fine he took her hand in his and calmly told her that Ben still had not returned from his day of trapping.

"Captain Ron called me about 8:00 p.m. and I made the decision to contact the Coast Guard," he told her. "I hope that was okay, Sarah, and I wasn't out of line to call Lieutenant Casey?"

Tears welled up in Martin's eyes as he continued. "Portland sent two boats out an hour or so ago, but it's too stormy and too dark for a chopper. If they haven't found Ben and Jeremy by morning, they'll send out a chopper then, plus two more boats."

Sarah, feeling anxious but showing incredible calm, shared with her father-in-law, Martin, that she was glad he had contacted the Port Authority and the Guard. She assured him that everything would be fine and for him not to worry. Her unborn child moved and kicked and she assured herself of the same thing. She patted her stomach with her left hand and continued holding Martin's hand with the other.

"I had a call from Ron earlier," she said, "and I'm so glad he called you next Martin." Looking into her father-in-law's deep blue, but sad puppy-like eyes, she tried to find the right words to comfort him. She was certain they would find both men safe, and find them soon. She couldn't understand why she felt so sure, so confident, but she did. Sarah thought to herself that maybe it was because she didn't wish to disturb her baby, or she thought, "It's because I do not want to go into labor without Ben at my side." If she got too upset she was afraid her contractions would start up again, and now was not the right time.

"I know Ben," she said, looking into Martin's strained but gentle face. "He is the best there is at what he does and at handling the boat on rough seas. If anyone can handle a boat in times like these, it's Ben. I know he'll be fine. I believe that with all my heart, and, Martin, you should believe it, too. After all, you are the one who taught him everything he knows, especially to be tough and to handle a boat on both calm and rough seas."

She smiled at him, gently touched his face with her soft warm hand and turned and kissed him on the cheek. As his hand came up to acknowledge her touch, he laid his hand over hers. "Smooth hands with long, slender fingers, such a beautiful woman you are, Sarah, and so much talent for the piano," he told her. "My son chose a wonderful woman to be his wife, and she will make a wonderful mother, too."

Sarah smiled at her father-in-law, clasped his hand a little harder and thanked him for those kind words.

Martin looked up into his daughter-in-law's eyes, amazed at this beautiful woman's calm demeanor. He felt a tinge of guilt for the way he had been acting the past year and a half after losing his beloved Jenny. He would apologize to her and Ben, and try in the future to be a better father, father-in-law and an even better grandfather. He smiled at the thought of a baby boy bouncing on his knee, just like he used to do with Ben.

Out loud and without thinking, Martin said, "A grandfather, imagine me as a grandfather."

Sarah, somewhat startled, began to laugh just as Martin looked upward, smiled and said in a soft, loving voice, "Jenny, I'm going to be a grandfather, Lord bless me, I'm going to be a grandpa!"

Sarah and Martin laughed together. She had no idea what he had been thinking, but if it made him laugh and it took his mind off of his son, then she was a little more at ease, too.

* * * * *

Martin Kestwick had loved Jenny like no man had loved a wife before him...or at least that's what he always told her. "I love you more than life itself. More than cherry pie or root beer floats or lobster and noodles," he would tell her. "I even love you more than my boat!" Jenny Lynn would laugh at him, give him a big kiss and a bear hug, and that's the way it had been for thirty some years. He even changed the name on the #2 boat to the JENNY LYNN and then, one day, the real Jenny Lynn was gone. Too soon, she was taken from him and from their sons, and Martin grieved. He grieved long and hard and continued to do so even now.

Martin Kestwick always considered himself a strong man, both physically and emotionally. He worked hard his entire life. When he was a child of maybe twelve or thirteen, his father put him to work on the docks for a few hours each day after school. He loved the water, cleaning up the docks, even at times helping to weigh in the loads. He made sure his homework was done every day, doing most of it at school, just to be able to spend more time at the harbor. As he got older, he had more chores to take care of at home, more studies and extracurricular activities to contend with, but he still found time to work for his father. He loved the fishing business, walking the docks and watching the sailboats come in and out of the harbor. He loved the sights and sounds and the smell of the sea. But most of all, he loved his father.

"You'll be as good a lobster trapper as me and your grand pappy," Martin's father had told him, and he had turned out to be just that, an excellent boat captain and an even better lobster trapper. When Martin's parents passed away, both within a year of each other, Martin and his brother Benjamin took over the Kestwick Fishing Company. Benjamin stayed on for about five years, married, had a family and moved to Seattle. Martin, however, met a beautiful young lady, married, had little Ben and his brother, and continued in the family fishing business. He never regretted his life. This small fishing town of Booth Bay Harbor was his home and his life. He never planned to leave. "I want to be buried here," he would tell Jenny. He just didn't realize that his beautiful Jenny would be buried so soon, and before him.

*   *   *   *   *

Martin watched Sarah, so filled with child, so calm, and as he turned to her, tears began streaming down his face. She asked again if he was okay and told him please not to worry.

At first, no words came out of his mouth. Then, tearfully, he told her how much she meant to him, how much he missed his wife, and how sorry he was for being in such a depressed state all of the time.

"I miss my wife so very much, Sarah," he said. Sobbing now, he let Sarah take him in her arms and comfort him. "I just can't lose my son, too, I just can't."

Sarah comforted her father-in-law for a few more minutes. When he was calmer and the tears had subsided, she asked if he would like a cup of tea. When he said yes, but said he would be happy to fix a cup for the both of them, she said that would be nice but suggested they do it together. Martin stood up first and assisted Sarah to an upright position and they walked into the kitchen. Sarah flipped on the light switch and noticed heavy beads of water still flowing down the outside of her kitchen window. As she pushed aside the lacy curtains and peered out into the blackness, she was positive she saw small, white flakes gently beginning to fall. Not wanting to alarm Martin, she said the weather looked about the same and put the blue flowered teakettle on to boil water. She took two coffee mugs from the cupboard, the bottle of lemon juice from the refrigerator and two bags of green tea from a canister on the counter. She set the three items on the table and waited for the kettle to whistle.

"How is the baby, Sarah?" Martin asked, hoping to change the somber mood. "Is it kicking and screaming to get out of there?"

He touched her stomach, gave the baby a little pat, and just then the baby kicked hard. Martin jerked back, somewhat startled, and said, "Goodness. It's been a long time since I felt an unborn baby move like that," and getting as close to her as he could without crushing her, he bent over and gave Sarah's tummy a sweet, loving little kiss.

"It likes the touch of his grandpa, I guess," Sarah said laughing. "This child has been kicking and moving all week long. I can hardly sleep at night anymore due to its movin'-n-shakin'! Yesterday and today all I have done is sleep during the daytime hours, and, yes, eat!" she said chuckling. "It's time for this little one to come into the world before I look like an elephant and have bags under both eyes."

The teakettle whistled, and Sarah took the kettle from the stove, poured steaming hot water into their mugs and added a tea bag and drop or two of lemon to each cup. She shared with Martin how her days were going, busy but happy. She told him about her and Ben's plans for the upcoming baby, her students and, as an after thought, suggested he see the nursery before he left. They talked for about twenty minutes over hot tea and lemon. Then looking at the clock, she realized she needed to call her parents and tell them about Ben. "I need to call my mother, Martin," she said calmly. "Mom is planning to come and stay with me on Wednesday and go with Ben and me to the hospital on Thursday. I better tell her about Ben. I know she will insist on coming yet tonight, perhaps I can talk her out of that. I'm okay, and you're here, close by."

"I think that's a good idea, Sarah," Martin said, "Your mom should be here with you. I don't think you should be alone at this time, both because of Ben and because you're so close to delivering my grandson."

"Grandson! Grandson!" Sarah laughed, as she reminded Martin as before that this baby just possibly was a girl. She asked Martin if he wanted more tea, and, when he said yes, she stood up, picked up the kettle and refilled both their cups. She picked up her cup and immediately excused herself to use the telephone in the other room. Knowing she needed some privacy, Martin enjoyed his second cup of tea but deep inside his stomach was churning. His heart was aching. He closed his eyes and murmured a short prayer, a prayer asking for the safety of his son. He had always been a religious person, maybe not as loyal as he should be to the church, but he believed in God and a hereafter. He had to believe in Heaven, because he wanted to see his dear Jenny again some day.

"Please God," he murmured, "Please calm the seas, as you did once before when your Son was on a fishing boat. Calm the seas, and stop this raging storm and bring my son back to his family. I believe in you, and I believe in my son, grant this, please, dear God, please." His eyes stayed closed and a sudden calm came over him. He had not felt this calm in a long, long time, not since before he buried Jenny. He had been angry then, angry with Jenny, angry with God and angry with himself. But now, Martin knew in his heart as Sarah did, Ben would come back to them and it would be soon. He continued to sip on his tea, thought of his Jenny, Ben, and closed his eyes one more time in thanksgiving. "God is good," he said to himself, "God is good."

Sarah picked the telephone up off its cradle and sat down in the brown and black upholstered rocking chair. She had sat in this old chair a few times at the Kestwick home, and after Jenny's death, Martin had insisted that she and Ben take the chair.

"Jenny used this chair when she was pregnant with Ben and his brother," he had told them proudly, "She would want you to use it when you have a child, Sarah." Sarah had accepted the gift, and, at the time, it seemed to lift Martin's spirits.

She dialed her parent's number and waited only a short time for an answer.

"Hello," came her father's voice on the line.

"Hi, daddy," Sarah said, her voice sounding like that of a little girl. "It's Sarah."

"Hi, my sweet girl," Jonas said sweetly. "How are you? Okay?" Knowing what she was about to tell them, Jonas tried to remain calm but his heart was already beating fast.

"I'm fine, daddy," she said calmly. "I'm calling because, well, it's just that Martin is here because Ben hasn't made it back to the harbor tonight. I thought I should let you know."

"Oh, my," Jonas said, his voice breaking. "Do you need your mom and me to come down right away?"

"No, not yet, dad," she said, her voice changing back to that of a grown woman. "Martin has been in touch with the Port Authority and with the Coast Guard in Portland. The weather is so very bad here. They can't do much until morning. I feel that he will be home soon though, dad, and I don't want you and mom to worry. Ben is good on the seas; he knows what he's doing. I really am doing okay, and the baby is doing okay, too." Then with a quick change of thought, she asked to speak with her mother.

"Okay, Sarah," Jonas replied, "Here's your mom."

Mary Anne had been leaning over Jonas' shoulder, listening in earnest to hear the conversation. When Jonas handed her the telephone, he motioned to his wife, smiled just a little to let her know that Sarah was okay, and, by his facial expressions, suggested to her she please stay calm for all their sakes.

"Hello, honey," her mom said, hand shaking on the receiver. "Is everything okay?"

"I'm fine, mom," she said, "But Ben, Jeremy and the SARAH JEANNE have not returned to port. There's a terrible storm here—rain, and some snow, and really high winds. Martin is here with me, and he and Ron at the Port Authority have contacted the Coast Guard. They have already sent out two Aid Boats to look for Ben and Jeremy, but it's only been a short while ago. I am sure Ben is all right."

"He just has to be," her mother thought, "Sarah and her baby don't need this trauma right now. She's about to give birth. She needs her husband."

"Your father and I will come down right away," she said sharply. "I am already packed, daddy can throw a few things together, and we can be in Booth Bay by 11:00 p.m."

"Mom, mom," Sarah said, trying to calm her mother down. "Please listen. Wait for a little while longer will you? I truly believe that Ben will be back tonight. I just know it. I want you to sit tight, and I will call you in a little while and let you know what's happening. Martin is here, like I said before, and he'll stay with me."

"Have you had any pain today, Sarah?" she asked her only daughter.

"I had a couple of contractions, I think," she said calmly. "I don't think they were the real thing though, and only two. I know the baby is kicking and squirming a lot, wants out into the world I think, but right now I'm okay. I still think you can come in the morning sometime, but I promise, I will call you in the next hour or so, and we can decide more then. Mom, I just know Ben will be back soon. Believe me, I know him. Please try not to worry."

"Mom, let me talk to dad again, please," she asked her mother. Sarah knew she could talk her father into staying put in Millinockett until Sarah called them back. When it came to Sarah, her mother had always been quite a worrier. When anything out of the ordinary happened, minor issues or problems of any sort, her mother panicked. Sarah knew her father would stay in control and control her mother as well.

Jonas came back on the telephone and Sarah asked him to convince her mother to wait for her to call back before they made any decisions. He agreed they would make no decisions until she knew more about Ben. With that, Sarah told them that she loved them, not to worry, and she hung up.

Sarah laid her head against the back of the rocking chair, began to rock back and forth and closed her eyes. The rocking not only soothed her, but it seemed to soothe her unborn child as well. For over ten minutes, Sarah rocked with the rhythm of the moving chair, and her baby never moved once. Patting her stomach, she spoke soft words to her child, calming words that seemed to set her mind more at ease even more than before.

"Your daddy will be home soon," she said, "He misses us and knows that he has to be home to see you come into this world. A rainy and wet world, I might add."

She looked out the window to the left of the piano. It was snowing harder now. Sarah stopped rocking, stood up and walked into the kitchen. Martin was still seated at the kitchen table, seemingly deep in thought, hands on his cold cup of tea. He glanced up as Sarah entered the room.

Sarah, are you okay?" he asked. "Are your parents coming down?"

I'm fine Martin, just fine," she answered. "My mom wants to come right away, but I convinced her to stay home until we know more. Plus, the weather hasn't improved any, Martin, it's beginning to snow."

Sarah walked over to the kitchen window, moved the curtains just slightly and peered out. She watched the gently falling snow seemingly swallowed up by the fierce thrashing sea. Long winged seagulls sailed gracefully above, ignoring the gigantic waves crashing against the rocks below. As far as she could see, there was blackness—only dark, total, blackness.

"Martin, should we call the Coast Guard and see if there's any news?" she asked.

"We can," Martin said, "but they'll contact Ron first if there is any news, and then I am sure they will contact me. I asked them to call me immediately if there was anything I should know. Ron has the land-sea radio and they'll get through to him easier than trying to get me. Plus, I'm not home now am I, Sarah? I can't answer the telephone if I'm not home to answer one."

They both chuckled as they looked at one another. It was good to laugh even in hard times. Sarah reminded Martin it was time for him to get a cellular phone, and he agreed.

"You're right, Martin," she said, still chuckling. "If you're not home, they can't contact you on the telephone. Maybe you should go home for a little while. I'll be fine here by myself, and if you hear anything, please call me right away. If this little one starts giving me any trouble, I will call you right away. Deal?"

Martin agreed. He placed his teacup in the kitchen sink, looked out the kitchen window one more time and went to look for his coat.

As he approached the door with Sarah close by, he turned to her and gave her and the baby a loving hug. He promised to call her as soon as he got home and to call immediately if he heard any news from the Port Authority.

"I think you should eat something, and get some rest," he said to his daughter-in-law. "Try to get some sleep, take the telephone with you into the bedroom; I promise I will call when I know something."

With that, Martin was gone. He walked to his car, got in, started the car and turned on the windshield wipers. He turned the heater to defrost and turned on the lights. He sat quietly for just a few minutes as the car warmed up.

"The snow seems to be coming down harder," he thought to himself, or maybe it was just the fact that it looked heavier in the bright beam of the headlights. He put the car in drive, stepped on the gas and headed for home.

Snow was starting to accumulate as he continued his drive home. The Kestwick place was thirteen miles out of town, on the northeast side of the bay, but he didn't worry about the distance. He had a good vehicle with four-wheel drive, and the snow was just now beginning to stick to the roads. The snow was, however, beginning to cover the grassy areas. He noticed only a few blades of summer green grass still sticking up here and there above the soft, white blanket of snow. He continued in deep thought and found himself almost hypnotized by the beauty of it all.

*   *   *   *   *

Memories of Jenny flooded his mind. It was another day, similar to this one when he and Jenny and Ben had been caught in a snowstorm. They were young then. Ben was maybe seven years old, and his brother Tim was four. They left Tim with his grandparents and they had set out for a weekend of camping in the Sugarloaf Mountains area. It had been nice weather all week, and when they left Booth Bay Harbor around 4:00 p.m. on a Friday afternoon, there had been no word of rain or snow either on the coast or in the high country.

Martin had taken off work early. He promised they would go camping for a weekend, and the time had finally come. Leaves on the trees were already highlighted with brown, yellow and gold, but the nighttime temperatures were staying unseasonably warm. Ben was excited. He helped Jenny pack food items, their sleeping bags and clean clothes. Jonas stored the small camp stove, a three-gallon jug of water, fishing poles and tackle boxes in the back of the truck. The four-man tent he used on occasional fishing and hunting trips with friends was strapped down in the back of the truck as well, and they set out for a great weekend.

About fifty miles into the mountains, they began munching on salty cheese chips and sipping on ice-cold bottles of Coke. They sang a few verses of "Three Blind Mice" and "Old MacDonald" all the while watching for wild life.

"I really want to see a bear," Ben said, "but not too close to the truck. Are they black or brown bears up here, dad?"

"I've never seen one close up," Martin replied. "Not sure I want to, but word is that most of them are brown up here in the Sugarloaf area. Closest I ever came to a bear was when Fred Mathison, Gerald Foosman and I came hunting up here, back when you were just a pup."

"A pup," Ben exclaimed, "I was a pup?"

"That's what they call little boys sometimes," Jenny chimed in, "Pups." Ben laughed.

"Well, anyway, Ben," Martin continued, "Fred was determined to get himself a moose that year, and he and Gerald and I had been hunting all morning and never saw one creature of any kind. All of a sudden, we heard a rustling in the bushes close by and Gerald turned to aim his gun straight at the sounds. Lo and behold, a brown bear came walking slowly out of the bushes."

"How big was it?" Ben asked, his eyes wide with curiosity.

"That was the funny thing, Ben," Martin said smiling. "Gerald got scared to death, couldn't even aim straight. Fred set his gun to fire, and out comes this brown bear cub, maybe five months old. We knew we had to get out of there quick, because we knew where there was a bear cub, there's always a great big mama bear close by."

"Wow," Ben said, "A baby bear huh, dad? I would have loved to have seen that bear. I bet he was cute."

"He was cute alright," Martin said, "but what was cuter and funnier was seeing the look on Gerald's and Fred's faces, scared silly over a baby bear cub."

As the family continued on their trip, they talked and sang more songs, but Martin noticed dark storm clouds closing in on the blue skies. Jenny noticed it right away, too, when she mentioned something to Martin about it, his only reply was that it rained often in the late afternoons up here. There was no need to worry.

A few more miles and a half hour later, they drove into the Sugarloaf Mountain campgrounds. They paid the $10.00 campsite fee and set up their tent in front of a natural rock wall. There were only two or three other campers in their area. Martin figured more campers would come in on Saturday. Jenny fixed a light supper and later they sat around a roaring campfire, singing more silly songs and telling spooky stories when they heard the first sounds of distant thunder.

"Wow, that was thunder," Martin said, a bit concerned. "We'd better make sure we're ready to get into the tent quickly if it starts to rain. It's still a way off, I think, but rain is definitely coming. How about it, Ben? We may be sleeping in the tent in the rain tonight. This should be great fun."

Jenny wasn't quite as certain as her men were about how great sleeping in the rain might be, but being with her family was definitely the greatest. So, if sleeping in a tent with the rain falling made her men happy, then she would be happy too.

* * * * *

Martin remembered back to that night with a light spirited heart. He pulled into his driveway knowing his life, too, with a little more effort on his part, would be much better from now on. He stopped in the driveway, pushed OPEN on the garage door's remote control and drove into the garage. It would be more pleasant to get into a warm and dry car when he headed out to Sarah's again later and, hopefully, to the docks to see Ben. There was no need to park outside in the elements.

He opened the back door, walked into the kitchen, hung up his coat and took some leftover ham and a few slices of bread out of the refrigerator. He also took out a can of Pepsi, opened it and took a long drink. As he made and then ate his sandwich, he thought again of that camping trip so long ago when Jenny was alive and Ben had not gone missing.

* * * * *

The thunder boomers were getting closer and closer to the campground. It also began to lightning. Martin suggested they put out the campfire, put the lawn chairs in the truck and get into the tent.

"Will we get hit by the lightning, dad?" Ben had asked in his boyish voice.

"No, not if we're careful, Ben," Martin had assured him, "so help me get your mom and me settled into the tent, okay?"

Just then, a lightning bolt hit very close to the campground and the rain began. They quickly scurried into their tent and snuggled into their individual sleeping bags. They talked, laughed and joked about what a great day it had been for camping and fishing and joked about how many fish they had caught and how big they were.

"Maybe tomorrow we can really fish and not just pretend," Martin said. "It was fun, though, even if our day was cut short by the rain, right Ben? Right, Jenny?"

They all agreed. Martin and Jenny talked for another hour or so, listening to the falling rain and watching their son sleeping peacefully beside them. They had no idea as they slept the night away that the snow would begin to fall and fall hard.

Luckily, the tent was strong, and they were sheltered from the winds in part due to the rock wall behind their camping space. When they awoke early in the morning, one side of the tent was sagging from the weight of the snow. They couldn't believe they had slept through the entire night, as the weight of the snow on the tent was almost level with the tops of their heads.

"Oh, my goodness," Jenny remarked. "Martin, it snowed, what do we do now? We can't possibly get out of the tent without all of that snow coming down on top of us or splitting the tent. We will be covered in snow! Everything will get wet!"

Ben thought it was awesome. What a story to tell his friends back in Booth Bay Harbor.

"Well, we do have a small dilemma here," Martin said. "We're all going to get snow dumped on us if we don't first have a plan on how to get out of here."

Martin eased out of his sleeping bag, so as not to hit his head on the top of the tent, pushed gently on the tent, attempting to push the snow off to the sides.

"Better give me some help here, Ben," Martin said, "You push ever so gently on the top of the tent, and I'll push on the other side. Then the snow will all fall off to the sides and not in the front. Then we can unzip the tent without getting snow on your mother."

They all laughed, and, surprisingly enough, it worked. There was about four inches of snow on the tent. Luckily, the stakes and ropes held the tent in place as they gently pushed the snow off, and there was no damage done to the tent. Martin unzipped the door, and they all peered out of the doorway.

"It looks like Christmas morning," Ben exclaimed, as he took a run in the snow. Jenny felt she should stop him, after all he had no snow boots, but she let him go.

They didn't catch any fish on that trip, but they did build snowmen and cook hotdogs on the old cook stove. They went back to the harbor a day earlier than planned with wet socks and shoes, muddy boots and ready for showers. It had been a camping trip to remember—a rather unusual camping trip, but fun.

* * * * *

Martin finished his light supper, picked up the telephone and called Ron at the Port Authority. There was no new information. They could not reach the SARAH JEANNE by radio; Ben and Jeremy had not been found, and they had stopped the search until Wednesday. The weather is too bad, Ron told him, to keep the Coast Guard out any later this evening. No sense in losing more boats if the SARAH JEANNE was indeed lost. They would begin the search again early the next morning with a helicopter and four boats. For now, that's all Ron could promise Martin, and he told his friend how sorry he was there was not better news.

Martin spoke with Ron for a few more minutes including asking how his daughter-in-law was holding up.

"She's doing remarkably well," Martin told him. "I'm headed back over there in just a few minutes. She shouldn't be alone, not with a baby coming any time."

Martin hung up the telephone, took his coat from the back of a kitchen chair and opened the door to the garage with the remote. He got in the car, put his key in the ignition, started the car and as he backed out of the garage he noticed that the snow seemed to be slowing down. He also could have sworn he heard a voice speaking to him. "Jenny, is that you, honey?" He looked up, surprising himself that he was even asking such a silly question. "If it is you, Jenny, I'm feeling so much better today. I know you're gone and living in Heaven, and I think now I can accept that and get on with my life."

Smiling, Martin took one look back as he drove the car into the street. The telephone in his kitchen began to ring, but he did not hear it.

CHAPTER NINE

Sarah turned the handle on the sanded but not yet varnished closet door. She stepped forward, reached up and felt along the top shelf until she found the white box tied with blue ribbon. She carefully lifted the box from the shelf, being careful to neither drop it nor cause herself to stumble as she walked to the bedroom. She turned on the lamp and moved it just slightly to the right on the antique table. She set the precious box down and, while bracing herself on the arm of the matching antique chair, she turned around and carefully sat down on the bed. Her unborn child, seemingly upset by all of Sarah's stretching and reaching, kicked hard against her insides, causing her to flinch.

She felt a little chilly, so she picked up her grandmother's hand-made quilt, placed it over her lap and legs and picked up the box. As if in a stupor, she untied the blue satin ribbons, letting them fall to the floor. She opened the box, removing the lid and took out the white lace handkerchief and the small family Bible, laying them on the bed beside her. She picked out one of several white envelopes lying on the bottom of the box. Her hands began to tremble as she opened the larger envelope, took out the enclosed document and began to read the words. Almost in a whisper, Sarah read, "Sarah Jeanne Waverly and Benjamin Arnold Kestwick. Joined in Holy Matrimony, the twenty-seventh day of June, 2008, Millinockett, Maine, witnessed by Jeannelle Garner and Timothy Kestwick." The document was signed by the Rev. Dr. Richard Willmer.

Sarah's fingers gently skimmed over the embossed writing, and this time she said, her voice breaking, "Benjamin Arnold Kestwick, Benjamin, Benj…Ben, Ben, Ben."

She laid down on the bed, closed her eyes and focused on Ben's face. Her beautiful Ben. She had loved him from that very first moment she saw him at the marina.

*   *   *   *   *

Sarah recalled that first incredible summer she spent in Booth Bay Harbor with Ben. Ben took the lobster boats out daily, and Sarah worked at the restaurant part time and gave a few lessons. Every free moment they spent together. They took sailboat rides and swam in the ocean; they walked hand-in-hand along the beautiful, but jagged edges overlooking the ocean at sunset and took late-night moonlight swims. They ate shrimp skewers in the park when Ben was in port at lunch and Lobster Elegante at least once a week at the Inn. They spent hours talking about their pasts and their futures. Sarah told Ben about her childhood and the story of her adoption, what great parents she had and how she would love to have a family of her own some day. Ben talked to her for hours about lobstering and trapping, about his mother and his infinite love for the sea.

When the summer was over she went back to Chelsea for her senior year. They spoke on the telephone every day and Sarah drove to the Harbor to spend quality time with Ben almost every weekend.

During one of those weekends in April when the trees began to bud out, baby ducks waddled behind their mamas and smells of spring filled the air, Ben asked Sarah to be his wife. They were taking a Sunday afternoon boat ride when Ben sat her down, portside. He slowed the engine and, as five beautiful white seagulls flew overhead and tipped their wings in a romantic salute, he brought out a bottle of champagne. He poured the bubbly liquid into two flowered Dixie paper cups.

"These are the only two cups in the galley," he said to her, smiling, a twinkle in his eye. "Here's to the most beautiful girl in Booth Bay Harbor, even though she's a Millinockett transplant!"

Sarah laughed, cheered him and took a sip of the bubbly liquid. She watched as Ben got down on one knee. He took her hand in his and placed a beautiful diamond and ruby ring on her finger.

Sarah gasped. She was not prepared for this. She had hoped and prayed for this day for so long she couldn't remember and now the day was finally here. She couldn't believe her eyes.

"It was my mother's ring," he told her lovingly, "and my grandmother's. My dad gave me both his permission and his blessing when I told him I was going to propose. I asked him for the ring two weeks ago, had it sized, and now I want you to have it."

"Sarah, I want you to marry me" he continued, tears filling his eyes. "Will you take this ring? The ring meant so much to my mother and to her mother. My grandparents and my parents loved each other so much, just like we love each other Sarah. I want you Sarah. Will you marry me?"

*   *   *   *   *

It was one of the most beautiful weddings ever held in Millinockett, Maine. The altar of the historic Methodist church was adorned with white wicker baskets filled with yellow daisies and powder blue mums. Green ivy and white baby's breath was everywhere, adding to the warmth and beauty of the age-old church. There were four massive candelabra, bearing a total of eighty blue candles draped in ivy and blue ribbon that stood between each tall pedestal of flower baskets. The aisle pews were decked out in yellow, blue and white ribbon and the flames from the flickering candles cast a romantic glow across the entire sanctuary.

"Nothing," Ben said later, "could hold a candle to the beautiful woman who walked down the aisle to become his bride." Sarah Jeanne Waverly walked down the aisle on the arm of her proud father wearing her grandmother Emma's off-white Victorian gown, including a five-foot-long train, and it took her mother and best friend, Jeannelle, over forty five minutes to fasten the 118 tiny satin covered buttons on the back of the gown.

"You are soooo beautiful," he told her at the reception, "so absolutely beautiful. You take my breath away."

"You didn't look too shabby yourself, Mr. Kestwick," she told Ben later on at the Inn in Booth Bay Harbor. "I always knew you were handsome, but in that black tuxedo, whoa, you were the most handsome man ever!" Lovingly she whispered in his ear and caressed his naked chest, "and without clothes, Mr. Kestwick, you are the most handsome, sexy man I have ever seen!"

*   *   *   *   *

For a moment Sarah wasn't exactly sure where she was. She looked around, realizing soon enough that she was in their bedroom. It was the room Ben and she slept in, made love in, shared their deepest, darkest secrets in, and Ben was not there.

'Ben's not here," she said to herself. But as before when Martin came over, she did not panic.

"How am I going to make it on my own if you don't come home, Ben?" she asked herself calmly. "If you don't come home, Ben, how am I going to raise our baby alone?"

Silly questions she thought to herself, Ben will be home soon, no need for me and this little one to worry.

She took a deep breath, realized that she needed to be strong for her baby's sake, and calmed down. She patted her swollen belly and quietly and sincerely said, "They will find you, my love, and I believe they will find you safe. This baby and I need you."

She rolled over onto her side, the wedding certificate still in her hand. As hard as she tried, she could no longer hold back the tears and they streamed down her face. She placed her hand on the unborn child stirring inside her and thought how badly she had always wanted a baby.

She remembered, too, how she shared the news of her pregnancy with Ben. This baby was not planned and she wasn't sure how Ben would take the news. She walked down to the docks about noon and called him on the Port Authority's land-sea radio. She told him sweetly that he'd better get home on time as she had a surprise for him. He asked no questions and assured her he would do his best. She set a romantic table for two, including candles and a bottle of red wine. She made one of his favorite seafood dishes and set a gift box and card at his plate. Upon his arrival home, she suggested he clean up a little and then come to the table. She poured wine into his glass but not into hers. He did not notice. She asked him lovingly to first open the gift and card, and then they would enjoy their meal.

"What are you up to?" he questioned, "It's not my birthday, and it's not our anniversary again, or is it?"

Inside the gift box was the pregnancy tester that had turned blue earlier that morning proving her pregnancy. At first, he didn't quite understand. "I guess it's a guy thing," he told her later. But, when he opened and read the card she wrote, he understood right away.

"Some babies come from the heart, and some baby's come from mommy's tummies," she wrote. "This baby will come from both our hearts and from a mommy's tummy. Congratulations, my love, my heartthrob, my best friend. You are about to be a daddy!"

"My gosh!" is all Ben could muster.

"My gosh, Sarah, is it true? We're pregnant?"

"Yes," she had assured him. "We are pregnant."

Ben quickly stood up from the table, knocked over the chair and almost knocked over his glass of wine. He went to her, first taking her hand and then taking her in his arms. He kissed her, then kissed her again and told her just how much he loved her, and kissed her again and gently put his hand on her stomach.

The candles burned completely out, their favorite seafood dish and red wine went untouched, and Ben was late to work the next morning.

*　*　*　*　*

Sarah's tears stopped and she smiled thinking of that evening several months ago. She moved around, tried to get comfortable, but there was just no comfortable way to rest any longer. She hoped this baby would come soon for her comfort as well as for her child's. She stood up, thinking perhaps some exercise would help, plus she was getting hungry again. She retrieved a snack from the kitchen cupboard, checked the weather outside, and returned to her bedroom. She put their marriage certificate back into the envelope and picked up the small white Bible. She opened it, turned a few pages and found a photo of her parents stuffed inside. She recalled putting it there after their twenty-fifth wedding anniversary. They looked so happy, so in love, and she remembered how excited they had been at the news of her pregnancy.

"I'm going to be a grand pappy," her father had said, "and I will teach him to be a fisherman just like his grand pappy."

"And what if it's a girl?" Sarah had asked him, laughing.

"Well, she can learn how to fish, too," he had said, smiling, "Just like her mama did."

As Sarah finished her snack, she laid down on the bed and thought of fishing boats and Ben, her parents, a possible name for the baby, and the time when Jonas and Mary Anne told her she was adopted.

*   *   *   *   *

Sarah went to Booth Bay Harbor many times over the years, either for a day at a time or during vacations with her parents. She came to this quaint little fishing town the first time when she was only five or at least that was the first time she remembered coming to the harbor. Her parents left Millinockett on a late Friday afternoon, drove the 150 or so miles to the harbor, stayed at the Aqua Marina Inn, and returned home on Sunday afternoon.

She loved watching the fishing boats or pleasure crafts go in and out of the harbor. She would wave at all of the people on board and jump up and down with excitement when someone would wave back. She enjoyed the days of walking on the beach, taking off her sandals, and then running barefoot in the sand with her mother. She loved picking up and collecting seashells, eating hot shrimp sticks from the local beach vendor, and then, after the sun went down, going into the village with her mother. They would try on and purchase colorful matching sun dresses in one of the local dress shops. They'd check out the wonderful sights and smells at the farmer's market, picking up a few items to take back to Millinockett, and then eat chocolate almond ice cream before heading back to the Inn for a late supper.

"You spoil her," Jonas said to his wife as he hugged her. "And that's okay as she is the only little one we will ever have."

Sarah never doubted how much her parents loved her, and she never suspected that she was not their birth child. She didn't remember very much of the first few years of her life, but her mother and father did take a lot of photos. Surprisingly enough, she never questioned why there were not any baby photos. All the photos in family albums seemed to be from the time she was around two or three years old.

Her parents decorated a beautiful bedroom for her in shades of pink and orange like the sunsets and blues and greens, like the ocean, a room she dearly loved. She would lie on her bed for hours doing homework or playing with her dolls or, as she got older, listening to music. There were seashells everywhere, those she collected and ones her parents or friends had given her. There were giant photos of the ocean with fishing boats and giant seashells adorning her walls. There was a giant pink teddy bear given to her on her fifth birthday and a special doll with eyes that blinked and said, "mama". There were pillows and stuffed animals of all kinds and colors covering her bed, including a beautiful princess doll sitting right in the middle of it all. Joe had given it to her on her thirteenth birthday.

"For my little princess," he said. He also made sure Jonas and Mary Anne approved. He asked their permission to give it to her, and then said, "I hope you don't mind my spoiling her, too." Since they realized Joe had no children of his own, and they knew he loved Sarah too, they told him they didn't mind at all.

The Waverlys made certain that Sarah saw a doctor and dentist for regular checkups. They made sure she did well in school and Mary Anne even joined the PTA. They signed her up for gymnastics because she claimed she just had to do gymnastics. They chuckled when she gave it up because she said it was boring. She wanted to play the piano, so they first rented and then bought a used one and took her to meet Mrs. Farthey, whom she adored, for lessons. She loved playing and she practiced often. When she was old enough to understand its true meaning, she was baptized at the Millinockett Methodist Church. All three of them attended church services almost every Sunday; Mary Anne took her to Sunday School classes, and when she was twelve, she played Mary in the seventh grade Christmas play and Mary Anne made her costume. Most of all, Jonas and Mary Anne showed Sarah unconditional love, and she loved them back in the same way.

One day, when Sarah just turned eight, she came home from school with a new friend. Melinda (Melly) Thornton and her family recently moved to Millinockett and Sarah and Melly became instant friends. They both loved playing the piano, as well as the outdoors, and neither of them had siblings. Sarah invited Melly to a sleepover one Friday night, and, as Mary Anne was tucking both girls into bed, Sarah calmly said, "Mom, do you know that Melly is adopted? Her parents got her when she was a baby, isn't that the coolest thing?'

"Yes, that's a very cool thing," Mary Anne said rather calmly and quickly changed the subject. The next afternoon, after they dropped Melly off at her own home, Sarah began to ask her mother questions about adoption. Mary Anne realized the time had come to tell Sarah about her own.

One of the questions the Waverlys had asked the case worker during their six weeks of pre-adoption classes was at what age they should tell an adopted child about the adoption. The caseworker shared with the entire class of possible adoptees that between the years of six and eight was the best time.

"Children have a fear of being left or deserted," she said, "Even your own birth child has that fear when they are young. So it's in the child's best interest, and in yours as a parent, to wait until the child feels that he or she is secure in their surroundings to tell them they are adopted."

"Just how do we go about this?" Jonas asked. "Is there a book to read or lessons we should take to do it correctly?" The class had all chuckled and then applauded Jonas for asking the question, as they were all wondering the same things.

"The most important thing," the caseworker advised, "is to be calm, loving, maybe have the entire family around you, or make it a special event of some type when you tell the child that he or she is adopted."

"Then," she continued, "make sure that the child knows he or she was born first and adopted second. It is a choice that the birth mother made first of all to give the child life. Your choice as adoptive parents is to choose the child to be yours. Make it special," the caseworker said. "Show the child photos of the day you all went to the court house and why this was a special day. Tell why you signed certain papers and show them to the child. Describe why the brown teddy bear she loves so dearly was a gift from the child welfare offices on that special day."

"Then," she said, "have a party, or go out to dinner with the family or with friends. Let the child know just how special she or he is, and what he or she means to you. Lastly, let the child know that some children come out of their mommy's tummies, but that your child came from your hearts. You chose the child to be yours forever."

"What if the child wants to know about his or her birth parents right away?" Jonas asked, "Just how much do we tell them?"

"That is a very good question," the caseworker replied. "Some children will ask right away, and others will wait years before they ask. You need to tell them as little as possible if they are younger. If they ask how old their mothers were when they gave birth, or why they gave up the child, tell them just a little bit of the history. Assure the child you will tell them more later on. You must assure the child that it was a good decision on the birth mother's part. Never, ever, bad mouth the birth mother or father. Just assure your child that she was loved by both parents, but due to problems or issues the birth parents had, it was in the child's best interest to give him or her up to another family. Make sure that the child knows that the birth parents never ever did not love them. Then, if you wish in later life, you can give your child more information."

And so the time came. On an afternoon when Jonas came home from the Mill earlier than usual and Sarah was on a school break, Mary Anne dished up chocolate almond ice cream in big yellow bowls, and they all sat down as a family to talk about her adoption. Mary Anne shared with her eight-year-old daughter that most of the time a mommy and a daddy can have their own baby, but they could not have one themselves even though the doctors had tried to help them have one. Jonas shared with her how he always wanted a little girl, wanted to teach her to fish and camp and that he had so much love inside his heart that he looked and looked everywhere until he found her. They shared with her about the courthouse in Augusta and showed her photos of the family that took care of her the first two years, and they were called foster parents. They showed her the adoption papers with the date of her adoption and told her how they came to name her Sarah Jeanne, that Sarah was the name of her great, great grandmother. They also showed her photos of other adopted children and their parents and they told her what a caseworker was. They talked to her about the hospital in Augusta where she was born and they assured her the birthday they helped her celebrate every year was her real birth date.

They gave her just a little information about her real mother and father. They were too young to be responsible for a child, and it was their decision to give her to a different family who would love and care for her better than they could.

Sarah seemed to accept all of this information, and Mary Anne and Jonas were so thankful. They also thought how much it helped to have Sarah's little friend, Melly, also be an adopted child. Sarah was proud she could be "adopted" just like her best friend.

"I'm going to tell Melly first thing tomorrow that I am adopted too," she said cheerfully. "This is so cool, mom, can I tell everybody at school I'm adopted?"

Her parents assured her it was just fine to tell she was adopted. They were so proud of her and told her so, and reminded her again of how much they loved her.

"Does Uncle Joe know I am adopted?" she asked her mother at the end of the conversation.

"Yes, dear, he knows," Mary Anne said, "Why did you ask?"

"No reason," Sarah commented, as she headed for the refrigerator for more ice cream.

* * * * *

Thinking of ice cream made Sarah hungry again. She grinned, sat up on the edge of the bed and the white Bible she was holding fell to the floor. She tried to bend over and pick it up, but it was a futile effort, so she left it where it fell.

"Ice cream, little one, doesn't that sound yummy?"

Sarah stood up and walked into the kitchen. She took a clean dish and spoon from the drainer in the sink and went to the freezer to get the container of ice cream. She lifted the lid, took a rounded spoonful from the container and placed it in the bowl. She first licked the frozen substance off the spoon and placed the spoon in the bowl. You will love chocolate almond delight ice cream, little one," she said, "It's your mama and daddy's favorite."

Sarah took a second spoonful and, as she put the spoon to her mouth, the baby kicked hard, and a hard contraction caused her to drop the spoon. She grabbed at her belly, bent over and let out a big painful moan.

"Oh, my!" she said, gasping and then taking a deep breath. She sat down on a kitchen chair, thinking she should possibly call Martin or her parents. "Oh, I think I had better call the doctor first, then my parents. I think we are getting close, little one."

She stood up after a few more minutes. She walked into the other room and picked up the telephone. She called Martin first, let the telephone ring and ring until the answering machine picked up.

"Grand pappy Martin is evidently not home," she said to her unborn child, taking several more deep breaths and hanging up the telephone.

Continuing to walk the floor, waiting for another contraction, she called and left a message for her doctor and began to dial her parent's number in Millinockett. She walked over to the window, telephone to her ear, and noticed Martin pulling his car up to her curb. She breathed a sigh of relief as she continued to wait for her parents to pick-up.

CHAPTER TEN

The strange, unfamiliar boat from early morning slowed down and approached the SARAH JEANNE and came portside. Jeremy stayed at the wheel while Ben walked outside along the outside railing. His left hand slid down along his waistband, touching the weapon hidden from sight. He waved to the tall man on board, wondering if he should take the weapon out, cock it, and be ready for whatever might be coming down?

"Hello," Ben called out, "What brings you back?"

"Hello," came a response back. "I'm here on business, sir."

"Did you ever find the Blue Lady?" Ben questioned as the boat came to a complete stop.

"Yes, we did," came the quick reply. "That's why I came back; we need to talk." Looking towards the north, the stranger added. "Looks like the weather is changing. This shouldn't take long. We'll both need to be on our way soon."

Ben asked his name and if he could please show him some identification. "Never can be too careful this far out at sea," he offered. "I don't know you or recognize your craft. Do you mind?"

"Not at all," the tall man replied. "I'm going to reach in my left jacket pocket, take out my I.D. I'm Richard McLeary with the Federal Bureau of Investigation, out of Boston." As he showed Ben his badge, he asked Ben if he could come aboard.

From a distance, Ben couldn't be sure if it was a legitimate identification or badge, but he took a chance and gave him permission to come aboard. After McLeary boarded, he showed Ben the badge. "Can I take a closer look at that Mr. McLeary?" he asked, holding out his hand but looking directly into his face.

Ben took the I.D. badge, looked it over and handed it back. Ben asked if he wanted to talk above deck or should they go below deck?

"Below deck would be fine, Mr. Kestwick," McLeary said in a calm professional manner. He looked around the boat, noticing the cages filled with squirming lobster. He nodded his head in recognition of Jeremy and touched a finger to his nose as the stench invaded his nostrils. He turned back to his boat and told his crewman to "drop anchor".

"How do you know my name?" Ben asked curiously, walking down the stairs to the galley. He reminded McLeary, who was at least six foot three inches tall, to watch his head. "I have to duck every time I come down here, too."

"I'll explain all of this to you shortly, Mr. Kestwick," McLeary politely responded again, being careful as he walked down stairs. He added, holding his nose, "Do you ever get used to this fish smell?"

Ben chuckled but didn't respond.

Jeremy stayed at the wheel and killed the engine. He frowned as he watched the two men disappear. He was not too certain about this encounter, this strange craft, or with Mr. McLeary. Ben did not introduce Jeremy to the investigator either, and he wondered why. He glanced across at the craft anchored next to the SARAH JEANNE and tipped his hat to the man at the wheel. The man nodded back.

"I'm going to keep an eye on you, my man," Jeremy said silently to the man at the wheel. "Just who is your boss down in our galley? I don't like this at all. You better know, I won't allow anything, not anything, to place this boat or my boss in jeopardy." He secretly wished Ben had given him a weapon, too, for more reasons than one.

Once downstairs, Ben asked the investigator to take a seat, offered him a soda, which he declined, and McLeary began.

"Before I begin, Mr. Kestwick," he said, "I want you to know what we are going to discuss may be difficult for you to comprehend or understand. Decisions I may ask you to make will also be very difficult and please know the choice will be yours. However, it could be in the best interest for everyone concerned if you cooperate with the FBI."

Ben first asked him to quit calling him Mr. Kestwick, and to please call him Ben. He then asked McLeary to continue.

Getting right to the point, McLeary continued.

"Two months ago, a child was kidnapped from her home in Portland. The mother had left the home for a dental appointment, and the father was in the back yard talking to a neighbor over the fence. The child was in the house for only a short time by herself, and, in those few minutes she was abducted from her bedroom. No one saw anything, but we are sure we know the kidnapper. We believe the kidnapper is your wife Sarah's birth mother.

"What?" Ben asked, quickly getting to his feet. What are you saying? My wife doesn't even know who her birth mother is. How do you know it's her?"

"That's why this is so critical, Mr. K...Ben," he caught himself. "Please sit down, won't you? I'll try my best to explain this entire situation to you and how your family is involved. Please try to stay calm."

Ben sat down, nervously playing with and poking holes into a paper cup at the galley table. McLeary continued.

"Two months ago, a woman named Natalie Pickford Andrews abducted a child from her home in Portland. She evidently watched the home daily, for weeks in fact. She visited the child's school, was seen at the school playground more than once, and we know she talked with the child at the local park once or twice before the abduction, even when her mother or father was at the park with her. She followed the father to work several times and followed the family to church and other events. She watched the mother's activities closely, as the mother did not work out of the home. She was trying to figure out the family's daily schedules, and when the time was right she kidnapped the child."

McLeary went on, "We know from many witnesses whom we interviewed after the kidnapping and from descriptions given that the woman, Natalie, is your wife Sarah's birth mother."

McLeary continued by saying, "Here's the reason, Ben, we believe this is all true. We've had Ms. Andrews under surveillance off and on for the past year or so on another matter, a drug related matter. Since October of last year, and just within the last month, we have proof she is Sarah's birth mother. It took a lot of time, obtaining warrants, digging into her past and miles of footwork for the FBI and the DEA. I'll explain all of this at a later time. Right now, we have more important matters to discuss. But Ben, believe me, no one knows there is a connection between the Andrews woman and your wife except the authorities and now you. No one will ever know!"

Ben could not believe what he was hearing. Sarah, his wife, the soon-to-be mother of his unborn child, was somehow involved in some abduction, in possible jeopardy herself, and all due to her biological mother? He stood up again, paced for a few minutes, picked up an orange from the basket, peeled it and began to eat.

"Ben, we know your wife is pregnant and is due to deliver any day. In no way do we wish to jeopardize her, the pregnancy, the birth of your child, or any of you. However, we need you both to work with us. Together, you, your wife and our agencies will be able to catch this woman if you cooperate with us."

"You have got to be kidding," Ben said, noticeably disgusted and raising his voice at the agent. Standing again, he continued, his hands raised, his voice cracking. "What can we possibly do, Sarah and I? We're just common, everyday, hardworking people starting a family. Sarah can't possibly have anything to do with this woman, this woman, what's her name, Natalie?" He sat back down.

The agent continued, "Ben, I know that. We've been watching you and your wife for several months now…"

Before McLeary could continue, Ben stood up again, grabbed McLeary by the shirt collar and yelled into his face. "What do you mean you've been watching us? What have we done, what does Sarah and our baby have to do with any of this? No more horsing around, McLeary, get to the real reason you're on my boat!"

Hearing the shouting, Jeremy rushed down the stairs to the galley.

"What's going on here?" he asked. "Boss, you okay?" Ben nodded to Jeremy and asked him to go back on deck. Jeremy hesitated, concerned about leaving Ben alone with the agent.

"Let go of my shirt, Ben," McLeary asked, placing his hands over the top of Ben's. "You're messing with a federal agent." Noticing the gun in Ben's trousers, he added, "I suggest you hand me the weapon too, Ben. Calm down, and let's start again, shall we?"

Ben took his hands from McLeary's shirt, took the gun out from his waistband and handed it handle first to the agent. McLeary checked it over, released the clip and laid both on the table opposite Ben. Jeremy asked Ben again if he should stay below, and Ben shook his head no. Jeremy, looking somewhat concerned, took his leave, walking slowly up the stairs. Ben sat back down, took a deep breath, and waited for McLeary to continue.

"Okay, Ben," McLeary began again. "We know positively that Natalie is your wife's birth mother. As I said before, I will tell you later why we know and how we found out. She has been looking for your wife for the past two years. She evidently does not mean to harm her, but rather wants your child."

Once again, Ben came up off his seat, and before he said a word, McLeary stood up too, walked over to Ben and placed a hand on his shoulder.

"Ben, please?" He gently took Ben's shoulder, led him back to the table and began again.

"I want you to know Ben, that your wife is and will be perfectly safe throughout this whole undercover investigation, your baby too. You need to believe me. We have someone watching your home and Sarah's every move. We'll have an undercover agent at the hospital when she goes to Portland. We also have an undercover agent watching Natalie in her neighborhood. She is living directly across the street from her, and Natalie has no idea her neighbor is an agent with the FBI."

McLeary continued to tell Ben how Natalie had been in prison when she was in high school and again after graduation. He told him about her drug habit, dealing drugs, and a little about her involvement with a drug ring. He told him how she spent time in a mental institution and how she suffers from severe depression and split personality disorders.

"This has been going on for over twenty years," McLeary shared, "since giving up her two illegitimate children."

"Now just hold on!" Ben yelled, standing again. "My wife is not to be called illegitimate; I hate that word! You understand me? Don't use that word when you talk of Sarah!"

"I understand, Ben," McLeary said, trying to calm Ben down again. "I'm sorry for using that term. Your wife was the second child born to Natalie out of wedlock. She gave the first, a boy, up for adoption when she was only sixteen and while using. She had a serious drug habit back then. She gave birth to your wife, Sarah, known as Melanie Anne from what we found on Portland birth records, when Natalie was a senior at Portland High School."

"Was she on drugs when she was pregnant with Sarah?" Ben asked anxiously. "Sarah is fine, really she's fine."

McLeary explained further that no, Natalie had stopped using years ago. She stayed clean because of the love and support of a high school classmate and the father of her child, Sarah's real father. He continued, telling Ben how Natalie and the boy's parents insisted she give the baby up for adoption. She was so upset about giving the baby away that she tried to kill herself while in the hospital. McLeary continued to share with Ben how Natalie never used drugs again, but hooked up with and has been a serious dealer for a major drug ring involved in the United States and Canada ever since.

"She incurred serious mental issues after giving up her children, and has split personality disorder as well." The agent continued. "She has major problems, the worse being her drug dealings, but she tried early on to kidnap a baby and failed, and a few months back she succeeded in kidnapping a little girl named Jacqueline Chipley."

"Now she is out of her mind about getting a child of her own, Ben," he continued. "We need to get her off the streets and get the child she kidnapped back before she harms her. We most certainly plan to keep Sarah safe before Natalie does something else drastic, Ben, but we need the both of you to help capture Natalie before anything else happens."

Ben sat stunned, speechless, but listening to every word coming from the agent's mouth. After a few moments he said, confused, "This doesn't make much sense to me. Who is the little girl she kidnapped? Do you know her? Do we know the family? Have you seen her, or her parents? Are they okay? What do you need from me, McLeary?"

Realizing Ben was getting more and more confused and frustrated, McLeary said, "Yes, Ben we know who she is, of course, and have been with her family in Portland, but we also know Sarah knows her, she just doesn't know who she really is, and we will never tell her either, Ben."

"What?" Ben said, looking up at McLeary with a skeptical frown. "What do you mean Sarah knows her? She knows the little girl, the family? How?"

Realizing how confused Ben was, McLeary said, "Sarah is giving the little girl piano lessons," McLeary continued in a softer tone. "Her name is Jacqueline. Natalie, Sarah's birth mother, has been in your home four times a month for the past two months for piano lessons."

Ben was speechless as he just looked at McLeary and made no comment. McLeary continued in a soft, low, professional voice to tell this confused, hurting husband and father-to-be, how Natalie came to find and worm her way into Sarah's life.

"Natalie Andrews lives in Brunswick, Ben, she comes to Booth Bay Harbor to bank, to check on you and your wife, and to give Jacqueline Chipley, the child she thinks is hers, piano lessons. She knows Sarah is musically talented, and she wants her daughter Jacqueline to be like Sarah. She does not want Sarah any longer, she wants Sarah's baby, that way Jacqueline will have a sibling. She's after your child, Ben," the agent continued, "but she's also after revenge for her parents taking Sarah away in the first place. Since she could not have Sarah, she will have the next best thing, Sarah's blood child, and her grandchild. She wants an infant because she never got to keep her own or raise her own babies. She believes with her "good woman personality" that her life will finally be complete when she gets two children back. However, we know her "bad woman personality" is coming out more and more. She is getting very dangerous."

Agent McLeary continued to tell Ben how Sarah's birth parent was acting. "Our undercover agents tell us that Natalie keeps Jacqueline out of school, supposedly home schools her, and she locks her up in her room and doesn't allow her outside. Her punishment for the child is not to feed her when she's unruly. She also is trying very hard to overtake Jacqueline's mind, brainwashing her if you will, hoping she will forget her past life and her parents and become her real child. This is typical behavior of a kidnapper and a woman with her mental problems. We have an FBI agent or DEA agent tailing her at all times and she has no idea she's being followed. Natalie moves around a lot, but we know where Natalie is holding little Jacqueline and while we want to get her away from Natalie, we also need to capture her at the same time. We are close Ben, we just need your help."

For a few minutes Ben said nothing. He could not believe this woman had been in their home, not only once, but several times. He had no idea what to say or what to do, so finally and quietly, hanging his head as if in shame, he asked McLeary in a low voice. "What is it you want from me?"

Thunder rumbled in the distance, and, due to the rocking of the boat, both men knew the weather was changing up top. Ben could not sit still any longer so he stood up. He went to the cooler and took out two bottles of water. He handed one to the agent and opened the other, taking a huge gulp.

Calmer now, he repeated the question. "What, Mr. McLeary, do you want from me and my wife? She's been a Waverly since she was two years old! She's never wanted to know her real mother or where she lives. She never looked for her birth mother or her birth father. She loves her adoptive parents, her real parents. Jonas and Mary Anne are wonderful parents. This is crazy, sir, this is just plain craziness."

McLeary no longer asked Ben to try to take it easy or to sit down. He continued giving Ben more information on Natalie and her past, and Ben asked more questions but received no acceptable answers. Finally, McLeary placed both hands on Ben's shoulders, looked directly into his face and said, "Ben, we need you and your wife to help us catch Natalie and put her away for a long, long time. We need you both to allow us to set you up as decoys to help the FBI."

Ben tried to interrupt the agent, but McLeary pushed hard on his shoulders and said, "Ben, listen to me, you need to temporarily disappear. Natalie has a plan in place. She had her husband 'try' to place an explosive device on this boat, just to disable it, but because he was under FBI surveillance too, our agents caught him and he's in custody. There is no explosive on this boat. Do you hear me, Ben, there is no explosive; we caught him, and you and your boat are not in jeopardy!"

Calmer now, McLeary continued, "Natalie, however, does not know that we have her husband in custody, and she is expecting to hear news tonight that your boat is missing, is lost or in trouble, and you are out of the picture, presumably drowned. This way, she is free to go after your unborn child without your interference, and the couple plan to use your boat in more drug dealings."

McLeary tried to continue telling Ben the plans, but Ben forcefully took McLeary's hands off his shoulders and, in protest, turned away from him, pounded his fists against the alley walls and began to cry.

"No! No! Oh my God, no!" Ben said sobbing, "this can't be happening to me and my family. You can't put Sarah through this, oh my God, what will happen to our baby?"

McLeary put his arm around Ben's shoulders and led him back to the galley table. He sat him down gently, told him to try to get his breath and to calm down as he continued with the FBI's plans. He assured Ben that he would be safe. The plan was to get him to Yarmouth, Nova Scotia, hide his boat at the Yarmouth docks and keep his haul safe and alive for later shipping. Within the next two days, the undercover agents should have Natalie in custody, and Sarah and the baby would be safe. They knew Sarah was going to the Portland hospital for delivery on Thursday, and even though Ben might not be there for the delivery, they would keep him abreast of everything that was going on.

"I know we are asking a great deal from you, Ben," McLeary said, "but with your help, we can not only crush a huge drug ring, but get this lunatic kidnapper off the streets. You do want that don't you, Ben, to get his woman away from young children? Little Jacqueline Chipley needs to be back with her parents, and you and Sarah will be safe from her, too, for the rest of your lives. You will help us do that, won't you Ben?"

Ben nodded his head in agreement, but no words came from his mouth. He was exhausted, worried, and sick to his stomach and missed Sarah so much. He just wanted her in his arms, to hold her, protect her and tell her how much he loved her.

Ben heaved a big sigh, stood up and said, he would do whatever it took to capture this woman. He only had one request, and the request was that no one, absolutely no one would ever tell Sarah that Natalie was her birth mother. "No matter what, she must never know who Natalie is, understood?" McLeary said yes, shook Ben's outstretched hand, and assured him again. No one would ever tell. It was confidential.

McLeary thanked Ben, and then said, "As soon as possible, the FBI will let Sarah know you're safe. We also plan to let the Port Authority in Booth Bay Harbor know that you are not lost at sea, but safe, but, for now, they too need to continue in the belief that you are lost. We will also contact the Coast Guard but need them to continue looking for you, to make this whole scenario seem real. This is the only way to make our years of work a success. We are so close to shutting Natalie and her drug dealers down, just so close. Do you understand, Ben? Do you realize how important you and your wife are to the success of this undercover scheme?"

Ben nodded his head again and asked the agent if he could go up top and talk to his crewman, Jeremy? McLeary assured him he could, and he would also go up with him and explain it all to him if need be. He promised, however, that he would not tell his crewman the name of the kidnapper—Natalie Andrews, or that she was Sarah's birth mother. He would also say nothing about the kidnapper being a possible drug dealer. Then, immediately, Ben would follow the other FBI boat to Nova Scotia, and the last part of this two-year old undercover, government-approved undertaking would enter its last stage.

Ben walked slowly up the stairs, spoke to Jeremy, checked his cages, and, as a bolt of lightning lit up the eastern skies, asked Jeremy to pull-up anchor.

* * * * *

Wednesday

* * * *

CHAPTER ELEVEN

A large white sign supported by three six-inch steel poles stood atop the four-story blue and gray building. On the sign were printed in large black letters, Department of Homeland Security-Department of the Treasury.

There were six steep cement stairs going into the front of the building, and at the bottom of the stairs, an arrow on a blue and white sign pointed left, for wheelchair access. Once inside, and at the first door to the left, a sign read, "Maine Coast Guard - Harbor Patrol - Search and Rescue – Portland". There were several small cubicles where uniformed men and women sat at small cluttered desks. Several were speaking on their telephones, one was engrossed in a journal on Coast Guard Regulations and two were working on a large map on the eastern wall of the room. At one of the front cubicles, Gerald Browning stood up from his desk and walked one cubicle over.

"Are you working on the Ben Kestwick case?" Gerald asked, as he walked over to where Lieutenant Casey sat, his nose buried in his computer.

"Yes," he said looking up. "Or at least I'm trying to make some sense of it all. I just can't figure this one out. The first report is that there are no signs of a boat, no lifeboat, no debris, nothing! How can a guy with so much boating experience get lost at sea with no trace of the boat? I've known the Kestwick family for years. Ben's dad is an accomplished fisherman and he trained Ben in exactly the same manner. Safety first, Martin Kestwick always says, safety first. I just can't figure this one out. There are no signs anywhere out there, no boat, no debris, and no sign of the two men on board. There's just nothing!"

Tom stood up, and facing Gerald, mentioned that there were choppers already in the air and had been since early morning. Search and Rescue was out in the area in the black aid boats, there were two rescue boats and still nothing was spotted as of two hours ago.

"The weather was bad last night," Tom continued, "but I'm sure Ben has been out in worse. I'm just at a loss right now, kind of bugs me, you know?"

Gerald was fairly new to the Guard, but Tom came on board right after he was commissioned and was his commander.

"The word on the harbor is that there may have been foul play," Gerald said, "Have you heard anything to support that?"

"Well, there's always gossip and hearsay," the Lieutenant responded, "but nothing we can use so far. Ben is a standup guy I can't imagine why there would be foul play, maybe pirating or something to do with the business, but not foul play."

Tom continued by telling Gerald that the last person to see Ben Kestwick and his crewman, Jeremy Brookings, was Ron at the Port Authority. Kestwick did the usual, filed his chart course, said he would be back late the same day, and provided the same daily information as always with the fishing business.

"Ben Kestwick always follows the rules," Tom continued. "This may turn out okay, and he may just show up this morning, and we all got excited for nothing."

Gerald and Ben continued their conversation and Gerald asked half-heartedly, "Any reason he might want to disappear, maybe Kestwick was having trouble at home, you know with the wife or kids, or financial woes?"

"That's the weird thing, Gerald," Tom said, "Ben and his wife Sarah are expecting a baby real soon, I understand this week maybe. Doesn't sound like a guy who would want to disappear with a baby coming, now does it?"

"Not unless he's not the daddy type, got himself into a situation, doesn't want the responsibility of a kid, you think, maybe?" Gerald chuckled, and then on a more serious note continued, "I personally don't know Ben Kestwick, just know his father, Martin, met him a few times at the harbor is all, never met the wife either. I hear they have a successful lobster business."

"Ben and his wife Sarah are good people, I think," Casey said,

"I knew Ben a little from middle school days before my folks moved away. He and Sarah have been married a little over a year, and she teaches piano to the local kids, guess she's quite the musician from what I hear. She's from up north by Millinockett. Martin's wife Jenny died a few years back, and he's not been down to the dock much since then, but that's all I know."

"I did hear that Jeremy called into the office on Tuesday, checking weather reports and so on, but the dispatcher didn't say he sounded alarmed or anything," Casey recalled, "Just making sure there were no storms or gale warnings out; I guess he was concerned about the cloudy weather and all. Not sure why he called here, he could have checked with the locals about the weather. Maybe that's something we should check into?"

Lieutenant Tom Casey stood up, stretched his arms over his head and headed over to the table for his third cup of java. Whoever had made the coffee this morning had done a bang-up job. Usually the coffee was so black you had to add at least three packets of sugar and half a pint of milk to make it drinkable, but today it was exceptional. He walked over to the window, peered out over the harbor, and noticed that within the past two hours the sun had appeared and it was no longer raining.

"I guess the weather guy was right on today. Going to make searching a little easier."

Tom Casey served four years in the Navy directly after high school. He had no desire to go to college, but wanted to get away from home for at least a few years, so he joined up. He served both on land and at sea, and when he got out decided to apply for entrance to the Coast Guard Academy. He was accepted and after four years and graduating with honors, he chose to go back to his home state and take the position offered him at the Portland based Coast Guard SAR offices. So far he had no regrets. He liked the job, liked most of the people he worked with, and had met a really nice young woman, Jill Goodwell, who was born and raised in the area. He was involved in just a few search and rescue operations over the past two years, most of which turned out positively, but this new case had him puzzled already. It was going on the second day, and there was something about this boat and two-man crew that bothered him.

"I think I will head up this case myself," he thought, "there's something just not quite right here."

"I'm headed up to Booth Bay Harbor," he told Gerald, "I want to hear and see for myself just what's going on with this case. I'll keep in touch, keep your phone close, okay? Let dispatch know where I'm headed," he continued, "I probably won't be back in until tomorrow. If the chopper pilot calls in or anything new develops, give me a ring."

Casey set down his coffee cup on the desk, picked up his newly starched and pressed uniform jacket, his Guard SAR hat and headed for the door. Once outside, he put on his jacket, buttoned it up and set his hat on top of his perfectly styled black hair. Touching his hat once again, he smiled, remembering how Jill loved his hat. She wore it on several occasions. She would tease him, salute him, and then seduce him into her bed with nothing else on but his Guard hat.

The rain had stopped but there were huge, deep puddles everywhere. He walked quickly to his SUV and wondered if and when the department would ever build an indoor or covered parking garage for the Treasury Department employees, or at least fix the potholes. Repairs were discussed, but as of now, rain or shine, everyone in the Department who drove parked in the open lot and put up with the substandard asphalt. There was security posted at the gate to make sure only government people got into the building, and God help you if you forgot your badge or used someone else's vehicle.

He unlocked the door to his SUV and took a look at the clock on another government building's watchtower across the street. It showed exactly 10:00 a.m. He took a look at his watch, and the watchtower clock was right on.

He got in, fastened his seat belt, turned on the radio to a local jazz station, and backed out of parking space #7. He headed for I-95. He figured it would take a little short of an hour to get from Portland to Booth Bay Harbor. At Brunswick he would take the highway into the Harbor, and this early in the day, hoped there would be little or no traffic.

Lieutenant Casey turned the heater of his SUV to "defrost", and wiped the inside of the windshield dry with a bar napkin out of the cup holder. He stopped at the security guard building, showed his badge and, as the guard waved him through, he thought about Jill.

* * * * *

He had seen her for the first time four months earlier. He was down at the docks on another Guard matter when he saw her disembarking from a cruise ship. She was with another cruise line employee and both were dressed in similar white and blue uniforms. He noticed her immediately, tipped his hat, and briefly said hello. When he returned from the docks a few hours later, he stopped in for dinner and saw her again coming out of the local shrimp joint, The Blue Lagoon. He smiled and said hello again. She stopped for a moment to respond to him and grinning, he asked if seeing her a third time today would be lucky for him?

"Third time's a charm," he said. "Would you consider having a drink with me sometime, maybe in five minutes?"

She laughed, said that having a drink with him was a possibility. He introduced himself, and since she could tell from the uniform he was military, she would take a chance and have a drink with him. She said goodbye to her coworker, telling her she would see her in a few days, and together they went back into The Blue Lagoon.

They saw each other twice that week, and each time she came back from a weeklong cruise they met somewhere for dinner or a drink. Two months later, she had invited him to her apartment for dinner. She set a beautiful table with white linens, fresh flowers and candles. She prepared pasta and salad, served red wine, and the evening had been nothing less than wonderful. She played jazz music on the stereo, they danced and had made love for the first time in her king size bed. Tom knew even before the night was over that he was falling in love with Jill and told her so.

They made plans to see each other again on her next days off, and, while pouring another glass of wine, he said, "No sense wasting this big beautiful bed by sleeping in it by yourself, Jill!"

She agreed.

After only four months, he had asked her to marry him. She asked him please not to rush her, as she needed a little more time. She shared with Tom about her childhood, the mean stepfathers she remembered, and how afraid she was for her mother each time one of them beat her. She was so thankful for how her mother had protected her from those men.

"I love you, Tom," she told him one evening after a romantic dinner in downtown Portland. Sitting at a candle-lit table, music softly playing in the background, she softly kissed him on the cheek, took his hand and continued. "When I marry, I want it to be forever Tom. I don't want you to think I don't trust you, I do. I know you would never hurt me, but I want to take just a little more time to get used to the idea of marriage and commitment. You are my first and I hope my only true love, please, will you wait for my answer?"

Tom had understood completely, told her once again how much he loved her, and that he was willing to wait forever. Deep inside, however, he hoped forever would come soon.

One weekend after she'd been out with Tom a couple of times, Jill drove over to Booth Bay Harbor to see her mother. She took her time driving to the Bay and waited until her mother closed the restaurant before surprising her with an unexpected visit. They drove to Loren's home, where over coffee and Jill's favorite cookies, they discussed Tom Casey.

"He's so incredibly handsome mom, and caring, and funny, and…" she said shaking her head, "that mop of black hair on his head…she didn't finish her description before looking into her mother's eyes and finishing, "I'm crazy about him, mom," she said, "and he's crazy about me."

She asked her mother how she was supposed to know he was the one. "Mom, you made so many mistakes, chose so many wrong men. What if he's not the right one? How will I know?"

"Your heart will tell you," her mother said. "I know that I thought your father was the right one, and thank the Lord, we loved each other enough in the beginning to bring you into the world."

Taking Jill's hand, she continued, "Your father just came with too much baggage. He liked his liquor, and I thought I could live with it, could help him overcome it, but I couldn't."

Jill saw tears welling up in her mother's eyes, and she gently touched her mother's hair and then her cheek.

"Sweetheart, when he started beating me, I had to make a decision." She continued, " It was a hard one, but I had to leave him to save you, and to save myself."

"I understand all of that," Jill said calmly to her mother, "But you knew he was a drinker when you married him, why did you marry him, knowing?"

"Because my heart told me he was the right one, Jill," she said, looking straight into her daughter's blue-green eyes. "I loved him so much, and I knew that he loved me too; he just loved the liquor more and wasn't willing to change. I didn't realize that until too late. I have no regrets, Jill, because I have you."

"Do you still love him, mom?" Jill asked gently.

"Yes, I guess I do." Loren said sadly, "I tried to find that same feeling in my heart with those other two bastards I married. I think I just needed someone to support me. Caring about me would have been nice too! I made big mistakes, Jill, I am so sorry."

Jill assured her mother that the past was history. "Everyone makes mistakes, mom," she said lovingly, "I understand, really I do." Loren took her daughter in her arms, hugged her, and told Jill how much she meant to her.

"I'm very happy for you, sweetheart," she told her beautiful daughter. "Just take your time, your heart will tell you if it's right. He sounds wonderful; bring him to the Bay sometime will you? I would love to meet him. We could go somewhere else beside the Hut and have dinner!"

They talked a while longer about the cruise lines, the Breakfast Hut, more about the past, and, before Jill knew it, it was time to go back to Portland. There was a two-week cruise scheduled and she had laundry and cleaning to do, and, of course she wanted to see Tom at least once more before she left town. Her mother wished her well, sent her home with a bag of cookies and told her to keep in touch.

Jill and her Lieutenant saw each other twice before she boarded the ship, once for dinner and once at her apartment. Tom brought her the cutest stuffed lion, told her she made him roar each time he made love with her, and she laughed and named the lion Casey. She even took

Casey along on the next cruise. He kept her company when the real Casey could not.

*   *   *   *   *

In less than thirty-five minutes, Tom was at the Brunswick exit. He exited I-95 to highway 218 to Bath and then to Booth Bay Harbor. He always loved driving to the Harbor. He knew it was faster to come by boat than it was to drive, but today was not a day to come by sea. He pulled in close to Captain Ron's, parked his SUV, locked it, and walked over to the docks. The rain was over, even the clouds were breaking up, and there was a hint of blue sky above. "At least one thing is in our favor," he said to himself, "the weather has improved."

"Morning," Tom said cheerfully, as he walked in the door at the Port Authority. "Anyone here?"

"Over here," came a deep voice. "What can I do for you?"

"It's me Ron, Tom Casey."

"Well, you got here fast," he said, a cup of coffee in one hand and a Danish in the other. "Want a cup?"

"Thanks but no," Tom said, "Already had three cups this morning. Can I use your restroom?"

"Sure thing," Ron pointed, "down the hall and to the right."

Captain Ron, as everyone in town called him, was the man in charge at the Booth Bay Harbor Port Authority. He was the authoritative figure on the docks and had been for over eighteen years. There were a couple of men working with him in the office, and one cute redheaded receptionist. She was sitting at a dark mahogany desk in front of the window and smiled a sexy little smile for Tom when he came in. Ron was the man, however, and everyone, including his staff, knew it, and the townspeople and fisherman respected his authority and his alone.

The Captain was about six foot eight inches tall, weighing about 245 pounds. He had a mop of unruly brownish black hair, slightly graying at the temples, and his face was covered with a matching eight-inch long beard. He was a people person, kind and jovial, but all business when he had to be. He loved the ocean, having spent four years in the Navy, and owned his own boat. He was proud of the Harbor and the Port Authority, and made sure all the traffic coming in and out of the Harbor was properly charted and legal. Ron was forty-eight years old, his wife Betty was forty-six, and together they had raised four daughters. The family now included two sons-in-law and three grandkids, and he never went anywhere, on land or on sea, without his faded US NAVY hat.

Tom returned to Ron's office, drying his hands on a paper towel. He tossed it into a trashcan and told Ron that the trashcan was missing in the bathroom.

"Not again!" Ron said grinning "Can't get any good cleaning help around here anymore. That woman must have absconded with it when she cleaned up the place last night. Been missing a few other items lately too; I'll have to see to her tonight. Maybe she needs a raise!"

Yup, Casey thought, a raise right out of the building to the unemployment office might be a good idea!

Ron motioned for Tom to sit down in the old leather chair in front of his desk that was piled high with folders and unopened letters, documents of all sorts, and a half eaten tuna fish sandwich. "Now, let's get down to business."

"So what do you think about Ben Keswick's missing boat? That's why you're here right?"

"Yes, I am," Tom said, looking down at his shoes, still wet from walking through the rain puddles. "I wonder what information you have, what's been done so far, and what else the Guard can do to help? I know we have choppers out, and SAR is out, but so far I haven't heard any good reports. Of course, the weather hasn't helped any."

Captain Ron told Tom Casey what he knew so far. Ben left on Tuesday morning about sunup, filed his chart course and was expected back by sundown. He or Jeremy had called in to check the weather report early in the morning. Later in the afternoon, Ron's receptionist took a call that disconnected soon after she answered. She recognized Jeremy's voice, but the message did not come through clear. She tried to call again soon after, but there was no signal so, of course, no answer.

"I tried to get a hold of the SARAH JEANNE until 7:30 p.m." he told Ben, "and then I called Ben's dad, Martin, and Ben's wife, Sarah. She's having a baby real soon, didn't want to alarm her, but figured she should know he wasn't back yet. We really have very little to go on,

Tom," Ron explained. "I wish I could tell you more. What do we do now? How can we help out of this office?"

Tom and Ron discussed the situation for another hour. They agreed to keep the helicopter out at least all day, and to keep the Search and Rescue boats out today and Thursday as well.

"We'll send them farther out west and northwest to look for any sign of a boat, debris, lifeboats, oil spill, anything that will give us some clue as to where Ben and Jeremy might be." In the meantime, Tom said he would check in town and talk to as many of Ben's friends and employees as he could find.

"Maybe I'll talk to the Kestwick's boat mechanic, the people at the weigh-in dock, and then make a point to go see Ben's wife, Sarah," Tom said as he stood up to leave.

He thanked Ron for his time, shook his hand and told him he would check in later in the day. In the meantime he hoped somewhere in town he would get a lead as to where Ben Kestwick, and Jeremy Brookings and the SARAH JEANNE might be.

CHAPTER TWELVE

Sandra Chipley opened the front door of her modest Portland home and greeted her best friends, Linda Jones and Betty Moore. "Come in, come in," she motioned to them both as they walked into the living room. "May I take your coats and umbrellas? Looks like the rain is over, doesn't it?"

They slipped off their wraps, handed them to Sandra, and watched as she hung their coats in the closet and set their umbrellas down. Together, the three women moved further into the room, where seven other women were seated drinking coffee and chatting. Greetings and hugs completed, the three women sat down on the empty chairs and waited for Sandra to begin.

Looking at her watch, she began. "I am so grateful to all of you for being here again, especially in this uncertain weather. This must seem mundane to some of you, but for my husband John and me it will never be. As long as our baby girl is missing, we will continue having evening vigils once a month, and these weekly prayer meetings on Wednesdays."

She continued, thanking them again for being there, for their constant prayers and for all the cards and notes the family continued to receive. She thanked them for the "Missing Child" posters being constantly printed, put up and mailed. She thanked them for continuing to spread the word about their missing daughter, and like John and her, never giving up on finding her.

"I would like to open up our work time and prayer vigil this morning with an opening prayer by a special new friend," she said cheerfully. "I am delighted to have Ginger Morrison here with us. She is the wife of the new pastor at the Neighborhood Baptist Church, two blocks to the north of us. Most of us do not know Ginger, but she called and wanted to be a part of our prayer vigil today. Many of us here belong to different denominations and faiths, but we're always open to welcome another Baptist in our midst." Everyone laughed and several stood up and introduced themselves. After a few minutes, Sandra continued by saying, "Ladies, if we can begin now? Ginger will lead us in prayer."

Ginger stood up, asked the others to do the same and for the women to hold hands. They all bowed their heads and Ginger began. She prayed for this moment, for all of the women gathered here, for John and Sandra Chipley, and for their daughter Jacqueline Suzanne. She also prayed, her voice breaking just a little, for the person or persons who had taken and were holding Jacqueline. She asked God to forgive the person responsible, to keep Jacqueline safe, and to bring her home soon.

She closed by asking God to help the FBI catch the kidnapper and that he or she be brought to justice. She prayed for her or his safety and well-being too, and again for forgiveness. When her prayer was completed, all of the women took a turn voicing their requests to God, their concerns and their abounding love for Him and the Chipley family. At the end, they all shared a loud amen, and sang a verse of "Jesus Loves Me". The women then moved to a large table where they worked on thank you letters and addressed more missing person notification letters.

Morning prayer meetings were held every Wednesday morning at the Chipley home with ten to twenty women in attendance. Several of the women were not regular churchgoers or even firm in their faith, but they became involved due to their love and concern for abducted children and their families. On the third Thursday of every month, ever since Jacqueline went missing, hundreds of people, both friends and strangers, gathered at the park near the Chipley home to pray and hope. For an hour or more, they prayed, lit candles and sang. It was everyone's hope and prayer that this precious little girl, Jacqueline, was somewhere safe and would be returned to her parents. "God's will abound" were the final words spoken each and every Wednesday morning and Thursday evenings.

*   *   *   *   *

It had been on a Wednesday, a little over two months prior, the 23rd of August, when Jacqueline Suzanne Chipley was taken from her home. Normally, she would have been on track in her third grade class at Jamison Elementary School, but she woke up with a slight fever and her mother insisted she remain at home. She wasn't happy about being sick, having to stay in bed, or being unable to play outdoors or attend school, but she did as her mother requested. Around noon, John Chipley called his wife to inform her he was not coming home for lunch, normally a daily routine. "Something's come up," he told his wife, "and I can't get away to come home."

Sandra, knowing she was scheduled for a dental appointment at noon, informed John of Jacqueline's fever. "What should I do?" Sandra asked her husband. "I kept her home from school today and I really need to keep this appointment, John, the toothache is getting worse every day."

John informed his wife that he would try to get out of the mandatory meeting, to give him just a few minutes to find someone to cover for him, and he would be home.

"I know your tooth has been bothering you," he said, "Just bad timing having to see the dentist today and having Jacqueline home sick, but I'll be home before you leave."

Sandra made herself ready, gave Jacqueline another baby aspirin and asked her to remain in bed to try to rest. She then turned on her small Barbie Doll radio for company.

"Do not get out of bed until I come back from the dentist," she requested. "Absolutely do not go outside, and do not answer the door if any one knocks or rings the bell. Do you understand, sweetheart? Here is the telephone. Daddy will be home shortly to watch you while I'm gone, okay?"

Jacqueline agreed. She cuddled with her Raggedy Ann doll, turned over in bed and closed her eyes. Sandra laid the telephone on the pillow next to Jacqueline's head, stepped out of the bedroom, leaving the door wide open, and left the house.

Sandra backed her car out of the garage, closing the door with the garage door opener as she backed down the driveway. She looked both ways before backing out into the street, and saw John's car coming towards her from the left. As he approached, she waved at him and pulled away.

"I could have made another appointment for later," she mumbled to herself as she drove the few miles to the Sunset Medical/Dental Center. "I hate leaving Jacqueline when she's sick. I know she's a big girl, but still a mother worries. I know John will watch her, but a sick baby girl needs her mama."

She arrived at the dental offices at noon sharp.

John had driven his vehicle into the driveway, turned off the engine and stepped out. He walked up to the front door and unlocked it. Walking inside, he laid his house and car keys on the small round table in the hallway and didn't bother re-locking the door. He peaked into the bedroom where Jacqueline lay sleeping, then walked into the kitchen and took the box of soda crackers from the lower cupboard. He opened the refrigerator and took out a carton of milk, took a swig directly from the carton and set it on the counter. Looking out his kitchen window and seeing his neighbor Jake Mitchell working on the fence separating their backyards, he walked out the door, munching on crackers and began to speak to him.

At 8:00 a.m. that morning, a woman dressed in blue jeans, gray t-shirt and a Red Sox ball cap on her head had parked her gray Chrysler one-quarter of a block to the west of the Chipley home. For three days she had watched the three of them during their early morning routines. Today, however, she had waited for over thirty minutes for Jacqueline and her mother to leave their home for the short walk to school, but they never came out of the house. At 11:30 a.m., she had returned to park down the street from the Chipley home, and when she saw Mrs. Chipley leave and Mr. Chipley come home, she assumed Jacqueline was at home for the day. She smiled, thinking today would be the perfect day to abduct the child, the child she had been watching at home and at school for weeks, the child that looked so much like herself at that age.

"This is going to be a good day," she said to herself. "Everything is falling into place so nicely. This beautiful little girl will soon be mine. I won't be childless much longer." She continued to watch the Chipley home and the surrounding area. There was very little activity as school was in session and most parents were at work. She noticed a stray dog crossing the street in front of her and a postal worker turned the corner to the north.

The woman in the Red Sox ball cap smiled and was pleased with her new plan. "I won't have to sneak up on the mother, knock her out or hurt her and steal the beautiful baby girl on the way to school," she said, assured of herself. "I can go into the house and take her with no problem. I wonder why she's home today, if she's sick or if it's a teacher's holiday or something?"

She convinced herself that this was the day to get herself a child. She had been planning abduction for months. She had scoped out schoolyards in Brunswick looking for the perfect little girl with no luck. One day, while driving through Portland after a "business" deal she had noticed Jacqueline in the playground at a local elementary school. She had driven by the school several times during the next few weeks, even stopped, parked and walked up to the fenced-in school yard and spoken with her and several other little girls playing dodge ball. She had picked out Jacqueline from the very start—her Melanie Anne.

She looked in the rearview mirror, making sure her freshly dyed long black hair was tucked neatly under the ball cap, and placed dark sunglasses on her face. She got out of the car, walked only a short distance before she noticed a man, presumably Jacqueline's father, leaning over the fence in the backyard of their home. She continued walking and climbed the three stairs to the front door of the Chipley home. She looked quickly to the right, then to the left, and immediately and without hesitation tried to open the front door. It surprised her when the door opened, as she had planned on it being locked. She had placed a small, black case of picks in her back pocket, but luck was with her and she didn't have to use them. She opened the door and walked right in. She quietly walked through the living room and into the kitchen. She looked out the window, noticing the man she presumed to be Jacqueline's father was still in the backyard and walked out of the kitchen to the first open door. There in the bedroom, she saw Jacqueline, her baby girl covered in pink and white bed covers. Taking a soft, white cloth sprayed with a sleeping agent out of her back jeans pocket, she cautiously approached the bed, leaned over and placed the cloth over Jacqueline's mouth and nose. After just a moment, she lifted the limp child into her arms, moved quietly out of the bedroom, lightly kicking the door shut behind her and carried her out the front door. The entire kidnapping took less than two minutes.

At 1:10 p.m. Sandra Chipley pulled her Oldsmobile into the driveway, turned off the engine and went inside their home. The telephone was ringing, and, as she headed to the kitchen to answer it, she passed Jacqueline's bedroom, remembering the telephone was with her daughter. "Strange," she thought, "I left her door open when I left for the dentist, now it's closed. She must have gotten up to use the bathroom and closed it after returning to bed."

Sandra walked into the room, goose bumps rising on her arms and panic filling her stomach. "Jacqueline? Jacqueline?" she called. "Jacqueline, where are you?" She also called for her husband. "John, John, are you in here?"

The constant ringing of the telephone irritated her and she finally answered it.

"Hello," She said sharply.

"Hi, Sandra, it's Linda. How are you?"

"I just walked in," she replied, a note of frustration in her voice. "I've been to the dentist, can I call you right back?" Linda assured her that would be fine, and, as she hung up the telephone, wondered at the concerned tone in her friend's voice.

Jacqueline was nowhere to be found. Hysterically, Sandra called her name over and over. She went into the garage, out to the back yard where she found John talking with the neighbor and yelled his name.

"John," Sandra screamed, "She's not here, she's not in the house. I can't find her anywhere!"

John turned away from the fence, asking his hysterical wife to calm down. "Sandra, Sandra!" he asked, grabbing her by the shoulders. "What's wrong? Who's not in the house?"

* * * * *

Sandra Chipley had been inconsolable for over a week after her daughter's abduction. John had tried everything he knew to help her, but with no success. Their pastor and their friends came over daily with food and words of faith and consolation, their mailbox overflowed with messages of hope and good cheer, but Sandra refused to eat, refused to read the messages and wanted no visitors. All she could think of was the children she had lost previously either to miscarriage or death, and there was no convincing her that Jacqueline's abduction would end on a positive note. Finally, eight days after Jacqueline's disappearance, and, after the story of the kidnapping appeared in the local newspaper, a woman, a stranger, called. She first spoke with John, then asked to speak with Sandra. After finally convincing her that taking the call would be a good idea Sandra took the telephone from John. When she answered, the woman introduced herself as Maralou Nielsen and said that she and her family had gone through exactly what the Chipley's were going through. She and her husband had also had a daughter taken from their home, and, their daughter had been found and the kidnapper was now incarcerated. After speaking with the woman, Sandra felt she had been given a new lease on life, that God was working through this stranger and in a little over a week's time Sandra changed her outlook, and, her attitude on the abduction.

* * * * *

After a little over an hour, the women who came to pray left and only Sandra and her friend Ginger remained. Sandra asked Ginger if she would like more coffee or perhaps join her for a sandwich, as it was lunchtime.

"I really appreciate the offer," Ginger replied, "But I have another meeting this afternoon, and I really do need to be on my way. I would love to meet with you again, though. May I join your group again next week?"

"Of course. I would love to have you come back every week until Jacqueline is found," Sandra responded positively.

"I really think the answer to getting your daughter back is prayer. God knows exactly where she is, and He will guide the FBI and they will bring her back to all of us. You have such a strong faith, Sandra, just keep on believing." With that she gave Sandra a hug and walked out of the Chipley's front door.

Sandra went back into her living room, collected a few more coffee cups and napkins, straightened up a few chairs and walked into the kitchen. Her kitchen was bright with high open ceilings, several sets of windows, and bright cheery wallpaper and curtains. As she set the dirty dishes in the sink and put the used napkins in the trash, she thought of how Jacqueline loved to sit by the kitchen windows to do her homework. "She was, no, she is such a wonderful little girl, my baby", Sandra said, looking out the window. "Where are you, baby, where are you?" Just then the telephone rang. Sandra answered it and recognized the voice right away. It was Richard McLeary with the FBI.

"Hello, Mrs. Chipley," McLeary said in his deep Irish voice. "I hope your day is going well. How was the weekly prayer meeting?"

"It was wonderful, agent McLeary. We just constantly pray and work towards our daughter's return. I have a good feeling she will be home soon." Then, continuing in a hopeful voice she asked, "Do you have news?"

"We have a lead ma'am," he said smiling to himself. "I do have fairly good news, but I don't want you to get your hopes up just yet, but we do have a good lead. I think we're getting close to finding out who it is that took your daughter. May I come over this afternoon, after your husband returns from the office, and talk about it with you both?"

Sandra Chipley assured him that 5:30 p.m. would be a good time, and once again she asked if he could give her any more information.

"Let's just wait until I come over later, okay? Again, don't get your hopes up too high, but I am anxious to speak with you. See you in a few hours."

With that, Sandra hung up and went to the kitchen. She tried very hard not to get too worked up or excited about Agent McLeary's telephone call, but she did stop for just a moment, folded her hands, and thanked God for the telephone call, and then asked Him for patience. Always, after a short prayer of thanksgiving, Sandra felt so much better, so much more at ease, and she thanked God often for always being there for her.

She finished cleaning up, walked into the living room and picked up a photo from off the end table. She sat down, gently running her fingers across the glass on the framed picture of Jacqueline. She was dressed in a white frilly dress, pink and yellow ribbons adorned her hair, and she held a huge Easter Bunny in her arms. It had been taken on Easter Sunday, several months before her abduction.

The Chipleys always planned for a large family, but after three miscarriages and one stillborn child, Jacqueline was their only living child. "God's will is for us to have only one child," Sandra would tell her husband, and looking at their daughter proudly she would tell him "and I am so thankful we have her. She is our gift from God. Our miracle baby."

Sandra recalled her pregnancy and delivery and the first time she saw her child. She weighed 8 pounds 7 ounces at birth and had absolutely no hair. "Baldy," John had said, laughing the first time he saw her. The birth had been difficult. When Jacqueline finally entered the world, covered with serious but temporary birthmarks from the forceps-aided birth and the long difficult delivery, she came out screaming and fighting. Sandra thought she was the most beautiful baby she had ever seen, hair or no hair.

Jacqueline grew fast, learned to talk early, walked before she was eleven months old and giggled and laughed non-stop. She was a polite, smart little girl with a sunny disposition and who enjoyed school. She most of all loved her Brownie Girl Scout Troop. Sandra volunteered her time as the Brownie's Scout leader and enjoyed the ten eight and nine year olds who met in their home once every week. On the weekends, the entire family would participate in events or outings involving the Brownies, as well as take part in community or church activities and enjoying their close friends and their children. Lately, Jacqueline's Brownie Scout Troop made up hand-drawn posters, each were about her kidnapping and, with the approval of the mayor and help and support from the Brownie's parents, placed them in businesses throughout the area. The principal at Jamison Elementary also brought in a grief counselor the first few weeks to help the children in Jacqueline's class handle all their questions and fear about the abduction. "Would they be kidnapped too?" they had asked.

Sandra recalled how quickly the police had arrived at their home the day of the abduction. After searching the neighborhood for only a few more minutes, John had called the Portland police department. Two squad cars arrived at the Chipley home within a few moments.

The police tried to assure the Chipleys that everything would be fine. They had called the department quickly and that would help the police in solving the case. The police officers spoke with all the neighbors and sent an officer to Jamison Elementary to talk to teachers and students. They dusted the house for fingerprints, cordoned off the entire home and yard, set up extra telephone lines in their home and waited for what they supposed would be a ransom call. The call never came.

Sergeant David Deerfield was in charge. He stationed an officer inside and outside their home the first three days and nights and, after a week with no major leads, Sgt. Deerfield had called in the FBI.

The police had questioned Sandra and John Chipley for hours, over and over again, asking them the same questions. Did they have money, could they pay a ransom, was their marriage good, did they have any enemies, had Jacqueline been threatened at school, what were her friends like, was she a problem child, could she have run away? They asked question after question, getting no feasible answers. Sandra Chipley felt horrible, she kept asking herself if she been a selfish mother, thinking only of herself and her terrible toothache. Should she have stayed home? Why wasn't John in the house instead of out back? Why wasn't he watching their daughter more closely? Would she ever be forgiven? Could she ever forgive her husband? Would God ever forgive them? What if they didn't get their precious daughter back? There were no immediate answers.

*   *   *   *   *

Sandra stood up, placed the framed photo back on the table. She touched her fingers to her mouth then touched the face on the photo. "I love you, Jacqueline," she said, "so much. Will you ever forgive mommy and daddy?"

With that, she called John to let him know Agent McLeary was coming over later with what she hoped was good news. John Chipley promised to be home by 5:30 p.m.

CHAPTER THIRTEEN

Joe Spencer was adding water to his coffee maker and reaching for the canister of coffee when his telephone rang. He set down the canister and picked up the phone.

"Hello," he said, trying to hold back a yawn.

"Joe, it's Jonas," he said, a concerned tone in his voice. "I'm not going to make it to work today, so no need for you to stop by. Sorry to call so early, but I guess you're up by now."

Joe automatically looked up at the kitchen clock noticing the time of 5:45 a.m.

"Yeh, Jonas, I usually get up around this time," he said, chuckling. "What's up? Anything wrong?"

"Yes," Jonas continued, "Our son-in-law Ben has gone missing at sea. He never returned to port last night. The Coast Guard's been called in and the boats and choppers are already out looking for his boat. Mary Anne and I are leaving in just a few minutes to head down to the harbor."

"I am so sorry, Jonas," Joe said, his voice changing to a more somber tone.

What he really wanted to ask Jonas was how Sarah and the baby were doing. Instead he asked a few more questions, asked Jonas to call him when he had more information on Ben, and then finally asked about Sarah. "Is Sarah okay? Does she know about Ben, Jonas?"

"Yes, she knows Joe, and she's holding up like the trooper she is. Her father-in-law, Martin Kestwick, is with her and stayed throughout the night. We wanted to go down last night, but Sarah insisted we wait until the weather cleared. I guess the rain and wind was real bad there last night. Sarah's had a few contractions, but so far her doctor wants her to wait until they are more regular before she heads to Portland."

Jonas talked with Joe for a few more minutes, told him he had already called in to work, and for Joe not to worry. "I'll call as soon as there's any news of Ben."

"Good Luck, Jonas," he said. "Please tell Sarah I'm thinking about her, and yes, please call me as soon as you know anything."

The two friends said their goodbyes. Joe hesitated a moment before hanging up the telephone. He moved toward the counter and continued to make the coffee. He sat down at his kitchen table, pondering what he just heard, recognizing the sadness and concern in his friend's voice. The Waverlys must be going through hell, he thought, but he felt more sadness and concern for Sarah. His Sarah.

Joe Spencer sat quietly, becoming mesmerized by the drip, drip, dripping of the coffee maker. His mind returned to years ago when he and a beautiful young woman shared coffee at the Cozy Corner Diner close to their school.

*   *   *   *   *

Natalie Pickford had been his one and only love. She came into his life shortly after he and his family moved to the Portland area. They had shared so much, had so much in common. They were both recovering drug users and had spent time in lockup. They both had wanted to improve themselves and prove that the bad years of their lives were over and the best part was yet to begin. They loved to listen to music and enjoyed school dances. She loved to watch him play basketball, and together they studied almost every day after school while drinking coffee at the diner. They both worked hard at their studies. He needed to improve his grade average to score a basketball scholarship, and she needed to get her grades back up just to graduate. They had mutual friends, most of them decent teenagers, with whom they hung out, but most of all they were in love and spent most of their time together, just the two of them. Most of the time she was sweet and loving. He saw the side of her he wanted to see and ignored the side of her that at times could become evil or unbecoming. He was so in love with her, and so young, he never saw her split personality or the really bad mood swings.

He knew then as he knew now, that Natalie's life had not been easy. She was a troubled teenager, her parents, who were into their mid-forties when they had her, tried to help but really had no clue what to do with a troubled teen, or any teenager for that matter. She disliked school, had low self-esteem, had only a few friends who were the wrong kind, and she had gotten herself pregnant and into drugs. By the time Joe met her, she had straightened out somewhat, was no longer using drugs, and was over the pregnancy and the loss of her son. She promised him and herself that she was ready to move forward and become a positive member of society. Neither Joe nor anyone else had any idea she had given up using drugs in order to deal drugs, and no one saw Natalie's dual personalities.

As Joe and Natalie's relationship grew, so did her drug dealing business. By the time she found out she was pregnant with Joe's baby, Natalie, only eighteen years of age, was becoming one of the major drug dealers in the Portland area. She was good at what she did, covered her tracks well and made significant money. No one suspected her about anything other than being a typical high school teenager.

*　*　*　*　*

Joe stood up, went to the coffee maker and poured himself a strong, black cup. He looked at the clock, making sure to get ready and leave for work on time, but first sat down to reminisce a little more.

*　*　*　*　*

Natalie was excited when she found out that she was pregnant with Joe's child. She had stayed clean throughout the past year so this baby would be drug free. She was making plenty of money, most of which she had stashed away, so she knew she could support the three of them. This way, they could get married, get a home together, and Joe could go to college after graduation. They would have their beautiful love child, and life would finally be good. When Joe would ask her about the abundance of money she always seemed to have, she would always tell him her parents were very generous as she was an only child.

Joe pondered. "How long had she planned on keeping the drug dealings from me?" he wondered again after all these years. She, no both of them, had lived in a fantasy world most of the time. They were kids, way too young to become parents, but they loved each other. She had been a child in a woman's body, physically able to meet all his needs, but mentally, he now realized she had been unstable. She had already been showing signs of the split personality disorder in high school. Most days she was kind, sweet and loving, and other times she would unleash cruelty and heartache upon him without any notice. She always apologized and made up to him in loving ways and he always forgave her.

* * * * *

Joe stood up, checked the clock once again and began to make his lunch. He took a brown bag from the upper cupboard, quickly made a sandwich, grabbed a banana from the counter and threw it in the bag. He turned off the kitchen light and headed for the door.

As he walked out the door to his truck, he remembered the heartache like it was yesterday. When Natalie had told him about the baby, they had both agreed to keep it a secret as long as possible. Natalie would have the baby and they would get married as soon as he graduated. Joe wasn't as certain as Natalie, however, that he would be able to still apply for a college basketball scholarship. Colleges frowned on freshmen with families, but he figured it would be worth the price, after all, he would have Natalie and their child. What could be more important?

His plan was to continue working hard, make good grades, apply to a local college, work part time and, although it would be tough, he and Natalie and their baby could make a go of it. Their love was strong enough and he was confident. When his parents found out, however, they did not agree. They insisted, as did Natalie's parents, that both of them were too young to start a family, and insisted that they wait, not marry, and give up the baby for adoption. Natalie, after all, was a year ahead of Joe in school, would graduate ahead of him, and who knew if they would still care about one another by the time Joe graduated. Most of all, the Spencers wanted their son to go to college and play basketball, even possibly make it as a professional in the big leagues some day. He had the talent and they insisted that if the two of them wished to continue dating, it was fine, but the baby needed to be put up for adoption immediately upon its birth. If in the future they still loved each other, they could marry and have more children. They also insisted that Joe was not to go to the hospital with Natalie, nor see the baby after the birth. Joe fought with his parents, but he was, after all, a minor, and his parents had the final say.

Natalie stayed in school and graduated, although not with her class. She received her diploma after giving birth to their little girl, Melanie Anne, two weeks after graduation. "It would be an embarrassment," the principal told them, "to have Natalie, who was nine months pregnant, walk across the stage with her classmates to receive her diploma."

Natalie's labor and delivery had been fairly easy, giving birth in less than nine hours. She saw her daughter for only a few moments before she was whisked away to the nursery. She cooperated with her doctors and the hospital staff, seemed cheerful and happy and even admitted to her parents they were right about giving the baby away. She asked her parents to take a photo of the baby if it was allowed, and she asked to see Ben. His parents did not allow a visit.

Twelve hours after giving birth and two hours after they told her the baby was being placed in a foster home, Natalie tried to commit suicide. Late into the evening, after the nurses had made their rounds, she went for a walk and sneaked into the staff kitchen area on the OB/GYN floor. She took a sharp paring knife from the drawer and used it to slit both of her wrists. She then stabbed herself in the stomach, fell to the floor and, had a nurse not come in for a late evening break, Natalie would have bled to death.

Natalie was immediately moved from the OB/GYN floor to intensive care where she was unresponsive to any and all contact. The doctors assured her parents that she would recover from her physical wounds, but her mental state was unstable at best. After physically improving, she spent fourteen days in the psychiatric ward of the Portland hospital, and after an in-depth psychiatric evaluation, Natalie was moved to the Mental Health Stabilization Center in Thomaston.

There, the doctors promised her parents she would be evaluated further, and this would be the most cost-effective way to handle her level of mental illness. Natalie Pickford spent over a year at the Center. Joe Spencer never saw Natalie again.

*　*　*　*　*

Joe drove his truck into the logging camp employees parking lot, parked and prepared to get out. He breathed a deep sigh, and, before getting out of the truck, took his wallet from his back left pants pocket. From behind his driver's license and buried in between scraps of paper and business cards, he pulled out a worn photo of a beautiful young woman dressed in jeans and a Portland High School sweatshirt. On the back of the photo, barely readable, it said, "To Joe, the love of my life. Natalie." He placed it back in his wallet and stepped out of his truck. A tear gently fell from his eye. He wiped it away with the sleeve of his jacket and proceeded through the gate marked "employees only" to begin his day.

He looked down at his watch, noticing he still had ten minutes before he needed to clock in. He walked to the office, picked up the "for employees only" telephone, and dialed a number in Cincinnati, Ohio. As he waited for an answer, his thoughts turned to Sarah. Was she okay? Had she started labor yet? Would they find Ben in time for him to share in the baby's birth? Would he ever have a chance to tell Sarah he was her birth father? He had never wanted her to know the truth. Being a friend of the family was enough for him, or was it? He thought of the time when he learned Sarah was his daughter.

He had been in Millinockett for almost two years. In that time he had spent many hours with the Waverlys. The more time he spent with them, the more attached he became to Sarah. There was something between them, but he just couldn't put his finger on it. It was like they shared something from the past, they had things in common, they both loved music, they both had blond hair and their facial features were similar. He kept telling himself all of these thoughts were absurd. However, as time went by, and he realized Sarah was the same age as his own daughter would have been, and since she was adopted, he wondered if there was the slightest possibility that she might be his and Natalie's child. The signs were all there. She was born in Portland, adopted from Augusta's Child Services Center, and the more he thought about it, the more he wanted to check into her adoption records. He knew looking into adoption records would take a court order, lawyers and a lot of money. Before he began secretly to look into Sarah's past, he had another idea. One night when he was babysitting for the Waverlys, he had brushed Sarah's hair, got her into her pajamas, helped her brush her teeth, read her a story and tucked her into bed. As always when Joe was at her house, she had given him hugs and kisses and told him she loved him. After she was asleep, he had taken strands of her hair from her pink hairbrush. He put them into a plastic bag and later that weekend had taken it into the police department in Portland for analysis. There had been a ton of forms to fill out, but lady luck had been on his side, and the investigators had approved his requests for a DNA analysis. The results were defining. His DNA and Sarah's DNA were a match. He was her birth father.

He had been thrilled and scared to death, all at the same time. He wanted her to know she was his daughter, but he could not break her heart or the hearts of the Waverlys. After long talks with himself and with God, he decided not to tell her but to continue to be her Uncle Joe, the way it had always been. This way he could love her from a distance, take care of her when needed, and no one would ever know… except, he thought now, except Natalie.

*   *   *   *   *

"Hello," the voice said, "Ball Music Company, this is Maurice." The voice startled Joe, bringing him back to reality and, as he looked at his watch, he knew he had to take care of this business transaction fast if he was to clock in on time.

CHAPTER FOURTEEN

Unbeknownst to Ben or Jeremy, Jack Currier and the BLUE LADY had been anchored within three nautical miles of the SARAH JEANNE. The boat came within range on Tuesday afternoon before sundown, dropped anchor and the crew was told to wait for further instructions. The wind was picking up, thunder rumbled through the skies, and the crew figured rain would be falling soon, but they waited. Special Agent Jack Currier, dressed in brown trousers, a dirty white t-shirt and waterproofed shoes, was at the helm. He looked like the normal fisherman he claimed to be. He was joined by two other DEA agents: Caroline DelMarco and Bill Sorenson, also similarly dressed. Sorenson currently lived in Booth Bay Harbor, working undercover as a part time boat mechanic/fisherman for a boat builder. He kept a low profile. His instructions were to keep tabs on Ben Kestwick. He followed his every move, as no one knew when Natalie Pickford Andrews would make a sudden or drastic move to harm him. Word was from the agency that she planned to first get rid of Ben and then get to Sarah and her baby. How she planned to do this, no one knew… explosion, bomb, sink or blow up the SARAH JEANNE, no one with the FBI or DEA knew for sure.

Because of ongoing tips and clues from those doing surveillance, Sorenson followed Ben to the docks, to the Breakfast Hut, and to the boat a few mornings each week. He would follow him in his craft at a close distance, watch him set traps and later pull them in, and follow him back to port. After dark he would watch the boat, making sure no suspicious characters tried to get on board. On more than one occasion, he had seen Natalie at the docks late at night in one or more of her disguises, but he had never caught her in a criminal act.

DelMarco worked as an undercover hair stylist first in Portland and now in Brunswick. She watched Natalie go to and from beauty shops in the area once a week. One week she would be a blond, then the next week she would dye her hair brunette or black. She also wore a number of multi colored wigs when she met with her contacts. DelMarco followed her as she moved from town to town, always staying one step ahead of the FBI. DelMarco watched as Natalie added more and more dealers to the drug ring.

DelMarco's primary employer was the DEA. She worked in drug enforcement. She was brought in by the FBI to watch for a break in catching Natalie in drug dealing and in the Jacqueline Chipley case. She hoped they could nail Natalie on both the drug and kidnapping charges, and soon.

She also watched Ben and Sarah's home on the days Natalie brought her daughter to Sarah's for a piano lesson. She had seen her just yesterday, Tuesday, and she was positive the child was Jacqueline Chipley. She matched the description and they knew for sure the woman was Natalie. The way things were moving, the FBI was expecting an arrest soon. As a woman and as a mother, the agent hoped and prayed for little Jacqueline Chipley and for Sarah and her baby's safety throughout this entire case. She pleaded with God to help her and the other agents bring Natalie Pickford Andrews quickly to justice.

Jack Currier had made a point of meeting Ben when the agent first went undercover. He set up an arranged-accidental meeting with Ben one night after they both docked. Jack just happened to back into him while walking away from the bar at the Inn, spilling beer all over him and the floor. Laughing and apologizing to one another, they introduced themselves, shared a beer or two and chatted for an hour.

Since that meeting a few months back, Jack and Ben met at the Inn once or twice but very seldom ran into each other on the docks. Ben was always up before dawn and got back to port late. Jack, he figured, wasn't an early riser and went out to sea on different shifts and to different locations. When they did meet back at the harbor, they would talk about work or hobbies or family. Ben shared about his family fishing business, how long they had been in Booth Bay Harbor, about his granddad and his father, but socially they did not see each other. Ben had never met Jack's wife or asked where he lived. He knew there were two small children in the Currier household, or at least Jack told him there were, and Ben told Jack about Sarah and that they were expecting their first child.

Of course, Ben had no clue that Jack Currier was an undercover agent with the DEA and the United States Department of Justice, Law Enforcement Agency based out of Quantico, VA. He did not know that, together, the FBI and DEA were sharing jurisdiction on a case in the area, and that their goal was to close down a huge drug distributer in the United States and Canada, as well as looking for and solving the kidnapping of little Jacqueline Chipley.

Both agencies had the proof they needed and were positive that Natalie Pickford Andrews was involved both in drug dealing, the US and Canadian drug ring and the kidnapping. Both agencies were hoping to bust the ring wide open, and at the same time get Jacqueline back to her parents. This would bring closure to two huge on-going cases.

The DEA knew several of Natalie's contacts. They knew she brought in her drugs from Canada because the Mobile Enforcement Team gave them continual information. They knew she started out by selling depressants and stimulants and then moved on to selling cocaine, marijuana and other drugs. They had already picked up a couple of dealers via information from FBI and DEA snitches, but their goal was to dismantle the entire drug ring and drug trafficking operations in this area of the United States. They needed to be patient, and their patience was about to pay off.

"MC3203, MC3203", the voice called over the boat's radio. "Come in MC3203, this is JC7878."

Jack Currier, anxious to hear if Richard McLeary made contact with the SARAH JEANNE, tried once, then twice before there was an answer.

"This is the BLUE LADY, come back."

"This is Jared," came the smooth voice on the other end, "MC3203 is unavailable."

Special Agent Currier knew to ask no more. He placed the phone back on the cradle on the wall and sat back down. He took another sip of his black, cold coffee, winced and set the cup down. He wondered how the meeting was going with Ben Kestwick and Richard McLeary. If it went well, this could be the end to a two-year battle to put a stop not only to a major drug ring, but also get Jacqueline Chipley back. They would also be able to put Natalie Pickford Andrews away for a very long time. He knew, however, they were also putting an innocent family in jeopardy.

Richard McLeary had contacted Jack Currier several months ago. Jack was already working on the Pickford-Andrews case, and, when the FBI fingered Natalie as a possible kidnapper as well as drug dealer, Jack was asked to go undercover. His wife, Janice, was not too keen about her husband going undercover again, but when Jack shared with her the story of a missing eight-year old, she changed her mind. Their daughter, Theresa, was eight years old, and Janice could not imagine life without her. She imagined the fear and sadness the family of this little girl must be going through, so she agreed to Jack going undercover. Not that it was Janice's decision, but agents and their families were always asked to discuss as much information as was allowed on a case and decide as a family whether or not to accept certain undercover assignments. It made the job easier and kept families feeling more content, happy and the agents safer.

Jack came home to Portland often during the first few months of the assignment, but during the last two months, he was living in the Booth Bay Harbor area. Jack could not tell his family exactly where. He called in weekly on private telephone lines, talked with Janice and his girls often, and the DEA sent his wife his paychecks. Richard McLeary covered his expenses.

Approximately an hour after agent Richard McLeary boarded the SARAH JEANNE, he called the Blue Lady. "JC7878, JC7878, come in. MC3203 calling JC7878, come in."

Thunder rumbled, lightning bolted through the afternoon skies, and, although a lot of static interrupted the telephone lines, McLeary heard the voice on the other end. "JC7878, come on."

"MC3203 here, all is ready and set to go forward," McLeary spoke clearly into the radio. "Go ahead with original plan. Meeting up with you at fifteen hundred hours at appointed location. MC3203 out."

Everything had gone according to plan. Agent McLeary stayed on board the SARAH JEANNE, followed closely by the unmarked FBI boat with DelMarco and Simonson aboard. Jared Jorgenson was at the helm.

The weather had been more than nasty. The winds blew in at about thirty-five knots, rocking the boat haphazardly, waves crashing in and over the railings, but through it all the mesh cages filled with lobster held firm. Down below, McLeary constantly talked with Ben, assuring him that he was doing the right thing. Two hours later while docking in Yarmouth, McLeary also shared with Ben that on Monday at about 3:00 a.m. two of his undercover agents had caught Carl Andrews placing an explosive device in the SARAH JEANNE'S engine compartment. They caught Andrews in time, took him into custody and the device into evidence, and right now Andrews was in jail in Yarmouth under the watchful eye of the Halifax police and two detectives.

"Now, Ben," he said looking at the forlorn and sad face of his new friend, "the police in Booth Bay Harbor, the Port Authority officials and the Coast Guard think you have gone missing due to the storm. More importantly, Natalie will think that Carl did his job and that you are dead, or at least incapacitated. That way she will go forward with the next step, trying to kidnap your new baby as soon as it is born."

Ben cringed, and then replied. "Whatever you say."

"Ben, there are Aid Boats already out looking for you and Jeremy, and tomorrow they are going to send out choppers. For right now, everyone involved, including your wife, needs to think the worse that you and the SARAH JEANNE have either been blown off course, disappeared somewhere due to the storm, or sunk. I promise, we will keep those in authority abreast of what is happening, what the real truth is, and we'll let your wife know as soon as we can. Are you okay, Ben? We just about have this case closed up and I guarantee everything will go well. We have incredible, experienced agents working on this case."

Ben nodded his head yes, and asked what next?

By the time the SARAH JEANNE and the FBI boat pulled into the Yarmouth Harbor on Tuesday night, the storm was in full force. Halifax police officers met them at the docks, helped them tie up and secure the boats, and drove them to the station. There, they informed Ben about the reports coming in from all the undercover agents, and, for now, that his wife was fine, his father Martin was with her, and, as he already knew, that Carl Andrews was in custody. In fact, he was being interrogated in a room down the hallway.

Ben would have liked nothing better than to get his hands on Andrews but kept those feelings to himself.

The officers at the Yarmouth station brought in some sandwiches and hot, black coffee for Ben and the agents. They were told they would be housed at a small cottage right off the coast, and Wednesday would hopefully bring more needed information to close the case. "A lot depends on Sarah," McLeary mentioned. "If she has this baby tomorrow or Thursday, we'll be able to close this case. I'm sure of it."

Ben looked at McLeary, made no comment but just thought of how much he missed Sarah and prayed she would go into labor tomorrow or Thursday as planned. He also prayed neither she nor the baby would have any blood problems and that her labor and delivery would go smoothly. Most of all, he prayed that no harm would come to either of them, and that deep down inside Sarah would know he was safe and would be back home soon.

Agent McLeary excused himself to use the telephone, but before leaving the room he promised Ben that two agents would be close by all night, and, although he had to head back to the harbor, he would be in touch. "I will be in close contact with my agents all night and all day Wednesday," he told Ben. "I'll be close to my private line all night. Call me at any time."

Tuesday night in Yarmouth had come and gone. Ben had not slept a wink, but no calls had come in either. He got up early Wednesday morning, showered, and, as he opened the door to exit the small cottage, agent Sorenson met him at the door with coffee.

"Morning," the agent said smiling. "Sleep well?"

Ben grumbled something the agent did not understand, accepted the coffee and walked back into the cottage. "I'm a prisoner," he thought to himself, "a damn prisoner."

Ben asked the agent if it was possible for him to talk with Agent McLeary. Sorenson took out his cell phone, dialed a number and handed Ben the phone. After two rings, the agent answered.

"Morning, Ben. How are you holding up?" he asked. "I've been in touch with my agents here. One has been outside your home all night. Your father is still with your wife. No one has come or gone, so we presume everything is fine with your wife. I promise you, I will call if there is any activity at your home at all."

"Also, Ben," he continued, "the FBI's plan is right on track. The Harbor Journal newspaper is reporting that you and your crewman are missing. This should make Natalie continue with her plan. She'll think everything is working out her way. I know it's difficult Ben, but this is exactly what we need to do to close this case. Within the next few hours, we're going to share what's been happening with the Port Authority and the Coast Guard, but we keep acting as though you are missing, you understand? They'll know the truth but not your wife yet. Ben, do you understand?"

Ben replied that he did, and once again asked to keep him informed as to what was going on at his home. "I expect my in-laws will be showing up soon. I'm sure my wife has called them. They were coming on Thursday anyway to go with us to the hospital in Portland, but I bet they'll come today." With those final words he handed the telephone back to the agent.

Sorenson asked his boss if there was anything else and closed the cellular telephone. He assured Ben that all was going according to plan and asked if he would go with him a few miles down the road for breakfast.

"You need to eat, Ben. Let's get into the car and head down for some food. I promise, McLeary can get a hold of us at any time." He continued by telling Ben that Richard McLeary was the best in the business, and for him to try not to worry. "Your wife is in very capable hands, Ben. I'm sure you don't believe me, but everything is going to turn out fine."

The two men got into the FBI vehicle, strapped in, and the agent turned on the radio. First, there was just a lot of local babble, but then the newsman talked about the boat missing from Booth Bay Harbor, who was aboard, and that the Coast Guard was on top of it.

The newsman was with the Lieutenant in charge of the case, and he assured everyone that everything possible was being done to find the two crewmen safe. He mentioned Ben and Jeremy's names and that Ben and his wife lived in Booth Bay Harbor. Once again, he assured the listeners that everything was going well with the case.

Ben wondered if Tom Casey already knew he was indeed safe, and he wondered if Ron at the Port knew the truth too. His concern was for Sarah. Her heart must be breaking by now. Oh, if he could only hold her in his arms.

Sorenson pulled up in front of the Eggery in Yarmouth, turned off the ignition and both men got out. They walked into the café and ordered coffee and breakfast. They waited only a few minutes for their food, and, as they were eating, Sorenson's phone rang. He answered, said just a second, and handed the phone to Ben.

"Ben, it's Tom Casey. I just heard. Richard McLeary called, and one of his agents was just in Booth Bay Harbor to see me in person. Are you okay?"

Ben assured the Lieutenant he was fine and told him it was good to hear a familiar voice. Tom continued to talk with Ben, asking him questions, telling him he was on his way to talk with Sarah to assure her every possible thing was being done to find him, and thanked him for his cooperation.

"Ben, this has got to be killing you, but believe me the FBI and DEA are on top of this case. I promise I will do all I can to assure your wife we're doing everything possible to find you. I can't tell her the truth right now, but shortly we will tell her that you are fine. Believe me, Ben, the Guard is there for you and your family. We will keep her safe and bring you home as soon as this case is under wraps. You believe me, Ben?"

Again, Ben said okay, and once again told Tom how much he appreciated the sound of a friendly voice. Talking with Tom Casey also calmed him down a little. He thanked Tom for calling, and asked him to call him with any news of Sarah. He finished his breakfast, drank another cup of coffee and took a deep breath. He relaxed just a little for the first time in the last several hours, but wondered just what the next twenty-four hours might bring.

CHAPTER FIFTEEN

In the bedroom of her Brunswick apartment, Natalie awoke with a start early Wednesday morning. She also had a horrendous headache. She sat up in bed, rubbed her temples, and blamed the headache on the difficult day she'd encountered yesterday. Jacqueline had cried and been a naughty little girl. "I must teach her to be a better little girl," she thought, her head pounding. "I'm not being a good mother, she must be disciplined more often."

Rubbing her temples harder now. she thought, "I can't believe I ran into Joe Spencer yesterday. At least I'm quite sure it was Joe. First, I saw him at the bank and then again at the docks. Unbelievable. After all these years!"

"I must make sure he doesn't interfere with my plans, my new baby," she said out loud. "I wonder if he recognized me? I doubt it. I look very different from high school days. Better. He would like me, no love me, more now than in high school." She smirked and through her immense head pain, evil penetrated her dark eyes.

To top it all off, she really hadn't slept that well. She'd had bad dreams again, the same dreams she'd been dreaming night after night. Horrible dreams of a baby crying. A baby without a face, a baby who kept reaching out to her. She would try to reach the crying baby, almost have the baby in her hands, and then it would slip from her fingers into deep black water. The dream haunted her this morning more than any morning before. "Maybe," she thought, "it's because I'm getting closer to getting a new baby and not being able to reach her in the dream upset me." Every night, however, the dream was the same. She never got to hold the faceless baby. Night after night, she kept trying to figure out what the dream meant, but she just couldn't grasp it. She was getting very frustrated and the dream hounded her night after night, never ending.

"I will have a baby soon, she said to herself, but it's never going to slip away from me. It will be mine for eternity. She'll be beautiful just like my Melanie Anne. No baby will ever slip away from me again."

Natalie believed in dreams, the moon, and the stars and in all things extraterrestrial. Three years ago she had gone to a psychic to learn more about the galaxies and their meaning for her life. The psychic had also talked to her about dreams. She truly believed afterward that her visit helped in her search for Sarah. The psychic told her that dreams were wishes that could quite possibly come true. If she imagined something long enough and strong enough, perhaps they would come to fruition. "I do believe," she told the psychic. "I know I believe. I'm going to have a baby soon, and my dreams tell me so."

Natalie believed completely and without reservation that the psychic could help her explain her dreams and help her with her future plans again. After all, she was the one who, years ago, told her the galaxies had taken a heavenly formation one evening, and the formations directed her to go to work in a college Child Care Center. Madame Madeline told her she would find a wonderful surprise at a college somewhere in the east and she should seriously look into the star's predictions.

A few months later, while looking on-line one day for a part time job, more for a cover than for the money, Natalie ran across an employment opportunity at the Chelsea College in Boston. The advertisement stated when parents attended classes, they would be given an opportunity to enroll their children in child care for three to five hours a day at no charge and they needed a director to take charge of the Chelsea Day Care Center. She had immediately sent in her resume. She wasn't, however, completely honest when she filled out the application concerning possible arrests or jail time, and the administrator at the college did not check further into her background. She had received a confirmation, and had been directed to contact the employment center within three days for an interview. The college administrator relayed to her that the nursery would be opening up within the month, and with her background, she would be perfect for the position. Of course she would have to move to Boston, but Natalie was used to moving. It would not be a problem, and within two weeks she and Carl moved to Boston and rented an apartment.

Unbeknownst to Natalie at the time, Sarah was a sophomore at Chelsea College. During her first few months at Chelsea, she had seen Sarah on more than one occasion in the coffee shop. It did not take her very long to realize that this beautiful woman looked very similar to Joe Spencer. She made sure Sarah never saw her at any time, and on two or three weekends she had followed Sarah to Millinockett. She had driven past her home, saw her adoptive parents in the front yard, even followed her to Booth Bay Harbor several times.

Natalie had the child care position at the college for over two years, giving her ample time to spy on Sarah, her supposed birth daughter. She had seen Sarah with Ben, been outside the church when they married, and she had watched Sarah blossom with child for the past several months. Everything had fallen into place since the time Madame Madeline proved to her the stars really were her friends and could predict her future.

Now, after all these years, she believed in her heart she was going to have a new baby in her life, Sarah's baby, and, since it was in the stars and in her dreams, she knew it would come true and was what the gods intended.

This latest dream, however, had her puzzled and frustrated. Was someone going to try to stop her from getting this baby? Why did she constantly slip away from her in the dream? What did the black water have to do with her dreams? Why was the baby always crying? Why couldn't she calm her? She made a mental note to herself to call Madeleine, the psychic, this afternoon.

Natalie gave up on sleeping any longer and got up confused and angry, her head still hurting. She turned on the television, hoping for news of a boat sinking off the harbor. "Hopefully, Carl took care of business," she said, mumbling through her headache pain.

She got dressed, took a couple of aspirin with her morning coffee and decided to wake Jacqueline up earlier than usual for her lessons.

She made a point of home schooling Jacqueline since her abduction. She couldn't take a chance on someone recognizing her even though she'd moved her several miles away from Portland to Brunswick. She could teach her enough to keep her on track, and then when she had the new baby, the three of them would move to another state. She always wanted to live in New York or New Jersey, and once there no one would recognize them, and Jacqueline could go back to a public school.

"I must teach her lessons today," she muttered to herself. "She needs to grow up to be an intelligent young woman. She will go far in life, and then she can help me teach her little sister. Just a little longer, I need just a little bit longer, and Jacqueline will have a baby sister, and I will have two smart and intelligent little girls. Everyone will be so proud of me."

Then almost immediately, as if someone pushed a button from ON to OFF, Natalie's personality changed from sweet, although confused, to angry and hateful. She walked briskly, straight into the extra room where Jacqueline slept soundly. She yanked off her bedcovers, pulled her up to a sitting position and yelled for her to get dressed. "You will study hard today, Jacqueline," she said. "Because tomorrow you will have a new baby sister to help me take care of, and we won't have time for your lessons!"

Startled and not completely awake, Jacqueline said nothing. She just looked at Natalie, got up from the bed and walked into the bathroom, Natalie following on her heels. "Use the bathroom," she said harshly "and get dressed. We won't have breakfast until after your lessons today. Do you hear me, Melanie Anne? No breakfast until after you study your numbers and practice the piano."

"J -ac -que- line…is my name," the girl stammered, "My name is not Melanie Anne, it's Jacqueline. You call me that name every time you get mad. Don't call me that name anymore; I don't like that name!"

Natalie picked up a pink hairbrush from the bathroom counter and smacked Jacqueline across the face with it. A welt swelled up instantly on the left side. Jacqueline, touching her cheek screamed, "I hate you, I hate you Natalie. You're not my mother. I want my mother. I want to go home. I'm going home!"

Rushing past Natalie and crying hysterically now, Jacqueline ran from the bathroom into the front room. She ran to the door, tried to open it but it was locked. After a few more seconds she unlocked it, released the dead bolt and, just as she opened the door, Natalie grabbed her by the back of her hair, dragging her to the floor. Screaming louder now and kicking hard, Jacqueline turned and kicked Natalie hard in the stomach, catching her off guard just for a moment. In that moment Jacqueline got to her feet, ran to the door, opened it and fled down the front steps into the street.

Someone would report later that they had seen a child in pajamas and bare feet running hysterically down the street. No, they didn't see which way she went or didn't try to stop her.

*   *   *   *   *

Natalie's neighbor, undercover agent Sally Benson, watched the activity unfurl at Natalie's home from her watch across the street. She watched as the child ran out of the red brick apartment house and down the street. She immediately dialed FBI dispatch, asked for one of three agents on the case and was told they were all out of the office on assignment. She left messages for all three. Phone in hand, Agent Benson opened her front door and walked calmly down her front sidewalk. She nonchalantly focused first on the red brick apartment house where Natalie stood in her front doorway, waved at her and continued to walk. As she continued walking and from the corner of her eye, she noticed that Natalie did not follow the child but went back inside, slamming the door behind her.

Natalie went to the kitchen, opened the refrigerator and took out a can of beer, and sitting down at the kitchen table, she popped the top on the can and drank half of the beer without stopping for a breath. "Damn! Damn!" She stood up, took another swig of the beer, threw it towards the trashcan, missing it by a good foot, splattering beer against the kitchen cupboards. "Think, Natalie, think! What do I do now?" she asked herself, pacing the floor.

"I should have given Jacqueline a sedative last night when I left. She would have slept longer and this would have never happened. "Damn!" she said again, slamming her fist into the refrigerator door.

Twice a week, normally after 10:00 p.m. Natalie left the apartment to meet up with other dealers or some of her buyers. She always gave Jacqueline an antihistamine to make her sleep. It was always a drug she would not become addicted to, but before she put her to bed for the night she would always drug her. Natalie was careful not to give the small child too much, but she couldn't take a chance on her waking up and wondering where she was or have her leave the house late at night. Last night, she had not gone out, choosing rather to stay with Jacqueline after their tumultuous day. However, a contact called later in the evening on her private line, and rather than causing a stir or losing a contact, she promised to meet up with him after midnight. She walked six blocks to where his car was parked, took care of business and, as far as she knew, no one spotted her. She hurried right back, even running part of the way. Jacqueline was still fast asleep in her bed when she checked in on her.

This morning, however, was a different story. Although slightly drowsy, Jacqueline got up upon demand and went into the bathroom. It was Natalie who had lost her cool. "Damn!" she said again. "I should have stayed calm and not have been so mean to her. It was that dream that damn dream. It's driving me crazy."

Holding her hands up to her head, Natalie walked the floor, trying to put her mind at ease. She was fighting her motherly instincts to go out and look for Jacqueline, but her mean, selfish inner-self was telling her to forget her, and the voices told her. "You only have one more day to go, and then you will have your baby, your own sweet baby girl. Don't bother with Jacqueline."

A normal woman with a healthy mind would have called the police, checked with the neighbors, gotten in the car and driven the neighborhood looking for her child. But Natalie's mind was far from healthy, and the only thing she could think of was a brand new baby. She chose to concentrate on Thursday, the day she would go to Portland and get her baby girl, Melanie Anne. Rather than worry today about someone else's child, all she said was, "Too bad, Jacqueline. Too bad. I'll have my own baby girl tomorrow. Too bad, too bad for you, Jacqueline!

*   *   *   *   *

Shortly after her release from the mental institution, Natalie moved back home to live with her parents. She told them it was only temporary and they welcomed her back.

In the time she had been locked away, she had learned so many things. The doctors and staff at the Stabilization Center taught her everything she needed to know about life again on the outside. After the first few months of being without Ben and her baby, she did as she was told but did not speak or carry on a conversation with anyone. She kept to herself. She, however, read every book they gave her on healing the mind and soul and body. Finally, after several months of silence, she asked for and received books on childcare, books on becoming a nanny, books on nurse's training and motherhood. She was determined to make something of herself when she got out of lock-up. She would show everyone on the outside how intelligent and capable she was. She would show them!

She participated in group therapy sessions and was always willing to share her story of heartache and pain. She told how she'd slit her wrists and stabbed herself but managed to survive. Now, because of the care at this place and the therapy she was receiving, she was well. She was ready to become a normal person, living on the outside.

Everyone, including Natalie, was convinced she was stable, as her doctor told her upon her release. He told her she would have to stay medicated for the rest of her life and see her psychiatrist at least twice a year. She needed to call immediately and let him know if she was starting to feel like she was "losing it" or felt her "old self" coming back. Most of all, and the most devastating news for Natalie to hear, was the self-inflicted knife wound had caused serious damage to her ovaries. She had no chance at all of ever getting pregnant again. Those words would remain embedded in her brain for the rest of her life.

* * * * *

Agent Benson walked at a normal pace until she was out of sight of the red brick apartment house. When she got to the corner she looked around, and, although she did not see anyone or see anything that looked out of the ordinary, she did see a woman in the next block, sweeping her sidewalks. She approached the woman, asking if she had seen a child clad only in pajamas run past, and the woman told her yes, she had.

"I tried to talk with her and ask her if she was okay," the woman replied, "but she just kept on running. You know kids these days," she continued, "I figured she was playing some kind of game."

Somewhat disgusted, the agent thanked her for the information, and asked which way the child was running.

"She went this way," the woman said, pointing to the left. "There's a church down there, you know, and then you run into the creek. She probably is meeting other kids down there. Kids like the creek."

Agent Benson walked left, and when she was out of sight of the woman, picked up her step and began to run towards the creek. She looked up and down the creek bed and then realized that if this little girl was smart enough to get away from her captor, she might just be smart enough to find shelter in a safe place—a church. She wondered if the church would be open this early in the morning and decided to check. She ran quickly to the front door, tried the door, and, thankfully, it opened. She walked quietly into the church, and, as she approached the altar, she heard the whimpering of a child. She approached her quietly and carefully and softly called her name. "Jacqueline, Jacqueline Chipley?"

Jacqueline jumped up, started to run, and Agent Benson grabbed her by the pajama top, spoke kind words to her, telling her she was a police officer and showing Jacqueline her badge. The frightened girl grabbed hold of Sally Benson, put both arms around the officer's waist and began crying hysterically again.

"It's okay, Jacqueline," the officer said over and over. "It's okay, you're safe now. Let's get you a blanket and get you warmed up, and then get you home to your mom and daddy, okay?"

She took the child by the hand, walked to a side door by the altar to try to locate a pastor or janitor. Just then, the side door opened. A very surprised laywoman appeared, asked what was happening just as Officer Benson showed the woman her badge. She asked for a blanket and perhaps some water for the child, then placed a phone call to the FBI and the local police. She gave dispatch the address of the church, asked for back up and for an extra squad car and the paramedics. She then asked to be put through to Agent Richard McLeary's private cell phone.

CHAPTER SIXTEEN

The cold brick room in the police station in Yarmouth, Nova Scotia was painted a dark gray. There were no windows, only the normal one way mirror, one door, and two shockingly bright lights. Sitting in a straight-back wooden chair at a long brown table, looking entirely too calm for the charges about to be brought against him, Carl Andrews was being interrogated by two Halifax detectives. He had been brought in earlier that afternoon in handcuffs, but now was free to move about the room if he so desired.

The FBI had captured him in Booth Bay Harbor, but because he lived in Nova Scotia now, the Halifax cops had first rights to him, and he was shipped over to the police station in Yarmouth.

Captain Lewis, Chief of Police in Halifax, had telephoned the station earlier, informing the two detectives, Bronson and Ford, to go slow and easy on Andrews until he arrived later in the day. "Got enough evidence to hold him for at least twenty-four hours or longer without pressing charges," he said. "And, I should be there later tonight and, if all goes right, we'll have him, cut and dried, and that wife of his, too."

"We got the warrant, chief," Bronson replied. "Just give us the word, and we're out to his place in Carleton."

"Hold tight, Bronson," the chief of police replied. "Don't want to mess this up. We got the goods on him now, and on his pesky little wife. Let's take this one slow. We still need the guy at the top, and we're close, but do this one by the book. I put a call into Agent McLeary, told him it's a go—to put his plan into overdrive and we are set to put these two away for a long, long time. Everything is falling into place right now, let's hope it continues that way. I'll call you in a few hours. Just keep Andrews under wraps until I get there. Savvy?"

Bronson agreed. This case had gone on for too long and needed to come to a positive end. Not positive for Carl Andrews and his wife, but good for the police department and the Specialized Unit on Violent Crimes in Nova Scotia. He was also glad for the boys with the DEA and FBI in the US. Everyone involved needed this case to be over, once and for all.

Ted Bronson and Bob Ford had been trying to shut down this drug ring for over two years. Every time they thought they had the Andrews' by the throat, something would go wrong either in Maine or here in Nova Scotia. There was never enough proof to bring them both in. Then a couple of months earlier, the case had taken a drastic turn when Andrews' wife, Natalie, had kidnapped a kid. The FBI in Maine and the Halifax police across the bay had enough evidence to prove she was involved both with the abducted child and had ties to the drug ring in Canada. Her husband Carl was just an added bonus. However, they couldn't bring both her and Carl in at the same time until they made sure the kid was somewhere safe. Bronson had commented to Ford earlier, "It's bad enough these two are drug runners, they have to involve an innocent kid, too? What do they need a kid for anyway?"

The two detectives got their answer when their chief informed them Natalie was not only dealing drugs, but she had kidnapped this child, Jacqueline Chipley, had tried to kidnap another little girl a few years earlier, and now was planning to kidnap another child as well…her own grandchild. The whole case made no sense to the two detectives, but then they didn't have all the facts. The chief had promised to fill them in soon. It looked like "soon" was going to be later tonight.

In the meantime, the two detectives worked on getting Carl Andrews to talk. He wasn't cooperating at all until they informed him they were about to take his little wife into custody too, and they knew she'd talk.

"She won't talk," he told them boldly. "She's nuts, anyhow, you won't be able to believe anything she tells you. Don't bother with her. Plus, she won't squeal on me."

"Well, we'll just see about that," Detective Ford suggested. "We should have her in custody in just a few hours, and you and she can spend some more time together over in the big house at Charleston.

You should like that, after all, you met at one of those facilities, why not spend the rest of your lives in one?" Ford smirked, looked over at Bronson, and told him he was going for coffee. Did he want some?

"Yup, and I'll just stay here with this scumbag until you get back," he answered, smiling. "Me and big dog here can have a nice conversation."

Carl Andrews crossed his arms across the front of his chest, said he had nothing more to say, wanted his lawyer and clammed up.

"Fine," the agent said, leaning up against the brick wall, and waiting for his partner to return with his coffee. "We got all day."

Detective Bronson had been watching Carl Andrews for months around the harbor areas with two or three other thugs as well. They would meet up at wee hours of the morning on the docks, in back alleys, even at times in local bars. They knew he was buying and selling from some locals, but they wanted the big boys at the top, the group bringing in the cocaine, marijuana and other drugs from New Jersey, New York, and Canada. Andrews was just a little fish; they needed to catch the big fish, and it was about to happen. They planned to get him first, then his wife and the big boys at the top.

Carl and Natalie were into more than just drug dealing. Even though they no longer lived together, he needed her. She got into his head and into his pants early on, and he was addicted to her, and because of that addiction and the money the drugs brought in, he had promised to help her steal a kid. Now, he promised he would help her steal another one. He couldn't figure out why she needed these brat kids so badly, but as long as he got what he needed from her, he'd go along with it.

He was now in custody because he had been stupid and had run off at the mouth one night in a Yarmouth bar. He was overheard bragging about how he was going to disable and steal a boat, kill the guy on board, and, with him out of the way, kidnap the guy's wife and kid. "I'm doing this all for the love of a good woman," he said in a drunken stupor. "You ought to see my baby," he said, "she's got a great body, no brains, but a great body and, whoa," he said making a shape with his hands like a woman's frame, "whoa, can she take care of this man's needs."

* * * * *

Carl Andrews had been a twenty-four year old guard at the women's correctional and mental facility when Natalie Pickford was incarcerated there. He noticed her right away. She was pretty, sassy, and played hard to get. But in lock-up, if they played their cards right, the guards usually got their way with any woman they chose. They had their pets on the inside, and with the right amount of money, bribery or threats, they helped the guards set up time in the back laundry room with their favorite inmate.

Carl Andrews had been with Natalie more than once, and rather than fighting him off, she let him have his way with her. She knew that in the end she would get her just reward and he would pay deeply. However, it didn't work out that way. She liked Carl and she cooperated with and encouraged his sexual advances.

When Natalie got out, she and Carl made arrangements to see each other. They dated for a year, started dealing drugs and making good money together, and ended up getting married. Natalie married more for security and for the money than for love. After all, there had only been one true love in her life, and he was gone forever. She knew with the drug money they brought in that their lives together would be comfortable, and, although there would never be any children, she could live with that. She didn't really love Carl Andrews anyway, but he loved her and he needed her, and she could use him.

She didn't tell her parents she was getting married. She had moved from her parents' home in Portland only a few months after she was released. They had been kind to her, but it was and always would be an uncomfortable situation due to their decision to give her babies away. She could not and would not ever forgive them for what they did. She also knew Joe Spencer was somewhere in the area, and she'd just as soon not run into him again either, too many bad memories. Carl quit his job at the prison, and they were married at a justice of the peace and remained in Brunswick. They rented a newly renovated apartment, and he worked for a local lumber company part time during the day and was a drug runner at night. Natalie, having taken child care classes in the women's correctional facility and having received a letter of good behavior and recommendation from the warden, got a job as an assistant in a day care program. She worked with Carl at night.

The money was great, and in the first two years they stayed in the same apartment, had no trouble with neighbors or with the cops and their lives seemed normal to everyone. Then one night about midnight, Carl met with one of his contacts about five miles out of town. Unbeknownst to him, the contact was working with a snitch and set Carl up. Carl, caught in the act of dealing, was found guilty and sent to prison for five years. The DEA found no drugs in his and Natalie's apartment; they found no fault or guilt with her, and her life continued as before, just without Carl.

Six months after Carl was sent up, Natalie moved to Campden into another apartment. She called herself Natasha instead of Natalie, colored and cut off her long blond hair and continued to work nights to find new contacts. She found a part time position at another day care center and visited Carl only a few times while in prison. When he was released from prison, they started up where they had left off, except in a different area of Maine.

As time passed, Natalie started to feel uncomfortable with Carl's dealing techniques. He was taking too many chances, didn't scrutinize his contacts very well, and when he was almost caught dealing a second time, she realized she needed to work alone. She was also contemplating finding a baby. Her heart ached for a child, but knowing that with a record, the system wouldn't allow her to adopt a child, she decided to find a way to get one on her own. When she told Carl her plans he was furious. "You just can't take someone else's kid," he told her, "What are you, crazy?"

Carl had been on the right track about her being crazy. Day by day, he watched her split personality disorder coming back. One day she was the happy, sassy and fun woman he remembered, and the next day she would be sad, forlorn, mean and hateful. After a few months of fighting and yelling and Carl being more and more careless with his contacts, Natalie moved out. She couldn't take a chance on getting caught dealing, and she could find a child better on her own. She set her plans up by herself, a plan to kidnap a child.

* * * * *

"Hey dingbat," Bronson hollered, poking Carl in the shoulder. "Got anything you want to say to me? How's that little woman treating you? What does she see in you anyway, you piece of crap! Did you help kidnap that kid, too?"

Carl Andrews didn't bat an eye but just sat there, arms crossed, waiting for his lawyer.

Carl thought about Natalie. She had been good for him, good sex, good drug money, but she had left him, moved out, left him high and dry. He didn't deal as well without her contacts, and a man had his vices after all.

She gave him what they both needed once in awhile. They would meet up either in Brunswick or she would take the ferry over to Yarmouth once every month or so. Since she kidnapped that brat kid, she hadn't called him at all. Then three weeks ago, she called. She asked him to do her a favor, and being the macho man he was, he told her, "You know sassy girl, a favor for a favor." She had obliged him and he promised to set explosives on the SARAH JEANNE.

"Make sure it's a small explosion and that the boat's far out at sea when the engine stalls. Make sure there are no witnesses," she had demanded. "We need that boat, but no witnesses, you got that Carl? Make sure you follow that boat and get rid of Ben Kestwick!"

In return, she had given him the explosion of his life, and more than once. There was something about that woman. "She may be nuts," he thought, "but, man, could she turn me on." She knew just what he needed and gave it to him.

But, once again, Carl Andrews had been careless. The Feds had been watching him. They saw him purchase the blasting caps and other explosive devices and had followed him to the docks night before last. They had caught him red-handed. Now he was busted and it was all that bitch's fault.

* * * * *

"Damn woman!" Andrews muttered.

"What's that, scumbag?" Ford asked, smiling. "You got something you want to say to me, huh, scumbag?"

Once again, Carl Andrews clammed up, rolled his eyes in Bronson's direction and said nothing else.

Bronson chuckled, hearing a knock at the interrogation room door. He walked to the door, opened it, and Agent Ford walked in with two coffees.

"How's the douche bag, Bronson?" he asked. "Has he spewed his guts yet?"

Agent Ford took the lid off his coffee, took a sip, and told his partner that Carl still wasn't talking, and he was going out for a minute to use the phone. "Got to call the boss," he said, "find out when we can throw the book at this jerk-off." With that, Ford left the room, closing the door behind him and headed for his desk and the telephone.

CHAPTER SEVENTEEN

Richard McLeary boarded the boat in a horrendous rainstorm and left Yarmouth late Tuesday night. He took Jared and DelMarco with him, and left Agent Sorenson with Ben Kestwick. Jack Currier stayed with Ben's boat and, with help from two police officers and a dockworker, they unloaded Ben's catch from the SARAH JEANNE for safekeeping and, hopefully, a next day shipment out of Yarmouth rather than Booth Bay Harbor. On Thursday, Agent Currier would be the contact between Ben Kestwick and the Portland hospital staff when his wife arrived and, hopefully, gave birth to their child.

On the trip back across the Bay from Yarmouth to Booth Bay Harbor, the weather had been treacherous. Due to rough seas and high winds, the boat thrashed back and forth, and although McLeary tried to snooze a little and finalize some paper work, it had been hopeless. He had eaten a stale sandwich, drank a bottle of water and, when they docked, it was past 3:00 a.m. and he had gone directly to his hotel. He stood upright long enough to take off his damp clothes and then fell onto the bed sound asleep. He had slept soundly until 9:00 a.m. when the ringing of his cell phone awakened him.

"McLeary here," he answered, half asleep.

"Sir, it's Agent Benson," came the excited voice on the other end of the telephone. "I have the Chipley girl!"

"What did you say, Benson? Did I hear you right?" he asked curiously. "You've got Jacqueline Chipley with you?"

"Yes sir," came the reply. "I'm in Brunswick at the Catholic Church on Bridgeport and Third Place, right down by the little river, or creek, that runs through town. Can you get down here right away? I've called the locals and the paramedics, but she's in pretty good shape, considering. What are your orders, sir?"

Richard McLeary sat up on the edge of the bed, thought for a few minutes, rubbing his free hand through his hair. "Good work Benson. Stay right where you are. Don't let anyone call the press. Anyone there with you?"

"Yes, sir, a Mrs. Thaddeus, she works in the church here."

"Make sure she stays with you. Don't let her out of your sight. We have to get all the information we can from the girl, call the parents and then the press. A lot is riding on this case, you understand?"

"Yes, sir, I do," Benson commented calmly.

"Okay," McLeary said, "You're in charge until we get some more agents down to Brunswick." Then as an afterthought he asked, "Where is Natalie Pickford? Is she within sight?"

"No sir, Jacqueline ran from her, escaped. I followed the child. As far as I know, Natalie is still in her apartment. She didn't go after her."

"Well, I'll be," McLeary thought, "isn't this something?"

"We don't want to jeopardize the case, Benson, make sure we keep this quiet as long as possible. You got me?" And then as an afterthought, he asked again, "You sure the child is unharmed?"

Agent Benson assured him the child was scared, had a large bruise on her face, but was otherwise fine, and she had the situation under control. Benson secretly hoped she could keep it that way.

Richard McLeary closed his cell phone, shook his head, and marveled at what he had just heard.

"Damn!" he said out loud. "Doesn't this beat all?"

He stood up, walked into the bathroom, cleaned himself up a little and got dressed. He left his hotel within fifteen minutes, got into his car and headed for Brunswick. On the way he stopped for gas, grabbed a cup of coffee and a poppy-seed muffin at the station, got back in his car and made three telephone calls while driving. He first called the FBI dispatcher and clued him in to the recent event and asked him to let the rest of his staff know, but to absolutely keep it from the press. He then dialed Agent Sorenson in Yarmouth and gave him the same information. "Go ahead and tell Kestwick what has happened," he told the agent. "It might give him more confidence in the FBI if he knows we have one part of this case in hand." His third call he decided would have to wait, the call to Jacqueline's parents. He needed to make sure everything was in perfect order before he let them know their daughter was safe. They weren't planning to hear from him until later today anyway, so he had plenty of time. He put the phone back in his pocket, breathed a big sigh of relief, and headed out of the gas station towards highway 27 leading to Brunswick.

After driving down highway 27 for just a few miles, he thought about the situation a little more. "If this was my kid, I would want to know right away that she was safe," he muttered to himself. He decided to call the parents as soon as he arrived at the Catholic church in Brunswick.

Agent Benson stayed close to Jacqueline while the paramedics checked her vital signs, attended to the bruise on her face, and checked for other signs of trauma. One of the paramedics gave her a bottle of orange juice, which she drank immediately and asked politely if she could have more. The paramedic in charge gave her another bottle of juice and promised she could have some breakfast soon. "What do you like for breakfast?" he asked.

"Scrambled eggs!"

The kind man in the blue uniform told her his name was Jackson, asked her if she was ready to move to the local medical center in a few minutes. He promised her she would see her parents very soon, too. Jacqueline smiled up at the medic but said nothing more.

"You have to keep an eye on her and keep her comfortable here for a few more minutes," Benson told Jackson and the other two paramedics. "She can't be moved until the FBI agent in charge arrives on the scene. Can you please get her another blanket?"

Sally Benson needed to make sure Jacqueline's pajamas were secured for evidence, but did not want to traumatize the child any further by taking them from her. She kept her warm with blankets and held her close to her own body when the paramedics finished checking her over. The local police department also knew this was an FBI case, so did not question Jacqueline at all. They knew to wait for the agent in charge and then they would do what was required of them.

Richard McLeary drove at least twenty miles over the posted speed limit and arrived at the St. Michael's Catholic Church by the river in a little over thirty minutes. By the time he arrived on the scene, there were four local cop cars in front of the church, an ambulance, a fire truck but, thank God, no news media. "Benson has done her job," he muttered to himself as he got out of his vehicle. He met Police Chief Carlson on the steps leading into the church, shook his outreached hand, and they walked into the sanctuary together. McLeary looked around, noticing the beautiful stained glass windows, the statues, and, being a practicing Catholic himself, stopped at the water fount, dipped his fingers in, crossed himself, and paused for just a moment. He then walked to the front of the church where several police officers and paramedics stood.

"Benson?" he asked, causing her to let go of Jacqueline Chipley. She stood up, turned around and faced him.

"Yes, sir?" she replied. Turning towards Jacqueline, she said to the little girl, "This is Agent McLeary, Jacqueline. He has been looking for you for a long time. Will you answer his questions if I stay right here with you?"

The little girl nodded her head in agreement, but hung tightly on to Agent Benson's arm.

McLeary sat down in the pew next to the agent and child, and for the next thirty minutes, he spoke kindly and softly with the little girl. She answered as many questions as she could, trying to remember everything that had happened to her since she escaped this morning. The agent asked if she was hungry and when she said yes, added, "and Jackson said I could have scrambled eggs." McLeary asked one of the police officers to go to the closest café and get her some scrambled eggs. She smiled at the agent, said thank you, and he continued to ask her more questions.

"Jacqueline," McLeary asked, "How is it you ran into this church this morning? Have you been in this church before?"

"No," came the meek reply. "My mama always told me if someone bad tries to take me or if I am scared, I should find a policeman or go to a school or to a church. I should run fast and find somewhere safe to go. I ran really fast from Natalie, but I couldn't find a policeman, so when I saw this church I went right in."

"Your mama is a very smart lady," he continued, touching her hair, "and you, sweetheart, are a very smart little girl, too."

McLeary was elated when the child mentioned Natalie's name. He knew the FBI was right where they wanted to be—the child safe in hand, and Natalie Pickford Andrews about to get her just due. He said nothing to anyone about his current feelings, just smiled, took his cell phone from his jacket pocket and dialed the Chipley's home telephone number.

By the time the police officer returned with scrambled eggs, the welt on Jacqueline's check had swelled up to the size of a large marble. The paramedics assured McLeary that it looked worse than it was, but she should definitely be checked out at the medical center. McLeary agreed and told the officers in charge to get her in the ambulance as soon as she finished her breakfast and have one patrol car escort the ambulance to the center. He was going to call the hospital and give them a heads up immediately. He would also call the Portland Police Department and tell them what was happening and for them to send a patrol car to the Chipley's home. He would then call one of the FBI agents in Portland and have them all meet at the Chipleys at the same time. A police officer and an FBI agent would bring the Chipleys to the hospital where they could meet up with their daughter.

"Just remember," he told everyone gathered there, "No press! No press until I give the word. Let's let the Chipley family have a little time together before we contact the press, understood?"

Everyone agreed, but by the time they moved Jacqueline into the ambulance, curious neighbors and those driving by had stopped to check out all of the commotion. McLeary knew it would be tough to keep this quiet much longer, but he would try his best.

He wished he could drive by Natalie's apartment, but knew he couldn't jeopardize the case. They needed one more day. One more day and Natalie would show her hand and they would catch her in her tracks. But right now he was excited for the Chipleys and for his department. One part of this case had turned out positively, and big and brawny Richard McLeary choked back a sob. He looked at his watch. It was 11:00 a.m.

CHAPTER EIGHTEEN

Sarah slept surprisingly well Tuesday night. She was still confident Ben would be found, and she found solace in praying for him and turning over her fears to God. The baby settled down around midnight, too, so she woke up refreshed. Martin stayed the night with her, which also made her feel safe and secure.

She hadn't said anything to Martin, but she knew the baby would be coming soon. Her contractions, although sporadic, were coming more and more often. One really strong pain had racked her body about 3:00 a.m. lasting over two minutes, but since then there were only light contractions. She made coffee, prepared hers and Martin's breakfast, and, after she cleaned up the kitchen, sat down to play the piano—an every morning ritual—there was a knock on the door.

'I'll get it," Martin called to her. "Stay where you are."

Martin opened the front door, noticed the sun was shining brightly this morning and welcomed Lt. Tom Casey into the house.

"I'm Ben's father, Martin," he said to Tom, shaking his hand. "Sarah said you would be stopping by."

"Yes, I know," Tom said politely, removing his hat. "I've seen you once or twice at the docks. Nice to see you again." As he stepped into the house, he asked if he could see Sarah, and Martin directed him into the living room where she remained at the piano.

"Mrs. Kestwick?" he inquired. "I'm Lieutenant Tom Casey with the Coast Guard. I've come to speak with you about your husband. I called earlier."

Sarah acknowledged him, carefully stood up from the piano bench, and asked him to have a seat and please to call her Sarah. She turned and said, "Please, Martin, join us, won't you? Would you like something to drink, coffee perhaps, Lieutenant?"

Tom said no to the coffee, wondered just how easy it was going to be to ask the father-in-law to leave the room and the three sat down.

"You look great, Sarah," he commented, "How are you feeling?"

"I'm fine," she said softly, patting her stomach. "But this baby is ready to come and I'm ready to have him or her come, too. We're just waiting for our daddy to come home first."

"It's so nice to finally meet you, Sarah. I've seen Ben a few times on the docks. We knew each other a long time ago," Tom shared. "He talks about you all of the time, and I know how excited he is about this baby. He can hardly wait for it to be born."

After a few more minutes of small talk, Tom Casey assured Sarah and her father-in-law that everyone in the Guard was doing all they could to find the SARAH JEANNE. He shared the details of a search and rescue with the both of them, said that due to the severe storm on Tuesday evening telephone lines were probably still out and he felt confident that the boat and the two men aboard were safe and docked somewhere.

"Perhaps Ben had engine problems or his land-to-sea telephone line is out," Tom Casey said in confidence, "I think it is just a matter of time and the boat and the men will be found."

Sarah asked Tom several more questions about the SAR and the Coast Guard, which Tom answered in a professional and timely manner, and when he and Sarah had finished their conversation, he asked Martin if he would mind leaving the two of them alone for just a few minutes?

"I really need to speak with Sarah, alone, Mr. Kestwick," he said. "I hope you don't mind."

Martin stood up, thanked Tom for his time, shook his hand and left the room. Martin picked up his jacket from the back of a chair, put it on and headed out the front door.

Sarah, understandably confused at Tom Casey's request, immediately but cautiously stood up, questioning Lieutenant Casey about their need to be alone. Tom stood up as well.

"What is going on Lieutenant?" she asked, a frown on her face. "Are you not telling me the whole truth? Is something wrong with Ben? Is my husband dead?"

Sarah began to waver, tears filling her eyes as she sat back down on the couch. She grabbed her belly as her unborn child kicked her hard, and she took several deep breaths to calm herself and her child.

"I am so sorry, Sarah," Tom began and sitting down beside her said, "I did not mean to upset you or the baby, Sarah, but please believe me, your husband, Ben, is fine."

Tom Casey sat down next to Sarah, took one of her hands in his, and began.

"I have been instructed to tell you," he said, "that your husband, Ben, is alive and being held in Yarmouth, Nova Scotia." Sarah, now visibly upset, tried to interrupt, but Tom asked her to please let him finish before she asked any more questions.

"There is a drug ring operating here in Booth Bay Harbor, in Brunswick and also in Yarmouth, Nova Scotia," Tom continued. "The FBI learned through a snitch that the drug ring was planning to steal the SARAH JEANNE and do away with Ben and Jeremy. The plan was to use Ben's boat for drug smuggling and, since the SARAH JEANNE is very well known in the bay area, the smugglers figured the Coast Guard or DEA would never stop Ben's boat. They could get across the bay to Canada with thousands of dollars worth of drugs without being detected."

Tom further explained to Sarah that undercover agents had been watching Ben and his boat for the last couple of weeks. "Night before last," Tom told Sarah, "two agents caught one of the drug dealers setting just enough explosives on Ben's boat to disable it when it got out to sea. The agents found a small detonator in the engine compartment set to explode about ten miles out. The boat's engine would have stopped and the smugglers who were in close proximity to the SARAH JEANNE would have pulled along side, overpowered Ben and Jeremy and most likely thrown them overboard. They would have taken over the boat and done whatever needed to get the SARAH JEANNE repaired, loaded the boat with drugs and head unnoticed up to Canada. The storm that night would also have helped them cover their tracks. However, the

FBI captured the culprit and gathered up the evidence before any harm was done. The man is now in custody in Yarmouth."

Tom continued to tell Sarah that in order for the FBI to successfully capture the rest of the drug dealers, the agents needed to pretend that the SARAH JEANNE and the crew were lost at sea. "The smugglers planned to take over the boat sometime today," Tom continued, "However, the FBI agents were one step ahead of the 'bad guys' yesterday afternoon and a boat piloted by three undercover agents boarded the SARAH JEANNE while out at sea, and, Ben was told the entire story. He had absolutely no idea of what had transpired in the past twenty-four hours."

"I have to tell you, Sarah," Tom told her, "your husband was not happy with the FBI and at first refused to cooperate with them. He is extremely worried about you and the baby's welfare and told the agents as much. He did finally agree to the FBI's plan, and, currently there is someone watching him in Yarmouth, and your house is being watched at all times. There will be an undercover FBI agent at the hospital when you arrive there as well. You will just not know who they are."

As Tom continued to hold Sarah's hand, he asked her if she needed water and was she doing okay? When she said, yes, she was fine she asked Tom to continue.

"Sarah," Tom continued, hating that he was only telling her a half-truth. "You and the baby are really at no risk, the smugglers only wanted your family's boat, but the FBI does not want to take any chances with your safety, so, when you are admitted into the hospital tomorrow, the FBI and the OB/GYN staff will have a direct telephone line to Ben in Yarmouth, and if this case is not over before you go into labor and deliver your baby, Ben will be with you the entire time by telephone."

"Now," Tom continued, "the catch here is that one of the big time drug pushers is also involved in a kidnapping case in Portland. The FBI knows where this person is holding the kidnapped child and hope to get the child back and capture the kidnapper/drug dealer at the same time. They cannot, however, let this person know that the plan to steal Ben's boat is a wash," Tom laughed at his choice of words, and even Sarah smiled just a little. "I know this is very complicated, Sarah," Tom said, holding her hand even more tightly, "but you and Ben may be the most important people in this case right now. You two could be heroes. You will be helping to get a kidnapped child back to her family and possibly help to stop a drug ring also."

Sarah agreed with most of what Tom Casey had to say, but admitted she didn't really understand all of it. All that really mattered was that Ben was safe.

"Will Ben be able to come home before I have the baby?" she asked.

Tom said sadly, "I don't think so, Sarah, unless the person of interest shows her hand, makes a move or a mistake before the allotted time. The FBI knows that a big drug deal is coming down on Thursday, and that is when they plan to take the suspect into custody. They will also, at the same time, get the kidnapped child back. I wish I could insure Ben's return right away, but I just can't."

Tom wondered if he was getting the story close enough to the truth for Sarah to believe it. He could not tell her anything about her and her baby possibly being in jeopardy, and he hoped and prayed that he had convinced her that she and her baby were not really involved. Deep down inside, however, he knew she and her child could be at serious risk on Thursday.

Sarah, although confused, seemed okay with what she had just heard. She didn't like it, wished it were not happening, but, once again, knew that God was in charge.

"I know this is all happening for a reason, Tom." She said, her voice cracking. "I just don't know why. I'll just continue to pray for guidance, for a healthy baby and for Ben to come home soon. Do you believe in a higher plan, Tom?" she asked Tom Casey? "Do you believe in a God who watches out for all of us?"

Tom assured her that he did, and told her he felt God was working in her and through her right now. "There has to be a God, Sarah," he said, "because no one, absolutely no one could be going through what you and Ben are going through and remain so calm if there were not a God. Yes, I do believe, Sarah."

Tom gave her a hug, helped her to a standing position, and said. "Sarah, you must not, I repeat, must not, tell Martin what is happening. The FBI allowed me to talk with you and you only, and only because of your condition. Can you handle Martin?" Realizing whom he was talking to, Tom chuckled and told Sarah that he had no doubt that she could handle it.

"You are a wonderfully strong woman, Sarah," he said, once again taking her hand in his. "I hope I can be as fortunate someday. Ben is a very lucky man."

Tom walked with Sarah to the front door of her home, walked out onto the porch where Martin was sitting. He spoke with the two family members for another few minutes. He then excused himself and took his leave.

"I'll be in touch often, Sarah, Martin," he said, acknowledging them both. "I promise to keep you abreast of the situation. I truly believe Ben will come home shortly and be fine. You and that baby just concentrate on yourselves, that's what Ben would want, right Martin?"

Martin put his arm around his daughter-in-law, thanked Tom again and together they started up the steps. Lieutenant Casey wished her luck, reminded her again to take care of herself, placed his hat on the top of his head and walked down the steps to the street. As he walked towards his vehicle, a woman in a gray Chrysler drove down the street very slowly. Tom Casey did not notice the woman at the wheel, but he did notice the unmarked vehicle parked a half block away. The vehicle pulled out directly in front of him as he got into his car. He presumed it was an undercover agent and that the FBI was watching all activities at the Kestwick home. "Good," he thought to himself. Everything is under control."

Natalie had driven by the Kestwick home twice during the night, and this was her first drive-by this morning. She watched for any unusual activity. If Sarah's or her father-in-law's car was gone, any sign that told her Sarah had gone into labor and was heading for the Portland hospital, she would be ready. She was elated to see a Coast Guard vehicle outside the home this morning. That surely meant Ben was missing, and she smiled, thinking how her plan was coming together.

"Poor Sarah," she said to herself, "first she loses her husband and soon she will lose her baby. I'll show her what it means to have your baby taken away from you. I'll show her. You just wait until tomorrow,

Sarah, you'll be all alone, just like I was!" Then, just like a light switch, she switched personalities and thought of Jacqueline.

"Poor Jacqueline, poor Jacqueline, I'm sorry I hit you this morning. I hope someone found you. I miss you Jacqueline, I really did love you, you know that, don't you baby? Maybe I can get you back. But you'll have to wait until tomorrow, first I have to get Melanie Anne."

Natalie drove a few blocks, stopped in front of a park, got out of her car and walked around for a few minutes. She noticed several mothers with their children. They were swinging on the swings, playing in the sandboxes, playing tag, laughing and hugging each other. She didn't, however, notice the car parked across the street a half a block away.

Exactly twenty minutes later, she returned to her car, drove back to the Kestwick neighborhood and, once again, drove slowly past the home Sarah and Ben shared. This time, another car was pulling up in front of the house. An older man and woman were getting out, and as the man opened the trunk and took out a suitcase, Natalie drove around the block to come back for a better look. As she came around the corner the second time, the older couple was walking up to the door. She recognized them. The Waverlys. The people who had taken her baby away from her, Sarah's adoptive parents. She was so agitated she almost drove into the curb. She had not only gotten rid of Ben Kestwick and would soon break Sarah's heart a second time, but now she could break the Waverly's hearts too.

"They will finally know what it is like to hurt, to feel your heart break," she thought, "I will finally have my revenge, finally, after all my years of heartache, I will get revenge and get my Melanie Anne too." She smiled and then laughed out loud as she headed for the park one more time.

Sarah greeted her parents with open arms. Her mother cried, her father tried to console her mother, and through it all Sarah stayed calm. "I'm fine, mom, really I'm fine," she assured her. "I know Ben is coming home soon, and I also know this baby is coming soon. So try to be calm, mom, okay? Your grandchild and I need you to be strong." Her mother nodded her head, wiped a tear from her eye, and before she sat down, handed Sarah the box of cookies and muffins she had made and told her she had made Ben his favorite lobster dish. "For when you are in the hospital, dear," she said. Talking about Ben and her famous lobster dish set off her emotions again. Sarah settled her mother down once more and set the food items down on the coffee table.

Calmly, Sarah shared with her parents everything that was happening. Ben supposedly lost at sea, the recent visit from Tom Casey, the contractions she'd had, how she had slept and, yes, she assured her mother, she was eating well. She realized she had not acknowledged Martin who was sitting in the kitchen drinking coffee and watching television. "I'm sorry, Martin," she called to him, "my parents have just arrived. Come out here will you?" Martin stood up, walked out to the living room, shook Jonas' hand, and gave Mary Anne a hug.

"Thanks for being here with Sarah," Jonas said, sitting down and motioning for Martin to sit as well. This is quite something, isn't it? Ben missing and all?"

"I just don't understand it, not at all," Martin scowled. "It's just not like Ben to get lost at sea; he's handled his boat in storms much worse that the one we had yesterday, and Jeremy too. I just can't figure it out. I keep expecting the telephone to ring and it will be him, all safe and sound back in port."

Martin asked Jonas if he would like coffee, and when he said yes, the two men got up and continued their conversation in the kitchen, allowing mother and daughter their own space. The two women sat together on the couch, and Sarah asked her mother how things were in Millinockett and how she and dad had been? Had they done anything fun or interesting in the last few weeks since she had seen them? Just idle talk mostly. She knew if she talked about Ben, her mother would get very upset, and Sarah did not need to be any more upset than she already was, not with this little one coming at any time.

She shared with her mother that her contractions were becoming more regular this morning, and she had called the doctor again. He suggested that, until they were consistent and she really couldn't handle the pain anymore, to wait it out. It was an hour's drive to the hospital in Portland and for her to use her own judgment when the time was right to leave Booth Bay Harbor. Her water had not broken, so she was just watching the clock, timing her contractions and biding her time. Most of all, she was waiting on word from Ben. She wished she could tell her mother that Ben was safe, but Sarah knew the truth, and in due time she would tell her family the truth as well.

Sarah told her mother she had packed her suitcase a few days earlier, Ben had filled the car with gas so they could take her car if they wanted and she was more than ready to deliver this baby. She told her mother what blood work would be done when she got to the hospital, how they would monitor her and the baby due to the Rh negative factor, and most of all, she tried to convince her mother that she and the baby would be fine. "Everything is in God's hands at this point, including Ben," Sarah told her mother. "Please, don't worry because I'm not overly concerned. Everything is going to be fine, mom. I really believe that."

Sarah's calming nature seemed to calm her mother as well. They talked about last night's storm, about Lieutenant Casey and that he used to live in the area, her piano lessons, her students and about names for the baby.

"I just feel for sure that it's a boy, mom," Sarah told her mother, taking her hand in her own. "Ben would love a little boy, and I would be happy with that, too. I guess we just have to wait and see, right? Right now, I just want it to be a healthy, happy baby. But if it is a boy, we like the name Seth, not sure about a middle name though, maybe Jonas, or maybe Martin. What do you think?"

Sarah and her mother both chuckled. "Doesn't sound like Seth Jonas or Seth Martin would be a very good middle name, does it to you, Sarah?" Her mother asked, smiling. "It doesn't really blend. Maybe you should name him Seth-Jonas-Martin-Benjamin Kestwick?"

Sarah laughed, "The poor little boy, that would be way too much name to remember." Still laughing, she continued, "I guess within the next twenty-four hours we'll make up our minds, won't we? Who knows, this little one may surprise us all and be a girl!"

Both women seemed to relax, and Sarah suggested that she fix some lunch for the five of them, and as she stood to go into the kitchen, another contraction almost took her to her knees. She sat back down, took deep breaths as her mother held her hand, spoke loving words to her, and mentioned they should possibly get ready to go to Portland.

"The last contraction was right before you and daddy came," Sarah mentioned in between her deep breathing exercise, "Let's wait and see how long before the next one comes, and then we can decide, okay?"

Her mother agreed, told her to stay sitting, and she would see to some lunch for everyone. Mary Anne walked into the kitchen, spoke a few words to Martin and Jonas and began to prepare a light lunch. She had never been in labor herself, but she was certain the time had come, the time for her grandchild to be born. As she stood by the kitchen counter preparing lunch, she stopped for just a moment, closed her eyes and prayed to the Father. She asked for safety for her daughter, for her unborn child and for her husband Ben. She also asked for forgiveness for her own weakness and asked that her doubts be swept away and her strong faith be restored. "Please God," she asked, "Give me the faith and strength that my daughter Sarah is showing right now, the faith to believe in you, and in only you. Amen."

CHAPTER NINETEEN

Sandra Chipley had called her husband John earlier in the day to tell him of Agent McLeary's telephone call and also shared with him how well the prayer vigil had gone. Around 3:00 p.m. John called his wife back to tell her he would be home early. He had asked for a few hours off, as he wanted to make sure he was home when Agent McLeary dropped by.

"Did he say anything, anything at all to make you believe Jacqueline is safe, or if they have found her?" he asked for the third time during this five-minute conversation.

"No, dear," Sandra said lovingly. "He just said there was a lead in the case, and like I told you before, he wants to come over and tell us in person. He was in Booth Bay Harbor, I believe. Please, John, be patient, this is in God's hands, and we must be patient. I will see you in a little while."

With that, Sandra hung up the telephone. She had barely begun to walk into the other room when the telephone rang again.

"Hello, Chipley residence."

"Mrs. Chipley? This is the Portland Police Department calling, Captain Ormand here," the deep voice said. "I am calling on behalf of FBI Agent Richard McLeary. He asked me to call you and inform you that he is on his way to your home, but it will take him a little longer than he planned. There will be an FBI agent from Portland coming and two squad cars coming to your home. He has very good news for you, your daughter has been located and he is on his way to Portland as we speak to give you all the information."

As the Captain tried to tell her more details, Sandra interrupted him, almost screaming into the telephone. "Can you repeat that please, sir?" she asked impatiently. Did you say they have found our daughter? Where is she? How is she? Is she okay? Is she hurt? Where did they find...?"

Captain Ormand tried twice to interrupt her and, finally with some success, got through to her, asked her to calm down, that everything, was fine and that a squad car should be pulling up in front of their home any minute.

"Is your husband at home, Mrs. Chipley?" he asked. She assured him he was on his way and could he tell her any thing else about Jacqueline?

"Mrs. Chipley," he said in that deep bass voice once again. "I have very little information other than that she is currently at the Brunswick Medical center...being..."

"What!" Sandra said, alarmed and interrupting the Captain again. "Why the Medical Center? I thought you said she was fine?"

"It's procedure, ma'am," the officer informed her. "Really, your daughter is doing very well. It's procedure ma'am."

"Also," the Captain continued, "Agent McLeary asked that you not make any telephone calls to anyone, don't talk to any of your neighbors, and please, do not contact the media until he gets to your home. Do you understand? We do not want to jeopardize this case, so please do not call anyone until he arrives."

Sandra told the officer that she understood completely, thanked him, hung up the telephone and rushed to the front door of their home. She opened the door just as a police unit pulled up in front and turned into their driveway. She ran out to the curb as another squad car pulled up, as well as a black SUV. In total, four men and one woman officer exited their vehicles and came towards her.

"Mrs. Chipley? Sandra?" the woman officer asked. "I'm Officer Jennings and this is Officer Bartells and Officer Landry. We are here to stay with you until Agent McLeary comes or calls from Brunswick."

Pointing to the gentleman getting out of the black SUV, she said, "and this is Agent Morrison with the FBI. He will fill you in as to what has just happened this morning concerning your daughter, Jacqueline."

Sandra nodded her head to each officer and before asking them into her home, asked again, "Is my little girl okay? Is she really all right? She's not hurt?"

Officer Jennings touched her gently on the shoulder, assuring her Jacqueline was safe, and then asked if they could all go inside. As they began to walk up to the Chipley's front door, John Chipley drove up and quickly got out of his car, ran to the front porch, reached out to his wife and asked the same old question from the past weeks and months. "Is it Jacqueline?" Tearing up now, he asked, "Is our little girl okay? Please, tell me, is she okay?"

Agent Richard McLeary was about ten minutes out of Portland when he called into Agent Morrison asking Morrison if he was clear to talk. Morrison excused himself from the Chipleys and the other officers and walked into the kitchen. Morrison informed him that all was in place at the Chipley home, so far no press was anywhere in sight, and the parents were anxiously awaiting more information on their daughter. Just how soon would he be showing up?

McLeary informed the Portland agent he was ten minutes out, but that the interstate was stop and go traffic, and he would be there as soon as possible. He asked him again to make sure no one called the media, and to assure the Chipleys he was on his way. When he had last checked, their daughter was still at the Brunswick Medical Center, being treated exceptionally well and had all the medical staff eating out of her hand.

"Make sure the parents know she's fine Morrison," he repeated again, "and she really is doing well, that's the incredible fact, she really is doing very well."

McLeary reminded the agent again to keep the press at bay if they showed up and he would try to be there in thirty minutes or less.

In her gracious manner, Sandra Chipley asked the officers if they would like coffee or sodas, and when they all said thank you but they were fine, she asked if they minded if she and her husband took a few minutes to be by themselves. The Chipleys walked into their bedroom, closed the door behind them and got down on their knees at the side of their queen size bed. They folded their hands, resting them on top of their bed, and bowed their heads. They began by thanking God for the good news, for the safety of their daughter, for all the officers involved, and for their never ending faith, faith that He had shown to them and continued to show them over the last few weeks. They asked for His blessings on their daughter, that she was indeed healthy and unharmed, for blessings for the medical staff attending to Jacqueline at the hospital in Brunswick, and, yes, for blessings on the person or persons who had abducted their baby.

With tears streaming down their faces, the Chipleys asked for further guidance for the FBI and the police department as they hopefully closed this case, and then thanked God for his grace and mercy. They asked that all missing children would be found and brought home to their families, just as their daughter was found and was about to be brought home. They thanked God again for His faithfulness, His goodness and told Him how much they loved Him, and how thankful they were for His Son, Jesus, who through His sacrifice, made all things possible. They said amen together, embraced one another, and as they stood up together, hands held, they kissed and said," I love you". Words that they shared with each other every day of their lives.

"I can't believe she is safe, John," Sandra said, looking lovingly at her husband. "I can't believe that just a few months ago I doubted God either, and now we are getting our little girl back. It is a miracle, John, a miracle and an answer to prayer."

As the Chipleys walked hand-in-hand and back into the living room, the officers all stood up, asked if they were okay, and the Chipleys, looking at each other, said yes, they were perfectly fine and thanked them for asking.

Thirty-five minutes later, Agent McLeary pulled up in front of the Chipley home. He took just a moment before opening his car door, looked up towards the heavens and said his own thank you to the God above. He crossed himself, pulled out the chain and kissed the attached silver cross, the cross he wore underneath his white shirt and tie every day. He smiled and got out of his car. This was turning out to be a wonderful day.

Agent McLeary spent just a few minutes in the Chipley home before telling them an officer would be taking them directly to the Brunswick Medical Center. In those few minutes, he filled them in on everything he knew about Jacqueline, her abductor (without using any names), and told them that the kidnapper was not yet in custody but would be soon. He chose not to go into too many details until he himself knew the whole story. He did, however, share the entire story of Jacqueline's escape, about Agent Benson, St. Michael's Church on the river, and how their daughter had asked for scrambled eggs.

"Sounds like her, doesn't it, dear?" Sandra said to her husband, still holding his hand and smiling, "She loves scrambled eggs."

McLeary told them their daughter had a slight injury to her face, but it was nothing serious. She was being completely checked out physically and mentally by the Brunswick Medical Center doctors, and being very well taken care of. He was sure Jacqueline was anxious to see them and told them so.

"We needed to talk with her first by herself and then with her and the officer who found her," he said calmly. "We hope she will give us the information we need to capture her abductor. There is a child advocate representative with her at all times, since you two are not with her yet."

McLeary continued to tell the parents that, sometimes it was easier on both the child and on the parents if they weren't present. "Jacqueline is speaking directly to the officers," he continued, looking directly into the Chipleys' eyes, "and she is much more able to tell them the entire story of her escape this morning without your distracting her. You do understand, don't you?" Without waiting for an answer, McLeary continued, "But we certainly understand that you wish to go to the Center immediately, and we will leave right now."

The Chipleys talked for a few more minutes among themselves. Sandra asked John to get their jackets from the hall closet and they exited their home, followed by the three officers. As they walked to a patrol car, agent McLeary thanked them for their cooperation and said he would be staying on the case as long as it was necessary. He asked Agent Morrison to accompany the Chipleys to Brunswick in his vehicle, but directed the two Portland police officers back to their stations. As he stood by watching Officer Landry open the back door of his patrol car and assist the Chipleys into the back seat, he noticed two vans approaching. Just as he guessed, the media had gotten word and were approaching the Chipley's home. He asked the police officers to remain at the scene after all and to report their current situation to the station.

"I do not want them speaking to the Chipleys just yet," he said, somewhat irritated, "just keep them at bay, and tell them I will make a statement in an hour or so. I'm sure they'll stick around until the child comes home. When the Chipleys bring her home, absolutely and positively do not let the media near her! Call in another squad car if one's available, and send it over here."

"Damn," he thought to himself, "I wonder who informed the media? If need be, we will give them a little information to satisfy them, but we need to keep Natalie's name out of this for now!"

McLeary introduced himself to the reporters, addressed just a few of their questions and promised to give them more information later. McLeary, knowing that the reporters had seen the Chipleys in the patrol car, told them specifically under threat of arrest, they were not to follow the patrol car. The two reporters agreed and, watched McLeary as he walked to the car and spoke with the Chipleys once more before being driven to Brunswick. McLeary informed them of what to expect when they got to the hospital.

"Are you two doing okay," he asked?

"Yes," John Chipley replied, "but we are anxious to see our daughter."

"I'm sure you are, and rightly so," the agent replied, "I just want you to know what to expect when you get to the medical center. The hospital personnel have been notified that you are on your way, and will let you in to see your daughter immediately. Upon arrival, and of course after you see Jacqueline, you will be asked to sign several papers—approval papers for Jacqueline's interrogation and medical treatment and, for her to be evaluated mentally before releasing her." He continued by telling them the doctors would most likely request further counseling and mental evaluations in the coming weeks, and the Chipley's agreed that further treatment would be a good idea and necessary for their daughter to return to a normal life.

John and Sarah asked McLeary a few other questions, and the agent answered them as best he could. He wished them "God speed", and said he would see them later on that evening or first thing in the morning. He closed the back door to the patrol car tapped on the window and watched as the patrol car pulled away and headed towards I-95 and Brunswick.

CHAPTER TWENTY

Mary Anne had prepared and served everyone soup and sandwiches, but Sarah ate very little. She was certain she was in labor and as soon as everyone finished lunch she would call Dr. Foster and tell him she was leaving for Portland. She knew the baby was ready to be born, and although Ben was still missing, she too was ready for the baby to come. She felt no panic or fear. She knew Ben was somewhere safe and would return soon. She also felt in her heart that this baby would be healthy, that she and the baby's blood problems would be minimal, and God, in His abounding grace, would see all of them through this trying but miraculous time in their lives.

"Are you sure you don't want anything else to eat, Sarah?" her mother asked. "This baby may take a little while to come, and you'll need your strength."

"No, mom, really I'm fine," Sarah said calmly. "I'm going to call the doctor though. I think the contractions are close enough together for us to leave for Portland."

Sarah picked up the kitchen telephone, dialed her doctor's number and talked with his nurse, Melissa. She told Melissa she would be leaving for the hospital within the next hour or so.

Melissa assured her she would contact the hospital so they could prepare for her arrival. She asked how far apart the contractions were, whether she had any discharge or bleeding, and did she have any other questions or concerns. Sarah said she was fine, was ready, knew exactly what to do, or hoped she did, laughed a little and thanked her.

As Sarah sat down on the couch, telephone in hand, she decided to call Ron at the Port Authority one last time before she left for Portland. She didn't know if Ron knew that Ben was actually safe or not. "I wonder if Tom Casey and the FBI agents are the only ones who know the truth," she asked herself. "I had better not ask him, just play along for right now. I certainly do not want to jeopardize the FBI's case."

As she dialed the number, she felt a small touch of panic go through her, the first bit of panic she had felt since this whole event concerning Ben began. "Oh, my darling, Ben," she said to herself, "I pray to God I can have this baby without you by my side." The telephone rang four times before there was an answer.

"Booth Bay Harbor, Port Authority, this is Mandy," came the sweet voice on the other end of the line. "How can I help you?"

"Hi Mandy," Sarah said, "This is Sarah Kestwick, Ben's wife."

"Oh Sarah. How are you holding up? I am so sorry about Ben and Jeremy," and as an after thought added, "I'm sure they'll be found real soon. Do you want to talk with Ron?"

Sarah thanked her, said yes, she would like to talk to Ron if he was available. Mandy put her through, and Ron cheerfully came on the telephone.

"Hi, Sarah, how are you?" he asked, "I'm sure your calling about Ben, and I wish I had some more information for you, but I don't. I've been in touch with the Coast Guard off and on all morning, and they still have the boats and choppers out, searching within twenty five miles of the east coast of Maine, both up and down the coast, but so far I don't have anything new to tell you." He added, "Are you feeling good, no baby at your house yet?"

Sarah shared with him that she was about to leave for Portland for the medical center and that her parent's and Ben's dad were driving her. "I just want to make sure you have my cellular telephone number," she said, "and also my mom's number. I want you to keep in touch with us, please Ron, will you do that?"

Ron felt so bad for Sarah but tried not to show his emotion over the telephone. He said, yes, he would call as soon as he heard anything, or Lieutenant Casey would call her as he was staying in town. Someone would call her mother's cell phone day or night, as soon as they had any news. He asked that she take care of herself and the baby. He told her he just knew for sure Ben and Jeremy would be found soon.

Ron did not tell her that he already knew Ben and Jeremy and the SARAH JEANNE were safe in Yarmouth. Lieutenant Casey had called him about 10:00 a.m. only a few hours earlier, but he could not tell her, and how he wished he could. He knew, as a member of law enforcement, that the first priority here was to stop the serious drug ring in the area.

Sarah told Ron goodbye, thanked him again, and as she walked into the bedroom to get her suitcase, a contraction racked her body. She made it to a chair, sat down, took several deep breaths, and a short time later the contractions stopped. She called for her mother, and Mary Anne immediately came in to check on her. One look at Sarah and her mother knew. Sarah suggested they all had better get into her car and leave. The time had come.

Mary Anne helped her daughter to her feet, told her she would collect her suitcase and an extra coat and anything else she had laid out. She called out to Jonas to get Sarah's car keys, and the close knit family calmly closed up the Kestwick home and walked out to the curb. Mary Anne helped Sarah into the back-seat of her car and Jonas loaded Sarah's belongings and another small overnight bag for himself and Mary Anne into the trunk. Martin climbed into the front passenger seat and Jonas drove. The only one missing was Ben.

The drive to Portland and to the hospital took about forty-five minutes. The traffic was lighter than usual due in part because it was early in the afternoon, and they arrived in better than usual time. Sarah had only endured one hard contraction during the drive and so far her water had not broken for which she was thankful. Her father pulled into the hospital driveway and asked Sarah if she could walk the short distance from the parking garage or did she want to get out at the front door? Typical of Sarah, she said she was fine, the short walk would do her good, and Jonas drove into the garage and parked close to the elevator door that read "General Admissions."

As they all prepared to exit the car, a driver in a gray Chrysler parked five or six spaces down from Sarah's car. A woman with reddish blond hair, bright red lipstick and wearing a nurse's uniform remained in her vehicle with the motor running, watching every move Sarah and her relatives made. On the next level of the parking garage another driver pulled his vehicle in and parked. An FBI agent in a black SUV with no markings got out, locked the vehicle and headed for the elevator. He too, pushed the elevator button for "General Admissions".

As Sarah and her family exited the car, a hospital service representative approached them. Seeing that Sarah was pregnant and in some discomfort, he asked her to wait for just a moment and he would bring her a wheelchair.

Upon his quick return the representative assisted Sarah into the wheelchair and pushed her to the elevator. She explained to the smiling, older man, who introduced himself as Randolph, that her husband was not with her, and her parents would be helping her out at admitting. "This will be a little different from your usual admission," she told him, although not wishing to share too much information about Ben, "I hope that's okay."

Randolph assured her that the staff would help her in any way they could. Sarah gave her father her insurance card and driver's license, and Jonas and Martin began filling out all of the proper forms at the Admittance Desk. Mary Anne accompanied her daughter and their new friend, Randolph, back onto the elevator and up to the OB/GYN on the sixth floor. Dr. Foster's offices had called ahead so the staff was waiting for Sarah when she checked in. Dr. Foster had also informed the staff about Sarah's situation concerning her missing husband, and, they not only had several nurses ready to assist her, but a pastor waiting for her as well.

Pastor Terry Dickinson introduced himself to Sarah and her mother, and suggested that, as soon as Sarah was checked in and was ready for him, he would like to have prayer with her, hear a little more about Ben and his disappearance, and assured her he would be available the entire time she was in labor. When she delivered or for any possible spiritual need she might have, he would be there for her and her family.

"Having a child is such a miracle in itself, Sarah," he said, also acknowledging her mother, "But in your situation, we are going to be praying in the next several hours for two miracles—a beautiful, healthy baby and for your husband to be found safe. I'll be outside your door and close by in the visitor's room for as long as you need me. God bless you Sarah!"

Pastor Terry left the room, Randolph said goodbye to everyone and wondered as he left the area just what the situation was all about. A nurse pushed Sarah's wheelchair into a room and asked her mother to please stay outside. After Mary Anne's simple explanation about Ben however, the nurse agreed to let Mary Anne stay with her daughter.

As Sarah began to undress, another contraction seized her body. "Oh, my!" she said, grasping her belly. "This is a bad one."

"Deep breaths, Sarah," the nurse said calmly, "calm, deep breaths, keep it up until the contraction subsides. You're doing fine."

Sarah had practiced breathing techniques over the past several weeks; she and Ben had even practiced them together. Doing the breathing exercise really did help with the pain and she was grateful.

Once the pain stopped, she continued to undress; the nurse took her vital signs, said everything was normal, and Sarah got into bed for a vaginal examination. The nurse informed Sarah that, she was dilated but since her water had not yet broken it might be a little while longer before she started into hard labor. She could walk around, go visit the nursery if she wished, and the doctor would be giving her more information when he arrived. The nurse assured Sarah that Dr. Foster had been notified of her arrival.

Sarah knew blood work would be on the immediate agenda, and she was anxious to get that over with. The twenty-week glucose test had been marginal, due to her being Rh negative but she did not need any Rhlg at twenty-eight weeks, so the doctor had been very pleased. Now, hopefully the tests would tell more good news; that her baby would not be Rh positive and there would be no chance of it getting hemolytic disease. She believed in God's presence through all of her pregnancy and blood tests, and now she just needed to be patient and wait for good test results.

At 5:00 p.m. Jonas asked Mary Anne if he should go and get them all some dinner and to find a hotel close by in case they needed to spend the night. It looked right now like staying overnight was a possibility. Sarah's contractions were coming every fifteen to twenty minutes, but they didn't last long, and so far she had only dilated to a four. Mary Anne agreed. "I will stay with Sarah, Jonas," she said smiling. "You can reserve a motel room close by, and just bring me a sandwich of some kind." Jonas asked Martin if he wanted something to eat, and did he want a hotel room also? Smiling, he stated that he would stay right here with Sarah, too, and he didn't need a hotel room or anything to eat. He informed everyone that sitting or sleeping in a comfortable chair was plenty comfortable for him for as long as it took this baby boy to be born.

"Baby boy!" Sarah exclaimed, laughing. "Martin, you are so sure this little one is a boy. You better not be disappointed when it's a little girl!" They both laughed, and it felt good.

No one had spoken of Ben the entire afternoon; and Sarah held her hand out to her father-in-law, and as he stood up, took his hand in hers. She said, "Martin, it really is going to be okay. Ben is safe somewhere, I just feel it in my heart. I know he will be here soon, maybe not in time to see this baby boy, or baby girl born, but he will be here." Sarah smiled to herself, gently touching her bulging belly. How she wished she could share the truth with her family, but for now, it was not to be. She would concentrate on giving birth to her and Ben's first child. God was in control right now; in control of her, the delivery of their child and of Ben.

CHAPTER TWENTY-ONE

Natalie turned off her car's engine and sat patiently waiting for Sarah and her family to get out of their car in the hospital's parking garage. She checked herself in the rearview mirror, added a little more lipstick to her already brightly painted lips and smoothed out her short, bobbed reddish-blond wig. Her pink and white freshly starched nurse's uniform looked perfect, and, as she added a pen and a stethoscope to her left-side uniform pocket, she smiled. She was wearing dark-rimmed heavy thick glasses, and she looked nothing like the woman from this morning. Thanks to one of her dealers who was into identity theft, she had even added an appropriate Maine Medical Hospital employee name badge to her nurse's uniform. She looked very professional, and she felt confident that this abduction would come off without a hitch.

Everything was going according to her well-organized plan. Natalie had been on her Wednesday afternoon drive by of the Kestwick home when she noticed Sarah and her family getting ready to leave. As she slowly drove by, she noticed one of the men loading bags into the trunk of Sarah's car. She smiled and chuckled an evil, snickering kind of laugh. "This is it," she said to herself. "Sarah is going to the hospital. I am about to get my Melanie Anne." She laughed again and her heart skipped a beat. She felt a nervous twinge go through her belly and, at the same time, she felt excited. She couldn't believe the time was finally here. All these years of waiting and wanting a baby of her own, all the years of being patient, all of the planning and all of the investigating and digging for information, the rotten jobs she'd had to endure, and worst of all, keeping that no-good husband of hers around to help her with the details. All this was about to end, and she would finally have her revenge and her own baby. Not once did Natalie show any feelings of motherly love or feelings of guilt for what she was about to do to her biological daughter. It was like Sarah never existed, she was just the surrogate for Natalie's own needs. Being Sarah's real mother, at this point in time no longer crossed her mind or mattered. What truly mattered was that she was about to have a baby of her own, one she could keep, and no one could ever take from her.

*   *   *   *   *

Natalie had slept only a few hours Tuesday night. She would sleep a few hours, get up and drive past the Kestwick home, then return to the park, sleep a few more hours in her car and start the routine over. She was getting slightly agitated when nothing seemed to be happening, but this time when she drove by she was thrilled as she noticed outside activity. She had been ready for the last few days to follow Sarah to Portland. She had two or three disguises packed, three different colored wigs, and she was positive no one would ever recognize her in Booth Bay Harbor or in Portland at the hospital. She had packed a suitcase with diapers, formula and bottles, baby clothes, blankets and a car seat for Melanie Anne, and had packed clothes, a few personal items and, of course several thousand dollars in a suitcase for herself. She had about three days worth of food and water in two coolers in the trunk, and had made sure her car was in good running condition. Her plan was to leave Portland with the baby and drive to either New Jersey or New York. She would get a hotel for a few days, then look for an apartment to rent. She had been in contact with her dealers as well as some of her buyers, and she would just start up where she left off, but in a different part of the country. Her plan was perfect.

As she sat in her car waiting for the right time to go into the hospital, she wondered why Carl had not telephoned. She was sure that her idiot husband had completed his assignment and blown the engine in Ben's boat. The newspapers were full of the "Missing Captain and his Crewman" stories, even mentioning Ben and Jeremy's names, the name of the boat, where they lived and worked, and so on. She just couldn't understand why Carl had not phoned her. She had tried calling his telephone on Wednesday evening, and again this morning and there was no answer. "Oh well," she said, "his loss, Melanie Anne and I will head out without him. I'm going to divorce him anyway. Had him around long enough. I don't need him anymore. I will find me a new husband in New York." She smiled to herself and, as she looked out the window of her Chrysler, she noticed a hospital employee bringing a wheelchair over to Sarah's car.

Natalie had thought long and hard about this abduction. When she had kidnapped Jacqueline it had been too easy. This time it would be a little more difficult, but she knew exactly how to do it, when to do it, and now everything just depended on when Sarah would actually deliver. The husband was out of the way. She had to admit Carl had done a good job on this assignment. Now, it was just up to Sarah. "Have a quick delivery and have a beautiful, healthy baby girl, Sarah," she said, smiling once again. "Then, I will take it from there! Yes", she laughed, "I will take it from there, literally, your baby from there—this hospital!" She almost cackled when she laughed, a wicked, evil laugh, thinking of her clever words.

As the hospital representative wheeled Sarah into the elevator followed by her family, Natalie checked herself one last time in the rearview mirror then got out of the car, locked it and waited until the elevator door closed. She walked over to the elevator, but decided instead to take the stairs. It was only one floor down, and she wanted to make certain no one in Sarah's family saw her this soon. She planned to walk around the first floor as if she was on her afternoon break, perhaps get coffee in the coffee shop, then take the elevator up to OB/GYN on the sixth floor. If anyone asked, she would pretend she had been sent up on an errand and find out Sarah's room number. Her employee badge looked quite convincing, and no one really ever looked closely at them anyway. She figured she would have a good hour to spare before heading up to labor and delivery. Then her mission to steal Sarah's newborn baby girl would go into effect.

Walking down the stairs and opening the door to the first floor, she remarked out loud, "What a smart cookie I am!" Smiling to herself and looking around she continued, "These people are all so stupid, I could steal three babies, and they would never figure it out."

As Natalie walked down the hallway to the hospital's coffee shop, she smiled and said hello to two doctors, smiled at a mother pushing a baby in a stroller and took a seat at the counter in the coffee shop, where she ordered black coffee and a roast beef sandwich. She hadn't eaten all day, and she figured she had some extra time before her final plans went into place. So far, she had fit right in to the hospital setting and she was feeling especially proud of herself. What she had not seen was the black SUV that pulled into the parking garage right behind her or the FBI agent, who got out of the car and followed her down the stairs.

Agent Yvonne Dixon, dressed professionally in a white pants suit, red scarf, earrings and matching high heeled shoes, a brief case setting next to her on the table, had gotten to the coffee shop before Natalie and was now seated at a booth in the coffee shop waiting for her to make her next move. Natalie did not notice her.

Agent Dixon had been assigned to the Kestwick case three weeks earlier. She was in charge of watching the Kestwick home during the night, and Agent Barry Cochrane watched the home during the day. Both agents had followed Natalie during her drive-bys of the Kestwick home day and night, followed her to and from the park every day and night, and parked a half block away from Sarah's home when they weren't chasing Natalie around town. It was a somewhat monotonous job, but they knew catching Natalie Pickford Andrews was a priority with the agency, and they were happy to help with bringing her to justice on kidnapping charges and shutting down her drug dealings.

Natalie looked at her watch, realizing that she had been sitting at the counter for almost forty-five minutes. She asked for her check, left the money on the counter, and left the area. She checked up and down the hallway and seeing nothing out of the ordinary, headed for the elevator and pushed the up button. Once inside, she pushed the sixth floor button. The elevator stopped on the third and fourth floors before making it to the sixth floor, which slightly irritated her. Once on the sixth floor, she passed the visitors' area, noticed two older men and a young man and small child in the room, and, as she passed, said hello to another nurse who pushed the button for the OB/GYN and nursery. It opened with no problem and Natalie followed her in. She walked through the area, slightly glancing into each opened door, and, as she passed Room 624, took a slightly longer look, noticing an older woman resting in a recliner. She could not see into the room far enough to see if Sarah Kestwick was there.

She had asked for Sarah's room number at the welcome desk prior to having coffee. She was told Mrs. Kestwick was in labor, and there had not been a baby born as far as they knew. The Pink Lady volunteer had noticed her badge, asked no further questions of her, and she had been given all the information she needed.

Natalie walked through the sixth floor labor/delivery area one more time and moved on to the nursery. She peered into the nursery windows, smiled at the beautiful babies in their pink and blue blankets and caps and wondered just how much longer it would be before she had her own baby girl to take home. She pondered for just a few moments more, acknowledged the nurse who was working with the new infants and left, going out the same swinging doors she had entered.

Natalie left the hospital, went back to her car in the parking garage, unlocked the door and sat down. She laid her head against the seat back, closed her eyes and smiled. Her plan was going very well. Soon, she would change her clothes, become a maintenance/cleaning employee, and initiate the second part of her plan. She was tired. She took a deep breath and slept for the better part of an hour. When she awoke it was dark in the parking garage except for a few overhead lights lighting the way to the elevator and stairs. She took off her wig, the glasses and the nurse's uniform, and stuffed them in a duffle bag. From the same bag she took out and put on a blue shirt, blue pants, and a pair of manly brown shoes. She pinned a new Maine Medical Maintenance Employee nametag on the front of her shirt and placed a short brown wig on her head. She took off all of her makeup with a wash-n-wipe, placed a pair of somewhat ugly glasses on her face, and when she looked in the mirror almost did not recognize herself. "Ugly," she mumbled, "I'm ugly, no one will recognize me in this get up." She got out of the car and threw the duffle bag with her clothes and wigs in the trunk.. She headed for the elevator and pushed the button marked "B" for the basement. As the elevator door opened, she stepped out, looked both ways and headed for the hospital's maintenance closet.

* * * * *

Thursday

* * * * *

CHAPTER TWENTY-TWO

John and Sandra Chipley held hands as they sat quietly in the back seat of the patrol car. There didn't seem to be any need for words. Their nightmare was about to come to an end. In just a few minutes she and John would have their daughter back, and perhaps life would return to normal. Sandra looked out of the window of the patrol car as it moved along I-95, noticing homes and businesses she had not previously seen or perhaps had been to busy to notice before. She saw children playing in their backyards, heard dogs barking loudly as they chased after them, and she was reminded of how short life could be. She promised herself that she would be more conscientious from this point on and not take her family for granted. Continuing to watch from the back seat window her mind went back to what had transpired in her own home within the past twenty-four hours.

*   *   *   *   *

Sandra had spent the early part of Wednesday afternoon cleaning and straightening up the house after the Morning Prayer meeting. She always felt so much better after she and her friends and neighbors had been together, having prayer and fellowship time. It was so uplifting for her. Later while cleaning up the kitchen, she had walked over to a calendar hanging on the kitchen wall next to the refrigerator. She and her husband had started this calendar, a check-off, day-by-day calendar the day their daughter was taken. Each day since Jacqueline's abduction they had written a word of hope or cheer, or on some days words of sadness or depression on the calendar. Depending on the kind of day they were having, they would make an X across the date and write one word describing their feelings on that particular day. Surprisingly, there were more words of gladness and hope than words of sadness. Sandra had taken the calendar from the wall and sat down at the kitchen table and turned the pages backward to August. She had read over each word written on each day until she had gotten to today's date. She remembered, she had taken a pen from the penholder on the table, and, looking up to the sky, she thanked God for today and wrote the word "thankful" across the date.

The call from Agent McLeary had unburdened her day. She had called her husband John immediately, told him McLeary was going to come over around 6:30 p.m. because there might be a lead in the case. She promised her husband she would try not to get her hopes up too high, but the agent had spoken in such a positive tone of voice. He would be coming this evening right after dinner to speak with them both. She asked John if he could he be home on time for dinner?

"I promise honey," he had told his wife. "I will even try to leave early. Is 5:00 p.m. okay? We can have dinner, and be ready for him when he comes by."

Sandra Chipley had said a prayer of thanks, hung the calendar back in its place on the wall and went back into the living room. She recalled looking around as if lost or in a trance, and, after another look at Jacqueline's photograph, had walked quickly into her daughter's room. The room was exactly as it had been on that fateful day in August. The only thing Sandra had done was make up the bed. She left every book, piece of clothing, dolls, stuffed animals or toys in their places. She had no doubts that her precious child would come back to her and leaving everything in its place seemed to calm her, and give her more hope. "If everything is as it was, maybe she will come home sooner," she had said, over and over.

Today, however, Sandra Chipley had felt differently. The phone call from Agent McLeary had given her more hope than she had been given in weeks. She had felt so positive today, she just knew that between the prayer vigil and the phone call, God was going to answer their prayers very soon. She had a feeling, a feeling only a mother could feel for her only child. She just knew Jacqueline was safe, and would be home soon.

Sandra started cleaning her daughter's room like she was a woman possessed. She stripped the bedding from the bed, brought it into the laundry room, placed the sheets and pillowslips in the washing machine, added detergent and turned the machine on. She returned to the bedroom, took everything from the shelves, dusted and polished them all, and took all the stuffed animals and dolls out to the patio to air them out. She took down the curtains, washed the windows, and took the curtains to the laundry room for the next load. She vacuumed the carpeted floors, rearranged every item in the closet and dresser drawers, throwing out every piece of clothing her child had not worn in several months prior to her kidnapping.

Sandra continued to clean. "I know my baby will have grown these past few months," Sandra said, "I will have to buy her new clothes, new shoes, so I might as well make some room right now. I want her back so badly, and I just know she is coming home soon. I just know it!"

Sandra continued to clean and scrub and throw things into plastic bags and boxes for pickup by the homeless shelter van and, finally when she finished, she had sat on Jacqueline's bed and cried. She had cried for her child, for herself and her husband, and cried because she was completely exhausted. She hadn't cried like this since the first week of Jacqueline's abduction. When she finally stopped crying and composed herself, she had taken two bags of clothing and a box of shoes to the garage, took a shower, and when she finished, realized how much better she felt. She had put on a little make-up, a bright pink blouse and tan slacks, and by the time she finished, her telephone had begun to ring and for the second time the news had been wonderful.

* * * * *

Sandra smiled thinking back on the day's activities. After the telephone call and throughout the entire afternoon she had been almost out of her mind with anticipation and when the Chipley family members were once again united, there were no words to describe the jubilation. McLeary recalled later that he had never seen such a reunion as the one he witnessed at the Brunswick Medical Center. He couldn't tell who was the most excited to see whom, parent or child. Sandra had fussed over and kissed Jacqueline's bruised face, kissed her hair, her eyes, her ears, hugged her over and over, and then began kissing her again. Jacqueline in her eight-year-old voice finally begged her mother to please stop. John Chipley cried, the two nurses in the ER cried, even a paramedic had tears in his eyes.

At 2:00 a.m. Thursday morning, Jacqueline was finally released from the medical center, with instructions for her parents to see their personal physician the next day and to set up counseling for all three of them in the next few days. The police promised to escort the happy family back to Portland, and Agent McLeary promised to make a statement on the family's behalf to all of the reporters waiting outside the medical center. In all of his years of investigations he would never understand how the media got their information so quickly, but he promised the reporters that Sandra and John would make a statement late Thursday morning in Portland after they had all rested. He would not however, allow them to question the child until the entire case was solved. Natalie's name did not come up, and McLeary wanted to make sure there was no mention of the possible kidnapper at least until she was in custody.

So, the two-month ordeal had ended. The Chipleys had their daughter back, unharmed, and the FBI was about to capture her abductor.

The Chipley's were dropped off at their Portland home around 3:30 a.m. Jacqueline had fallen asleep on the drive back and John had gently carried her into the house. Together, Sandra and John had tucked their daughter into her own bed, kissed her gently on the cheek and knelt beside her bed to pray. They thanked God for His grace and mercy, thanked Him for all of the people involved in the case, thanked Him for His love and kindness, and thanked Him for their family, once again whole. Together they said a soft "amen", kissed each other and walked towards the door. Before Sandra Chipley closed Jacqueline's bedroom door part way she turned and took one more look at her beautiful sleeping daughter. "Oh my God, thank you!" she said solemnly looking up towards the heavens. "Thank you for bringing our baby girl back to us."

Two hours later, at 5:30 a.m., Sandra sat up on the edge of the bed, got up and walked into her daughter's room just to make sure she was still there. She opened the partially closed door, walked slowly over to the bed and touched Jacqueline's cheek. She then kissed her on the forehead and knelt down beside her daughter's bed to give thanks once more. She offered thanks to the God of love and laughter, to the God of little children and thankful parents, and to the God who planned all things and most of all, thanks to His Son who died so long ago to make miracles like this one happen. Sandra Chipley said a quiet amen, and, instead of going to her own bedroom and joining her husband, sat down in a rocking chair in Jacqueline's room, covered herself with a pink blanket and fell sound asleep, the most sound sleep she had slept in over two months.

CHAPTER TWENTY-THREE

Around 5:00 p.m. on Wednesday, Lieutenant Tom Casey called the police chief in Yarmouth, Nova Scotia and informed him that Sarah Kestwick was in labor, had left for the hospital in Portland around 1:30 p.m. and asked whether he could speak to Ben. Chief Lewis said he would call his officer and the FBI agent at the motel and let them know Tom had called, and have Ben call him back as soon as he located him.

"Mr. Kestwick has been out and about today, I understand from my officers," he said hesitantly. "I believe he is struggling hard with this entire investigation and the way it is being handled. I imagine if it were I being put through this ordeal, I would be struggling too. My officers are sticking with him wherever he wanders and he's handling that okay, but he'll be happy, I'm sure, to hear some positive news about his wife." Pausing for a moment, the Chief continued, "Although it might make him more upset knowing he's not with his wife during her labor and delivery. After this is all over, we ought to give the guy a medal!"

The Chief continued speaking with Tom Casey, telling him what Ben had done throughout the day on Wednesday, including getting his load shipped out under a different name. "No sense in him losing money because of us," he continued. "He had a large load of lobster to deal with, and we saw to it that it was shipped out today. He seemed to be pleased with the help we offered. I'm hoping once this case is over, he will change his attitude towards all of us here in Yarmouth, at least I hope so."

The two men talked a little longer, and Tom thanked him and said he would be in touch throughout the next few days. Tom also asked him about Natalie's husband, Carl.

"What's going on with Carl Andrews, has he talked much? Has he been booked?"

"He's been waiting for his lawyer," the Chief replied, "Now that the lawyer has been here, they talked long into the night, and they both know Carl Andrews was caught red-handed trying to place explosives on the SARAH JEANNE, he's spilling his guts. He's putting all the blame on his wife, saying she threatened to turn him in on drug trafficking if he didn't do exactly as she requested—disable the boat, kill Ben Kestwick, on and on. He's been charged with a number of felonies, we got him good, no doubt about that. I think he'll also turn on his wife, give us all the information we need on her—the kidnapping, the drug dealings, and now this kidnapping attempt on the Kestwick baby. Now, we have to decide who has jurisdiction and where to try him, here in Yarmouth or back in Maine. I'm sure the judge will set a hearing in a few weeks, and then we'll know. Until then, we're stuck with him."

Ben did call Tom Casey back around 7:00 p.m. The FBI agent and the Yarmouth police officer staying with him at the hotel listened in to every word he said, and, after he hung up, they all encouraged him, empathized with him, and congratulated him on becoming a father in a few more hours. Ben was elated to get word on Sarah's condition and very upset that he was not able to be with her, but he understood. He had made a commitment to work with the police and the FBI to save his child, and, catch a crazy kidnapping drug dealer, and he would do just that.

At 11:00 p.m. Tom Casey called the Yarmouth police again. He informed them that the FBI had called in, and Ben's wife was in hard labor, but she and the baby were doing just fine, her parents and Ben's father were with her. He also wanted to make sure to let Ben know that there were FBI agents all over the hospital, in the OB/GYN area, stationed undercover at all entrances and in the parking garage close to Natalie's vehicle. They were watching her every move. The police once again put him through to the cottages and notified Ben there was another call from Tom Casey.

"Not to worry Ben," Tom said to his friend, "everything is going according to plan, and Sarah, I understand, is doing very well." He shared with Ben what he knew, that Sarah was in hard labor, her parents were with her, and the hospital representative appointed to work with the FBI and one who knew the situation well, was keeping close tabs on Sarah and giving the undercover agents updates every thirty-minutes.

Ben thanked Tom for the telephone call, asked about Jill, and Ben was thrilled when Tom told him that there were definite marriage plans in their future. "I have asked her Ben," Tom told him willingly, "but she's a little hesitant to marry right away, but I think within six months or so, she'll say yes. Do you know Loren, her mother, very well?"

Ben said yes, he did. "I eat at the Breakfast Hut often and know Loren quite well. She's a really nice woman, has had some troubles in her past, but one thing for sure, she loves Jill, and has seen to it that she gets the very best of everything."

"Well, then, you know Loren's history with men, don't you?" he asked. "Jill just wants to make certain she and I are right for each other. I guess I 'm not a very patient man, Ben, I love her so much, and I want us to get married right away."

Ben chuckled, and it felt good to laugh with a friend. "Just be patient then, Lieutenant Casey," he told Tom, "she'll come around. Has Loren checked you out, made sure you are the best thing for her daughter?"

Tom laughed, said he had met her a few times, and was sure he would pass the soon-to-be-son-in-law test. The two men said their goodbyes, Tom saying he would be in touch throughout the night, or when Ben's child was born.

Ben knew he wouldn't sleep a wink until he got word about Sarah, a new son or daughter, and that Natalie was finally captured. He wondered what her plans were, just how did she plan to try to kidnap his new baby. Would the FBI be close enough to catch her in the act? Would Sarah know what was going on with her baby and Natalie? The more his mind worked, the more questions he asked himself, and the more he worried. He just couldn't help himself.

He made another pot of coffee, played gin rummy with the officer staying with him round the clock, until almost 1:00 a.m. He then asked the officer if he would contact the hospital for him once again.

The officer said he would call one of the FBI agents at the hospital, but he could not call anyone on the labor/delivery floor, as everything was strictly undercover. He was instructed not in any way to jeopardize the case or Sarah or the new baby. Ben thanked him, watched as he made the call and waited for an answer and further information on Sarah.

"Hello, Yvonne Dixon," came the answer.

"Agent Dixon, this is officer Stearn, with Ben Kestwick, are you able to talk openly?"

"Yes, officer, I can. How is Mr. Kestwick doing?"

Officer Stearn handed Ben the telephone, and Agent Dixon shared with him that as of thirty minutes ago, Sarah's contractions were about five minutes apart, the hospital representative, Jeri Blanchard, had informed her she was doing fine, hanging in there like the trooper everyone said she was. "Her mother is with her all the time, Mr. Kestwick. The doctor thinks about another hour and she should deliver. All of her vital signs and those of the baby are good and all in all, things are going very well."

The Agent and the anxious father-to-be talked for about fifteen more minutes. Ben asked if there had been signs of Natalie, and she hesitantly said yes, but not to worry, as the FBI and the police were watching her every move, and so far all was going well. She was sure that this entire case would be closed and Natalie taken into custody by early morning. "We are just waiting for the baby to be born, and then we are certain Natalie will make her move Mr. Kestwick," she said politely. "How are you holding up? Everyone treating you okay?" she asked Ben.

He assured her he was fine, it was his wife and child he was concerned about. "I can't sleep, can't eat, can't turn my mind off," he told Yvonne. "I just want this nightmare to be over, and get our lives back to normal."

Agent Dixon assured him everything was going well, promised that everything would end positively, and try not to worry. She said she would call Lieutenant Casey the minute Sarah gave birth, and he in turn would call Ben. She knew how much he must be hurting, and the thought of someone trying to kidnap his newborn, must be heart wrenching. She hoped everything would turn out okay, just as she had promised him it would.

Much later, Ben finally laid down on the bed, closed his eyes and tried to sleep. Sleep would not come. He thought of when he and Sarah had first met, their first date, their engagement and wedding, and when Sarah had told him she was pregnant. He thought of his own mother and her fight to survive, her death and how many times he had seen his father cry. He thought of their house overlooking the bay, how much work they had put into making it a home, the nursery, the work they still had to do to finish it. He thought of the business, his brother, his life, everything he had ever done in his life, the good things and the not so good things. His life had been full of surprises and happy memories, of sadness and a few hard times, but all in all, his life had been wonderful, and if anything happened to Sarah or their new baby, he wondered if he could go on.

As a tear fell from Ben's eye and ran down his cheek onto the bed pillow, the telephone rang. Officer Stearn picked up the telephone, said hello, and walked over to where Ben lay. "It's for you, Ben," he said calmly, "It's Lieutenant Casey.

CHAPTER TWENTY-FOUR

On Wednesday, Joe Spencer had introduced himself to Maurice, at the music company and told him he had a few questions about pianos, but he only had a few minutes before he was due to be on the job.

"Can you take down my telephone number first thing?" he asked Maurice, "that way if I have to get to work, you can call me back with the information I am needing, will that be okay?"

Maurice assured him that would be fine, took down Joe's telephone number, and asked what he could help him with.

"I'm looking for a piano, preferably a used one, but it needs to be a very good one," Joe told the salesman. "I need it to be a Baldwin, a grand if you have one, and it needs to be in perfect condition, have perfect tones, and in other words, I need a perfect used piano." He chuckled, and asked Maurice if that was possible.

Maurice said Joe might not believe him, but yes, they had two or three Baldwin grand's. They were in very good condition, a company policy on all their used pianos, and asked what price was he looking for?

"We have one used one right now that has been completely gone through, newly tuned, all new keys, black in color, comes with a new padded bench and is selling for $14,095.00." He continued by telling Joe it would be a good idea for him to come down and take a look at it, and to play it. When Joe told him where he lived, and that he only played a little, the salesman was taken aback for a moment. "You do not play Mr. Spencer?" he asked, "Then, may I ask what the piano is for, a gift perhaps?"

Joe looked at his watch, realized he needed to hang up, and asked Maurice if he would call him back during his lunch hour. "Could you call me back at 11:30 a.m?" Joe asked. "And would you call me immediately and have me paged if someone else comes into your store and shows an interest. I really think this is the piano I need, but I want to ask you a few more questions."

Somewhat puzzled, Maurice said yes, he would call him in a few hours, and repeated Joe's telephone number at work once again. "There is a possibility I will not be back at 11:30 a.m.," the salesman continued, "but I will call you for sure either this afternoon or Thursday morning at the latest, if that is all right?"

Joe, sounding a little disappointed, assured Maurice today or tomorrow would work out fine, and he ended their conversation.

Maurice also hung up the telephone and walked directly over to where the beautiful piano sat on the showroom floor. He wrote out a '"Sale Pending" sign, added his name to the sign, and placed it on top of the Baldwin grand piano. This will be a nice commission, he thought to himself, very nice.

Joe smiled as he hung up the office employee telephone. He mentioned to the secretary sitting at the front desk about the expected telephone call coming in around 11:30 a.m. and he would drop by at that time, but in case he was delayed would she page him. She nodded her head, and Joe left the office and headed to his logging truck. As he drove towards the logging camp and lake where he was scheduled to work today, he thought of Sarah and how she would feel about his opening a music studio for her. The building he had recently agreed to purchase was perfect. It had a good size room for the piano, room for a small chair and couch, perhaps a nice table and lamp, and her computer. It needed a new coat of paint; maybe a light blue would be nice. He would see to purchasing some artwork maybe with photos of some of the great pianists/musicians of the world: Ernest Schelling, Liberace, Aaron Copeland or more of her favorites to add to the décor.

There was a smaller room where she could put a baby crib or play pen, so she could keep the baby with her some days. It would also need a fresh coat of paint and maybe new shades on the windows so the baby could sleep in darkness. There was a cute little bathroom and a small kitchen area with a refrigerator and a hotplate. He would buy a coffee pot, some decorative mugs and plates, and make the entire studio beautiful and functional for his Sarah. He smiled, thinking of his plans and how they were coming together. He had saved his money for the last ten years or so just for this purpose. His grandpa James had passed away a few years earlier, and his parents had given him and his sister some of the inheritance money. He really had few wants or needs and so had saved most of the money for the music studio. He wanted to do something for Sarah, his birth daughter, and knowing how badly she wanted her own music studio, this would be perfect, the perfect gift for her and her future. He wondered again how Sarah would accept this type of gift. He knew she loved him, like an Uncle, but he was curious about her acceptance of a gift this large from him. After all, this was not just an ordinary gift. He also wondered if the time was right to tell her that he was her real father. He thought about this often and always his answer to himself was no. He would not upset what was so good in everyone's life right now. He would never hurt Sarah or her parents, but still he wondered. Should I tell her who I really am? He would have to think about it some more before making his decision.

Joe jumped in his truck and headed for the lake with a lighthearted feeling in his mind and a refreshing feeling in his soul. He worked extra hard throughout the morning, looked at his watch often, and at 11:20 a.m. clocked out for lunch and headed back to the office. He parked, got out of the truck and walked in the front door. The secretary, smiling, motioned to him that the telephone call he was expecting had just come in and the caller was on hold. She said she would put it through to the employee line, and, after only one ring, Joe picked it up.

"Maurice?" Joe asked politely.

"No, Mr. Spencer, this is Jordan Holloway from Ball Music Company." Maurice asked me to let you know he will not be back into the office until Thursday. He asked me to tell you, however, that the piano you talked about is on hold for now."

"Thank you, thank you so much, Jordan," Joe replied. "I appreciate your call, and I'll wait for Maurice's call in the morning. He will call in the morning, won't he?"

Jordan Holloway told Joe Spencer that Maurice Burns would call him first thing in the morning, and they could finalize the sale then.

He finished the conversation by asking Joe if there was anything else he could do for him until then?

"Perhaps you could fax me a photo of the piano, here at the office, is that possible?" Joe asked.

Jordan said yes, asked for the fax number and said he would fax photos within the next few minutes. Joe thanked him, and the two men ended their conversation.

Joe worked the rest of the day in high spirits, and it wasn't until right before he left the lake to clock out that the receptionist gave him the fax and said that there was also a note for Joe to call the music company as soon as possible.

There were three photos of the grand and he visualized what it would look like in Sarah's new studio. "What a beautiful, beautiful piano," he said aloud. The receptionist glanced his way when she heard him speak, and she smiled when Joe thanked her and he headed over to use the phone.

When he finally got through to Maurice at the music company in Cincinnati on Thursday, Joe was as excited as a little boy on Christmas morning. Joe explained to Maurice that yes, he definitely wanted the piano, had not been able to find the exact grand anywhere in Maine, told him about the building he was purchasing in Booth Bay Harbor but that it needed some construction work and painting done before the piano could be shipped. He would give him a delivery date as soon as he could. He asked about a warranty on the piano, if there was a piano repairs service in the Booth Bay Harbor area in case he needed one, and how much did he need to send for him to hold the piano for delivery.

Maurice asked for Joe's identification, telephone and address, two references, and said he would need at least one-half of the money upfront to hold the piano, either a money order or he could use his credit card. He would fax him the contract/sales agreement, and would he sign it and send it back immediately by mail. Yes, he continued to tell him there was a five-year warrantee on the piano, and he could ship the piano out whenever Joe requested.

"You know we are located in Ohio?" he reminded Joe. "It will be quite costly to ship this piano, are you sure this is the way you wish to handle the sale?"

Joe said absolutely and asked if there was a guarantee or insurance on the shipping. Maurice told Joe it was fully covered by insurance and to check the piano over thoroughly when it came. "Do you play at all, Joe?" Maurice asked again. "You can play it and see how the tone is when it's delivered. Make sure there is nothing broken."

Joe said, that he played a little, and he would check the piano out thoroughly when it was delivered. Joe once again went over all of his previous requests. He wanted Maurice to send him several close-up color photos of the grand by mail, copies of the paperwork proving the repairs and restoration work had all been completed, a copy of the warranty, a sales agreement that he would sign and return, and any other paperwork he thought Joe might need.

"I want all of this proof, first," Joe said, "then once I get all of this paperwork, I will send you a certified check for one-half of the price. I will need confirmation that you received the money and a receipt, and I think that will do it. Is this all okay with you Maurice?"

Maurice said he would speak with his supervisor but was sure this would all work out fine. He would get papers in the mail today or tomorrow, and once again verified Joe's mailing address, and the address of the studio where the piano would be shipped.

"We do a lot of transactions by mail and have to ship a lot of Baldwin pianos across the United States," Maurice continued, "I know you'll be very happy with this purchase sir, and I wish you every success with this new studio. Thank you for working with us, and good luck. We will be in touch."

Joe thanked him as well, hung up, and stayed sitting for just a few more minutes. The office secretary looked up at him, smiled, and said nothing. Just seeing the satisfied look on Joe Spencer's face was enough. Joe Spencer didn't always look happy, so she hoped this was a good day for him.

Joe thanked the secretary once again and headed for the door and headed out the door. Before starting up the truck he also thought of Sarah. "This is turning out to be a good day," he said to no one in particular, "a very good day. I hope, Sarah, that your day is going well too."

Joe headed for home. He was elated with the way the piano deal had gone. Now, his next priority would be to go into the harbor on

Saturday, sign off on the final papers for the new studio, and look into a contractor who would add a few shelves, cupboards, do a few repairs and paint the entire inside of the building. He would check out some art galleries for artwork and find someone who could help him order artwork or photos of famous musicians or pianists. It would take almost all of his savings to get this project completed, but the rewards would be so satisfying. He hoped to have the music studio completed within a month or so. He would have a surprise open house for Sarah, her families and all her friends and townspeople. It would be a spectacular grand opening for his beautiful daughter.

As Joe pulled onto the highway leading towards Millinocket, he suddenly remembered Ben. "I wonder if Ben has returned to port by now. I have been thinking solely of Sarah and my plans for her today, I have forgotten completely about Ben. I need to call Sarah tonight, tell her she is in my thoughts and prayers."

"My God," Joe thought. "I hope Ben is okay. All of these plans for the music studio will be in vain if Sarah's husband doesn't return. She will be heartbroken and so lost without him. She might not even care about her music or a studio. Oh my beautiful Sarah, God help you."

*   *   *   *   *

Joe returned to Millinockett purposely driving by the Waverly place before going to his place. It looked quiet and deserted at the Waverly home, and there were no lights on anywhere in the house. Joe was certain Jonas and Mary Anne were either still with Sarah in Booth Bay Harbor or in Portland waiting for her to deliver. As he looked at his watch, he thought it was possible she had already delivered and he was curious to how things had gone. He hoped there would be a message on his telephone from Jonas sharing what he hoped would be good news. Good news about Ben and about a new baby. He didn't bother to park in the garage, but rather parked his truck in the driveway and quickly entered his front door. Upon entering the dining area, he immediately noticed the red blinking light on his telephone. He quickly walked over and picked up the phone, playing back the message.

CHAPTER TWENTY-FIVE

At 3:37 a.m. Thursday morning, Sarah Jeanne Kestwick gave birth to a nine-pound three-ounce baby boy. Her labor had lasted almost twelve hours and she was exhausted. She had begun hard labor around midnight, and although she tried to have her son by natural childbirth, she finally gave in to having an epidural, and asked for medications to help with the pain.

"I thought I could do this on my own, without Ben, without medication," she told her mother who held her hand throughout the entire delivery. "But I just can't mom, I just can't. I need Ben so badly. I can't be strong any longer, mom, I need something for the pain."

The nurse had immediately given her something for pain, and, although she could still feel the contractions, at least the pain was more tolerable. The delivery had taken a good twenty minutes. The baby was very large and, although seemingly a perfect little boy with a healthy cry, the birth had caused Sarah to bleed profusely. The doctor had anticipated this happening but not this severely. She had passed the afterbirth, but still she continued to hemorrhage. He had ordered one blood transfusion, and, although the bleeding had slowed down some, he ordered one more transfusion. She was much improved, but he presumed she would need more blood before the night was over. The doctor had ordered more of her blood type from the local blood bank, but they were temporarily out. As Mary Anne had been with Sarah during labor and delivery, Dr. Foster had asked Mary Anne about her blood type first. She told him that neither she nor Jonas was a match.

The nurse had come out of delivery and spoken to Martin about it as well.

"I know neither you or your wife can give her blood," Dr. Foster's nurse had said to Jonas. "Sarah, I know is adopted, and has a rare blood type so you won't be able to help. What about you Mr. Kestwick? "

Martin sadly said, that he was not her blood type either. Jonas informed the nurse that Sarah had never had to have a blood transfusion before so they had never incurred this problem. Dr. Foster, knowing Sarah's condition, had ordered blood for her just in case she needed a transfusion at delivery but he was sure orders for two transfusions would have been plenty.

"What can we do to help her?" Jonas asked the nurse, knowing full well that he already had an answer.

"Do you have any friends or relatives who might be a match?" she asked. "Anyone willing to come to the hospital right away and let us take a sample of his or her blood? Right now Sarah is doing okay, but in case Dr. Foster needs to give her another transfusion soon, we would need a blood donor right away."

Jonas said that possibly an employee at the Mill could help out his daughter. Mary Anne looked at her husband a little quizzically, but did not ask any questions. He said he would make a few telephone calls and be right back.

Jonas had placed a call to Joe Spencer earlier in the evening just to let him know Sarah's condition. He knew Joe would be concerned about Sarah, but when he tried to call there had been no answer. Jonas had left Joe a message on his answering machine.

Jonas left the visitor's room on the sixth floor, took the elevator down to the first floor, and placed a call to Joe Spencer. Jonas was almost positive Joe Spencer was Sarah's birth father. He had suspected it for a few years now, but had chosen never to speak about his suspicions, either to Joe or to Mary Anne and for sure not to Sarah. Now, however, it could be a matter of life or death, and he would approach Joe about giving blood, knowing full well that his blood would match Sarah's.

It took five rings before Joe answered. "Hello!" he said in a sleepy and somewhat irritated voice. "Who is this?"

"Joe, it's Jonas. I'm sorry to call you at this hour, but Sarah needs you."

"What? Jonas? What did you say?" Joe asked again, this time more awake and less irritated.

Jonas explained the situation to him. There was a beautiful new baby boy, doing very well; Sarah had had a rough go of it all, she needed blood and she needed Joe's help.

"What can I do, Jonas?" he asked. "My blood would not be a match for her. I'm not a blood relative."

Jonas said calmly and lovingly. "Joe, we can discuss all of this at a later date, but right now Sarah needs blood. There is none of her type in the blood bank in Portland, and Joe, I have known for a long time that you are Sarah's birth father. Will you please get dressed, get in the car and drive as quickly as you can to get to Portland. Sarah's life may depend on you."

Joe was speechless. How did Jonas find out that Sarah was his birth child? How long had he known? God, did Sarah know?

"Yes, Jonas, of course." he said, "I'll leave in fifteen minutes."

He asked for the address of the hospital. Jonas gave him the address and directions, said he could make it in approximately two and one half hours or less, and to please hurry.

Jonas went back to the OB/GYN visitor's room but checked in with the nurse's desk first. He gave the nurse at the desk the information on Joe, asked after Sarah, and whether he could go in to see her and his wife. The nurse assured him it was fine to visit Sarah, and they would give the doctor the information regarding the blood donor as well. They asked the blood donor's full name, and Jonas gave it to them. He asked if Joe could go directly to the blood bank in the basement of the hospital to give his blood, and asked that the donor's name remain anonymous. The nurses agreed, they asked to please let them know as soon as Joe arrived, and they would make it all as discreet as possible. Jonas looked at his watch, took note of the time and headed for the room where Sarah had just delivered his first grandchild. He stopped for a moment, bowed his head and thanked God for this new baby boy, for his continued health, and, prayed that Joe would get to Portland in time in case Sarah needed another transfusion. He then asked God for Ben's safe return and for continued strength for him and Mary Anne. As he opened his eyes and began to open the door into Sarah's room, he noticed the cleaning woman mopping the floor a few doors down from

Sarah's. Thinking it was a normal cleaning routine in the hospital, he thought no more of it, and went into the room to see his daughter and his new grandson.

Sarah looked beautiful as always, but very worn out, and very pale. She was hooked up to two intravenous feeding tubes and next to her bed in a plastic bassinette was a red-faced, blond haired, kicking, crying, naked baby boy. As Jonas watched a pediatric nurse washing him, lathering him up with some kind of cream, he choked back a sob, looked at his wife and daughter, as tears filled his dark blue eyes. He walked over, took Sarah's hand in his, and, as she softly said "Hi daddy," he gently kissed her forehead.

"I am so very, very proud of you, Sarah," he said kissing her again, "...so very proud."

Agent Yvonne Dixon watched Jonas Waverly enter his daughter's room, and, as soon as he was behind closed doors, walked up to the nurse's station, showing her badge, she asked for information on Sarah Kestwick and the baby, then walked towards the elevator. "So far, so good," she said to herself, "all the nurses are cooperating, and as long as everyone keeps silent as to what is going on with Sarah Kestwick, we should have Natalie Andrews in custody by morning." She did worry about the baby just a little. He would be staying in his mother's room as long as her blood levels remained stable. They would move the baby out of her room and into the nursery if she started bleeding again. Sarah needed more attention right now than the baby did. It would be easier to nab Natalie in Sarah's room than in the nursery. They did not want to jeopardize any other mothers and babies. She hoped this would all turn out the way McLeary and the other agents presumed it would. "You never know," she mumbled to herself as she pushed the DOWN elevator button.

She immediately radioed the other agents at the hospital entrances, and in the parking garage. She told them the baby was born and the mother was in a somewhat unstable condition. Natalie, she was certain, was in a cleaning woman's disguise working right outside Sarah's room, and, also, she needed a replacement for about fifteen minutes.

"I need a short break," she told a counterpart. "I will wait for another agent, and then I am headed down on the elevator, send someone up right away please."

Agent Dixon made a mental note to call Lt. Casey right away. Casey could call Sarah's husband, which should put him at least a little at ease knowing his son was born. She wasn't sure whether to tell Lt. Casey about the wife's blood problem or not, no sense worrying the husband any more than necessary. She walked out of the elevator towards the coffee shop, spotted another agent and tipped her head in acknowledgement. She first used the women's restroom, and then went into the coffee shop and ordered black coffee. While she sipped on the coffee, she dialed Tom Casey's telephone number and gave him the latest information. She chose not to tell him when he answered about Sarah's blood transfusions.

CHAPTER TWENTY-SIX

Joe Spencer quickly changed his clothes, grabbed a jacket and his keys and headed out to his truck. His heart was beating twice as fast as it should be beating, he was getting a headache, and he was sure his blood pressure was completely off the charts. He hoped he didn't have a stroke or a heart attack on the way to Portland. Luckily, it was the middle of the night, and there was no traffic between Millinocket and the interstate. Once on I-95 there were several semi trucks, as always, drivers liked driving during nighttime, but other than truckers, there was very little traffic. He drove at 85mph the entire one hundred and ninety miles and said a big thank you to the man upstairs when he arrived at Maine Medical in a little over two hours.

"I can't believe there were no cops on the highway," he said thankfully, as he parked in the hospital's parking garage and headed for the main entrances.

An FBI agent waiting at the hospital's main entrance had been given a description of Joe Spencer, and as Joe approached the automatic doors a little after 6:00 a.m. the agent approached him.

"Mr. Joe Spencer?" the agent asked. "Are you Joe Spencer, sir?"

Joe replied yes, asked if there was a problem, and, as the agent showed his badge, was escorted to a private room in the hospital's admittance area. He was told they needed his blood sample immediately, then, if it proved to be a match to Sarah's, he would be taken to the hospital's blood bank area where his blood would be drawn and taken up for Sarah. The agent shared with him that Sarah's family had asked him to be discreet; to not speak with anyone and that Sarah's father would be down shortly to speak with him. Joe asked about Sarah and the baby, and the agent replied that he had little or no information about either, but he was sure someone would be down to talk with him in the next few minutes.

Joe wasn't exactly sure what all the requests for discretion was about. He realized no one knew he was Sarah's real father, but he wasn't going to tell anyone, and evidently Jonas Waverly already knew anyway. He wondered what else might be going on here in the hospital. Why an FBI agent? Had Ben been found? Was he dead? Were Sarah and the baby really okay? His mind was throwing questions at him, and no one he asked wanted to give him any answers. As he was about to try to find someone who would possibly give him some answers, a laboratory technician came into the room with her little tray of needles and vials and asked him politely to take off his jacket and roll up his sleeve. She asked if he had good veins and did he ever have trouble giving blood?

He did as he was asked, answered the technician's questions, and, within seconds, she had taken a vial of blood, said she would be back within a few minutes, and would he like any juice or water? He said no, that he was fine, and he tried to start up a conversation with the FBI agent. Joe wanted to talk, but the agent didn't. He assured Joe that everything was fine, he would be informed as to the situation soon, and please just sit tight and wait. A half an hour later, a nurse came into the room and asked if he and the agent would follow her to the blood bank area.

Once there, Joe had two pints of blood drawn and was given juice and donuts to keep his blood sugar levels up and to keep him from becoming dizzy. The nurse asked him to stay sitting for a while longer. The FBI agent stayed with him to keep him company. About fifteen minutes passed, and Jonas Waverly knocked on the door and came into the room. The FBI agent excused himself, said he would be directly outside the door if they needed anything.

"Hello, Joe," Jonas said, smiling and reaching out to shake Joe's hand. "Thank you so much for coming to help out Sarah. I will never be able to repay you for possibly saving her life. You'll be able to see her and her baby soon, I promise, but now I think you and I should have a talk."

*   *   *   *   *

Dr. Foster had been in to see Sarah at 4:30 a.m. again at 5:30 a.m. and he was pleased that she was steadily improving. The color was returning to her face, her blood pressure was coming back up, and her outlook was very good. "You are doing much better, Sarah," he said, "and your little guy here is doing very well too. Have you held him yet?" Dr. Foster stepped closer to the bassinette, took a good look at the baby, and said what a great job she had done during the difficult delivery.

Sarah softly replied that she had not held him; she felt so weak, she was afraid she would drop him, but she wanted to hold him very soon. She said she was feeling some better, and asked what her prognosis was?

"You will most likely need at least one more pint of blood," he said optimistically. "You will also need to stay in the hospital a little longer than normal, maybe two or three days. You've lost quite a lot of blood, you need to get your strength back, and you will need to eat and drink a little bit, often, so you can feed this little guy here. We want to monitor you for a few days and make sure you are completely on the mend before we send you home."

Sarah agreed, said she was very tired, and how soon did she need to try and feed the baby for the first time? "I want to nurse him, Dr. Foster," she said, "can I do that now, the way I am feeling and with the blood transfusions and all?"

Dr. Foster assured her to at least try letting him suckle a little, that way her milk would come in more quickly. He told her, however, not to get tired, to just try nursing a little every few hours, the nurses would help her, and in the meantime they would give the baby formula. "It is very important to nurse him, Sarah," he said, "But our concern right now is your health. You need to be healthy in order for your baby to be healthy."

She assured him she would do everything she was told to do. Then she asked if it would be okay for her to see Pastor Terry? Dr. Foster said he would put in a call for him, that he had been in and out all night visiting with her father and father-in-law, but that she had been a little too busy for visitors. Sarah chuckled a little, thanked him, and he was gone.

Dr. Foster was pleased with Sarah's improvement, but he was worried about her mental state. He felt she needed some guidance right now and was glad she had asked for the pastor. He knew she had been through rough times the last few days, not only being in a long labor and having a difficult delivery, but doing it all without her husband. He would see to getting the pastor to her room first thing. He took out his cell phone and called the pastor directly. Pastor Terry promised to come to Sarah's room within the next thirty minutes.

*   *   *   *   *

Natalie finished scrubbing the floors on the sixth floor, cleaned one empty room twice, was asked no questions about who she was or why she hadn't been on the sixth floor before and was feeling very confident when she saw a minister going into Sarah's room.

"I hope she's okay or that the baby is okay," Natalie thought. "I should be able to clean her room within the next fifteen minutes, then I'll put the next part of my plan into place. I will be able to see exactly how Sarah is, how that beautiful baby girl is doing, and, within a few hours I'll be able to get rid of Sarah, take the baby and be on my way to New York City." Natalie smiled and went into the next room to clean. She walked into the room, said hello to the lady lying in the bed, remarked about how sweet her baby was, asked if it was a boy or girl and continued to clean. Her heart skipped a beat when she thought of the new life she and Melanie Anne were about to embark on.

CHAPTER TWENTY-SEVEN

The agent in the Yarmouth hotel had been sleeping soundly until his telephone rang. He looked at the alarm clock on the bedside table, noticing it was 4:30 a.m. Even before he located his cell phone and said hello he figured this call would be for Ben Kestwick and that he had just become a father.

"Hello, Sorenson here," the sleepy voice came on the line.

"Hey, Sorenson," Tom Casey said cheerfully, "You asleep?"

"I was Casey, until you phoned, what's up? We got a baby in your neck of the woods?"

"Yes we do, can I speak with Ben?" Casey asked.

Agent Sorenson turned on the light, but Ben was already sitting on the edge of the second double bed in the motel room. Sharing a motel room with another guy was not his thing, but at this point in his life, it was the least of his problems. "It's Casey," the agent said, half asleep, I think he has good news for you."

"Tom?" Ben anxiously asked. "Is Sarah okay, has she had the baby, what is it, a boy or a girl, when was it born?"

"Whoa, whoa!" Tom told Ben, "One question at a time, please, my friend. Yes, Sarah is fine, you have a son, he was a big guy, nine pounds and something, and as far as I know mother and son are just fine. He was born a little after 3:00 a.m. this morning." Tom continued by congratulating Ben and trying to get a word in every once in a while.

"You sure everything is okay, Tom?" Ben asked again, anxious to get as much information as possible. Tom assured him that all was going well. He would call back when he heard more, but for now, Ben should get some sleep, and he would call when they had Natalie in custody, and he and Jeremy could come home.

"How is Jeremy by the way?" Tom asked. Is he with you?"

Ben informed Tom that the FBI had Jeremy staying somewhere else in Yarmouth. He wasn't sure why or where, and that he had not been there yesterday to help him ship out their lobster haul, in fact, he hadn't seen him since they both came to Yarmouth. Tom asked if Jeremy had a wife or kids, and, once again, Ben said no, he didn't think Jeremy had any family, he was a loaner, but a good worker, and had been for many years. "I'm sorry Tom, I really don't know what's going on with Jeremy right now, or where he is. It figures, these FBI guys aren't telling me anything about nothing, thank goodness, they are letting you call me, or I'd be going crazy for sure."

Before Tom hung up, he told Ben he would try to call every hour or so, and as soon as Sarah and the baby were out of danger and Natalie was in custody, he would let him know. "If there is any change at all at the hospital that concerns you and your family, Ben, I'll call you immediately. Hang in there, okay?"

Ben thanked him again, handed the telephone back to agent Sorenson, and laid back on the bed. Sorenson congratulated him and wanted to talk to Ben more, but decided against it. He would talk to him later.

A baby boy, Ben couldn't believe it. He had wanted a boy so badly, but he would have been happy with a girl, too. He felt so happy, so thankful, and yet so lost and empty. He had missed out on one of the most important events in a man's life, the birth of his first child. He had not been there for Sarah. How could this have happened to his family? He rolled over onto his side and cried. Ben cried like he had never cried in his life. He didn't care that Agent Sorenson was in the room and heard him, a grown man, crying like a baby; he didn't care about anything but Sarah and his new baby boy. "My God," he cried, "Why did this have to happen to me and my family? Why?"

Agent Sorenson wanted so badly to console Ben. After all, he had four kids of his own, and he recalled how excited he and his wife had been when their first child, Nicholas, was born. It was a time when a husband and a wife should be together, to share in the birth, the naming of the child, sharing the news with family and friends, and Ben had missed all of this. Sorenson understood and didn't make a sound or say a word. He just let Ben cry it out. He needed this type of healing right now.

Ben actually slept for three hours. No one had called, so when he woke up, he presumed everything was going well with Sarah and the baby, and Natalie had either not made a move or was already in custody. He was in his motel room alone when he got up. He shaved and showered. He put on new underwear, a pair of new jeans and t-shirt, compliments of the FBI, combed his long blond hair, tied it back in a pony tail, and peered out the door. Sorenson was speaking with a police officer at the end of the walkway, and he waved at Ben as he closed the motel room door behind him.

"Hey, big daddy," the agent said, "Congrats on your little boy. I'm glad all went well and that you got a few hours of sleep. Want something to eat? I've got coffee and breakfast rolls over here."

Ben approached the agent and the Yarmouth police officer. He shook each of their hands, the officer left, and Ben said he really needed some real food, could they go and get breakfast. Sorenson said yes, and they walked to the agent's SUV. Over breakfast, Agent Sorenson talked with Ben about his own wife and children. He had been married fourteen years, had two boys and two girls, his wife was a stay-at-home mom, and the FBI had been very good to his family. "Only one time did we have a small problem," he told Ben. "I was gone for almost a year, got shot, almost died, and my wife asked me, no begged me, to leave the agency. I thought about it but just couldn't leave. I love this job, and most of the time we get the bad guys so it's very rewarding."

"Do you think you will get the bad guys this time," Ben quietly asked as they ate their breakfasts. "Are my wife and child really safe, and is that evil woman going to be caught?"

Sorenson saw the sadness in Ben Kestwick's eyes, and he felt sorry for him, truly sorry. "Yes, Ben, we will bring Natalie in. The latest telephone call, within the last hour or so from Agent Dixon was that everything is going according to plan, and there are four agents watching her and waiting for her to make her final move."

"Final move?" Ben asked, "You mean when she tries to steal my son, that's the final move isn't it?"

Sorenson nodded his head, looked at Ben, and wished there was something he could say to make everything all right, but there were no appropriate words. They finished their breakfasts' in silence, paid the bill and left in Sorenson's SUV. Upon arriving back at the motel, Ben exited the SUV, slammed the door shut and walked into his motel room. No, Ben thought, there is nothing anyone can say to make this all right. I just have to hope and pray that Sarah, our little boy and I will make it through this ordeal safely.

CHAPTER TWENTY-EIGHT

Natalie Pickford Andrews finished cleaning the rooms on the sixth floor, including the room where Sarah was resting comfortably. The baby had evidently been taken from the room for newborn testing, and, since the baby was not in the bassinette, Natalie did not read or notice the card that read "Baby Boy Kestwick." on the top of the bassinette. As she cleaned, she checked out the layout of the room, how many intravenous tubes Sarah had in her arms and exactly where the bassinette was in comparison to Sarah's bed. Sarah's mother was asleep in the overstuffed chair in the room, and she had not awakened the entire time Natalie cleaned. She was thrilled to get into the room undetected but disappointed that she could not see the baby, the baby she would be mothering in just a few hours.

She finished cleaning two more rooms, the two public restrooms and left the sixth floor on the elevator. Once in the basement, she placed her buckets, mops and brooms, as well as her uniform, in the basement maintenance closet and checked to see if the regular sixth floor cleaning woman was still unconscious. She was. Natalie had sneaked up behind her earlier in the afternoon, stabbed her in the neck with a syringe full of strong sleeping medication, tied her up and dragged her to a back room closet where she had left her. Checking her pulse then feeling her forehead, Natalie figured she'd be out cold for a few more hours, but she would be fine other than having a serious headache. Natalie had no intention of hurting anyone, she just needed to temporarily get out of the way all those who might stop her from getting her baby.

Agent Dixon had watched Natalie go in and out of the maintenance closet in the afternoon, but she had no idea this deranged woman had drugged the regular nightshift employee and taken her place as a cleaning woman. Now, watching Natalie leave the area in a nurse's uniform, she had an uneasy feeling. She radioed ahead to the agent in the parking garage, asking him to take over for her, telling him that Natalie was on her way to the garage, and that she was staying inside to check out a lead. She went into the maintenance closet hand on the gun in her waistband.

She found the uniform Natalie had worn, the fake badge still pinned to the shirt, and, having a feeling of something gone terribly wrong, she checked all of the lockers and closets until she found Loretta Thompson, the cleaning woman, bound and unconscious in the closet. She felt for a pulse, found one, tried to awaken her, but with no results called for backup. Within a few minutes, two agents came into the area, followed by an intern. The agents first took photographs, and then took off Loretta's bindings; the intern took the woman's vital signs, called for a pram, and Loretta was taken to the emergency room. Natalie had no idea Loretta had been found, and the intern was sworn to talk to no one but his immediate supervisor. One of the FBI agents accompanied him to the ER.

Once in the parking garage, Natalie opened her trunk, brought out a duffle bag and got into her car. Once inside she ate a sandwich and apple from a brown paper bag in her duffle bag, drank a warm bottle of water, locked the car doors and laid down on the back seat of her Chrysler for a few hours sleep. She covered herself completely with a blanket and smiled as she thought how the day had gone. So far so good, she thought. No one suspects who I am or what I am doing, except doing my job. Sarah gave birth, and in a few hours I will have my baby and be on my way to New York. She fell asleep with a smile on her face thinking of the next step in her kidnapping plan.

Agents Blom, Stewart, and Silverman came on early Thursday morning to replace two of the undercover agents, plus Agent Dixon. The three agents left for breakfast and to get a few hours sleep, and promised they would be back later in the afternoon. The undercover detectives were also replaced for a few hours, and Agent Richard McLeary came to the medical center to speak with the hospital's administration, security personnel and the sixth floor staff. He had called a meeting of all those involved, and now was addressing them on the issues at hand in a downstairs conference room.

He first thanked the hospital's supervisor and those involved in this surveillance for their cooperation, told them what had happened during the last twelve hours, and shared with them what to expect in the next twelve hours.

"I expect Mrs. Andrews to make her move within the next twelve hours," he explained. She has been under surveillance the entire time, our agents know where she is and what she is doing at all times, even where she is right now. However, the next few hours are critical, she will most likely make her move, try to steal the Kestwick baby, then try to escape with him, and your staff's cooperation is crucial." McLeary continued by asking the supervisors on the sixth floor to make sure the next shift of nurses taking care of Sarah and her child were also made aware of what might happen, but in no way should they let the mother or grandmother know that they were possibly in jeopardy.

"Your discretion is very important right now," he told the entire gathering, "the security of Mrs. Kestwick and her child are of the greatest priority for the next few hours. We have no idea what disguise Mrs. Andrews will appear in next or how she will attempt to steal the baby, but you must be aware and observant at all times. There will be four undercover FBI agents on the sixth floor, you may not recognize or notice them, and that is in everyone's favor. Once again, thank you all for working with the FBI on this case. You have no idea how important catching this woman is to the FBI, the DEA and the residents of this great state of Maine."

One of the nurses asked McLeary how they would know who was a good guy and who wasn't. "If we don't know the suspect, and we don't know the FBI agents, how will we know who to watch or report on?"

McLeary assured her and all in attendance that the FBI would know, and for neither her nor anyone else in the room to worry. They had the situation well in hand.

The staff's 7:30 a.m. shift change came and went, and there was no suspicious activity on the sixth floor. After the 6:00 a.m. nurse's rounds, Sarah used the bathroom, took her medications, tried to nurse the baby, and, although her milk had begun to come in she still gave the baby two ounces of formula and they both went back to sleep. The nurse checked on them, and changed the baby's diaper around 8:30 a.m. and Mary Anne left around the same time. She told the nurse she was going to the motel to shower and perhaps sleep for a few hours, and Sarah's dad would be back to stay with their daughter around 10:00 a.m. "Our phone number is on Sarah's records," she said, "Please call if you need us and we will be right over. Her father-in-law is asleep in the visitor's room, you can arouse him, too, if need be."

The nurse assured her they would, and knowing about Sarah's missing husband, the day nurse asked Mary Anne if there had been any word about Mr. Kestwick? Her face saddened when Mary Anne told her there had been no word.

Mary Anne Waverly walked the two blocks to the motel where she and Jonas were staying. She was very tired, but also relieved that Sarah's baby was doing well, and that Sarah, after having a third transfusion, was doing much, much better, at least physically; she wasn't to sure about her emotional state.

She arrived at the hotel, used her key to open the room door and quietly opened it. It was dark in the room, the television was on but there was no sound, and Jonas was fast asleep on top of the bed covers. "Oh, my," Mary Anne said softly, "He never even made it out of his clothes." She took off her jacket, laid down beside her husband and after a short prayer of thanksgiving, within seconds she too was asleep.

At 9:45 a.m. Natalie woke from a troubled sleep. She was uncomfortable on the back seat of her car, needed to use the restroom, and her head ached from the horrible dreams she'd had again—dreams of black water swallowing her up, and of a baby reaching out to her from that same black water.

She sat up, tried to stretch out a little, took a sip of water from the water bottle, and crawled out of the car. She opened the trunk, took out another duffle bag and got back into the car. "This is it," she said somewhat cranky and disoriented. "This is the day all my dreams come true, and Melanie Anne and I will start our new life."

Natalie returned to the back seat of her car, took off her clothes and pulled new ones from the bag and began to put them on. She put on a pair of new blue jeans, a t-shirt, socks and tennis shoes. She combed out her long hair, put on a baseball hat, added just a little makeup and got out of the car. She took the duffle bag with her, locked the car and headed for the stairs. She opened the door to the stairs, walked up two flights of stairs, exited and went directly into the ladies restroom. Once inside, she entered the larger handicapped stall, used the toilet, and began to once again change her clothes.

FBI agent Blom, covering for Agent Dixon in the parking garage, had followed Natalie down the stairs. He watched her enter the restroom and then waited for her to exit. He waited and watched for over ten minutes, and the only women he saw leaving the restroom were a tall woman in a business suit, talking on her cellular phone, a candy striper with bright red, braided hair, and a woman carrying a baby in front of her chest in a baby pack and a large diaper bag. He never noticed Natalie exit the restroom. Three more women entered and exited the restroom before the agent contacted undercover agents, giving them all the news.

"Send me a female agent," he demanded into his walkie-talkie. "I need a female agent in the women's restroom on the east end of the third floor, ASAP!"

He had lost track of Natalie Pickford Andrews.

CHAPTER TWENTY-NINE

At 10:30 a.m. Sarah asked her nurse if she could take a shower, and would she assist her? "I think I am strong enough to walk over to the shower," Sarah said smiling. "I think I can handle the IVs if you would help me. Can I sit in the shower, instead of stand, or is it too soon for all of this?"

She swung her feet over the edge of the bed, and her day nurse Wilma VanSteen steadied her as she stood up. "It's only been a few hours, Mrs. Kestwick," she answered, "since you gave birth but if you're up to it, I think it will be fine. There is a shower bench, and sitting might be a good option for you."

Before she took even one step, Sarah took a peek at her beautiful, sleeping baby boy. She lightly touched his cheek and thought how much he looked like Ben.

"He looks like you Ben," she said aloud. "You need to come home soon so you can see your son and so we can name this little one." She touched her fingers to her mouth, and then placed them on the small pink lips of her son. "I love you, little one," she said smiling, "and your daddy loves you to, and soon your daddy will be back, and we will give you a name, I promise."

Wilma assisted her into the bathroom and placed the shower bench in the wide shower stall. Although it took a few minutes to get Sarah undressed, and her IVs in a comfortable position and covered with plastic so they would not get wet, she sat her down slowly on a rubber donut on the shower bench. Although extremely sore and very tired, the warm water falling gently over her body felt wonderful and invigorated Sarah. She still felt rather large, but not nearly as large and bulky as she had felt the day before. "I hope I can get my belly back to normal size," she said to the nurse looking down. "I still feel like I'm pregnant!"

As the nurse helped her wash and rinse her long blond hair, she assured Sarah that in a few months she would be as she was before, slender and back in fine shape. She started to say something about how her husband would love the new woman she would be in a few months, but stopped, realizing Sarah's husband was missing at sea.

When Sarah finished with her shower, she felt so much better, so much more alive. The nurse asked if after she dried her hair, would she like to sit in the overstuffed chair or get back in bed? "I can change your bedding," she said, "That will make you feel even better. I can bring you the baby and you can try nursing again while you are sitting upright. Shall we try that?"

Sarah agreed and when she finished drying herself off the nurse assisted her into a clean hospital gown and shoe-socks, and helped her to a standing position. She opened the bathroom door, backed out of it, leading Sarah and her IV stand in front of her. She began to turn and sit in the large brown chair, when Sarah, a puzzled look on her face said to the nurse. "The baby is gone, were there more tests scheduled for him this morning?"

The nurse said she was not certain but she would check his chart immediately, and she was sure that must be the case. Then she helped Sarah sit down asked if she was comfortable, and told Sarah she would be back in just a minute. "I'll go check, and be right back. Are you okay for a minute?"

Sarah said yes, she was fine, and the nurse hastily left the room. The nurse was positive there were no orders for the baby to be taken from the room for more tests. As she rushed to the nurse's desk, her heart began to beat harder, sweat appeared on her forehead, and she began to panic. She knew she should have wheeled the baby's bassinette into the bathroom with Sarah, but it wasn't the normal procedure. She feared she had messed up big time.

Nurse Colleen Parker was supervisor on 6-West on Thursday and had been supervising the same staff for over eight years. She was pleased with her staff, they were a tight group, and she knew almost all of them personally. She had been informed early this morning by FBI Agent McLeary about the situation with Sarah Kestwick, her baby and her missing husband. She was told not to tell anyone else on staff, other than Sarah's nurse, about the situation. McLeary had pointed out two of the undercover agents on the floor and had given her his private cellular telephone number. "You contact one of the undercover agents immediately if anything disturbing or out of the ordinary happens today," he told her. "Or you can call me directly, but I will be off and on this floor, and we have a better chance of stopping the suspect if you contact the agents up here." He told her who they were, where they were located, what they were wearing, and to only contact them if they saw any suspicious women on the sixth floor or around Mrs. Kestwick's room.

Wilma looked for Colleen, but she was not at the front desk. She went into the nurse's kitchen, the staff's restroom, but she was in neither place. As she hurried down the corridor of the sixth floor, she spotted her coming out of a room, five doors down from Sarah's room. "Coleen," she called softly, "Colleen." She walked briskly towards her supervisor, asked if they could speak in the nurses' kitchen, told her the Kestwick baby was missing, and was he in the nursery having more lab work done?

Colleen, her eyes suddenly darkening, hurried to the nursery, noticed one of the FBI agents walking the hall with crutches and a fake limp coming the same direction, held up her hand and motioned for him to follow her, which he did. Colleen put in the entry code, and, once inside the nursery, asked the nursery's head nurse if the Kestwick baby was there. When she said no, the agent ditched the crutches, picked up his cellular telephone from his pocket, and called McLeary, the other agents in the hospital and hospital security.

"Keep this quiet right now," McLeary radioed his agents. "Only agents and hospital security involved right now. Shut down the hospital, put out a Code Green. This will keep all patients in their rooms; the hospital staff will know what to do. Make sure there are two agents at Natalie's car. No one gets out of the hospital or the parking garage, everyone understand?"

All the agents checked in by telephone, everyone took their appropriate places, and the final comment from McLeary was, "No one tells Sarah Kestwick about the baby, no one!! Get a hold of the supervisor on the sixth floor and Sarah's nurse. Make sure they assure Sarah Kestwick that the baby is fine, being taken care of, make up a story, I don't care what it is, but Sarah Kestwick must think her baby is fine!"

On the first floor of the hospital, McLeary was literally screaming into the telephone as he rushed to the stairs leading to the hospital's parking garage. "You all know your places, you all know what to do. No harm comes to that baby, you understand? No harm comes to that baby! I want Natalie in one piece, try not to harm her or you will harm the baby, everyone got that, get Natalie, but keep that baby safe!"

The second undercover agent on the OB/GYN floor was disguised as a fireman. He had been checking fire alarms, doorways, working and talking with the staff, and, when he got the call, he immediately went to find Supervisor Parker. He gave her McLeary's message and she and Wilma went immediately into Sarah's room. Sarah, although somewhat concerned as to the location of her child, had remained seated in the overstuffed chair and anxiously asked if her baby was okay.

Taking a deep breath before answering, Colleen said, smiling, "he's fine, Mrs. Kestwick." She assured Sarah again and said, "I'm so sorry we did not tell you that he would be gone for a little while this morning. He is having a few more blood tests. It's nothing to worry about, but due to your blood problems, your pediatrician, Dr. Flood, wanted to make sure he's okay. It's normal procedure, and once again, I apologize for not telling you before hand." She asked how Sarah was doing, was she eating well, that Wilma had said she had such a great attitude and outlook. She asked about Ben, was there any news, and just talked idle talk with her for about fifteen minutes. Wilma started changing the bedding, getting her fresh water, and then asked if she wanted to continue sitting up or take the opportunity to have a nap before the baby came back?

"I'm really very comfortable thank you," Sarah answered. "I'll just stay up for a little while longer. Just let me know when the baby's tests are completed, and I'll try to nurse him again. Is that okay?" Colleen and Wilma assured her whatever she wished to do was fine with them. Wilma left Colleen and Sarah to talk for a while longer; Colleen asked if she wanted to see her father-in-law, as he was now awake in the visitor's room, and a short time later, Colleen left as well. She went down to the visitor's area, told Martin that Sarah would like to have some company, and returned to the nurse's area. She stepped behind the desk, sat down in a chair, folded her hands on top of the desk, laid her head down for just a few moments and sighed a deep sigh. "What have we done?" she asked herself, "What have we done?"

CHAPTER THIRTY

Natalie had entered the ladies restroom on the third floor of the hospital in regular street clothes, baseball cap and tennis shoes. She almost looked like a teenager, carrying a huge purse and an even larger duffle bag. She suspected that there was either a cop or an FBI agent tailing her when she left the parking garage. She wasn't sure why, it was just a gut feeling she had. Twice during the past several hours she had passed a man and a women who gave her a creepy, suspicious feeling. She had been involved with cops several times over the past twenty years, including while in jail, and she could sense when they were in the area. It was like they gave off a certain aura or smell. She hated cops and Carl hated them too! She wondered, however, why they were in the hospital parking garage. She had slowed down her drug sales in the last weeks, had been careful and was sure no one had seen her dealing. Her dingy ex-jail guard husband wouldn't be stupid enough to snitch on her; besides, she hadn't heard from him in a few days. He did, however, know what she was up to, but no way would he jeopardize her plans. He needed her too badly. Still, she wondered why he hadn't been in contact with her.

Once in the ladies room, she had gone into a stall, put the lid down on the toilet, sat down, and gone over her plans to take Sarah's baby. If all went well, she would follow someone who had been buzzed in through the OB/GYN doorway, and if asked who she was there to see, say she was a friend looking for Jeannette in Room 623. She had cleaned that room the previous day and memorized the name on the door. She should have no problems getting onto the sixth floor, and into Sarah's room.

She would go into Sarah's room, if necessary sneak up on her and put a pillow to her face to keep her from calling out, stick her with a drug-filled syringe causing her to fall asleep instantly, and then she would steal her baby. She did not want to harm Sarah; after all, she was her daughter. She hoped Sarah would already be asleep, that no one else would be in the room this morning, and that she would pick up the baby, replace it with the doll in the baby carrier from the large duffle bag, cover her up, and be on her way. She figured she could complete this abduction in less than five minutes.

As she continued to review the plans in her head, she took out another disguise from her duffle bag. She took off her clothing and, dressed in a pink skirt with white blouse, added a light pink sweater, a curly brown wig and placed the baby carrier with a life-like baby doll inside the carrier and placed it in front of her. Over the doll's head, she placed a pink and yellow receiving blanket. She placed her previous clothes in her bag, adjusted the baby carrier and left the stall. She took one look at herself in the restroom mirror, smiled at what she saw, and, after about ten minutes left the restroom and headed to the elevator, smiling. She got out on the sixth floor. She followed and spoke to a proud, new father into the OB/GYN area wished him good luck and headed for Sarah's room. No one spoke to her or asked to see her fake baby in the carrier and getting into the area went smoothly. The most incredible part of the abduction was that she did not have to subdue Sarah and did not have to hurt her or fight her in any way. She was not even in the room. She had heard voices in the bathroom and presumed Sarah was taking a shower.

Natalie truly thought the gods were with her, that the moon and stars and all the galaxies were in the right formation and on her side today.

"The psychic has been right all along," she commented softly, "I am meant to have this baby." Her excitement, however, was short-lived. As she went to the bassinette to gently pick up the sleeping child, she realized Sarah's baby was wrapped in blue blankets, with a blue crocheted cap on its head. "Oh my god! Where is my Melanie

Anne?" Natalie gasped. "This is a boy baby, I need a girl baby!" She took a quick glance at the nametag on the bassinette.

"Baby Boy Kestwick! This cannot be! I need a baby girl to take home, not a baby boy!" She looked around, thought just for a moment, plucked the doll from her carrier, stuffed it into her duffle bag, and hastily picked up the sleeping baby. Her mind immediately skipped from sanity to craziness, almost madness. She opened the door, looked to the right and the left, took a deep breath, and started walking out of the area. She walked slowly to the stairs, opened the door and, once on the stairs, walked swiftly down two floors then took the elevator to the parking garage. Once inside the garage, she took a peek at the baby. He was sleeping soundly, but she was so upset that it was a boy. "I don't want this baby!" she said, looking down at the carrier. "I need my Melanie Anne, not a boy baby. Boys are always in trouble. They grow up to become men, and men mean nothing to me. They hurt you, they use you, they are rotten excuses for human beings. I do not want this baby boy! He'll grow up to be nothing but a dirty old man. I have to get rid of him, he's no good to anyone, not anyone!"

As she walked hastily towards her car, a man approached her from behind. Joe Spencer, who had been resting in his car, had seen her coming out of the elevator, and even with the disguise, he knew it was Natalie. He had watched her for a moment, then got out of his car and went after her.

"Natalie? Natalie, is that you?"

She turned completely around and stared into the soft, caring eyes of Joe Spencer.

"Joe?"

She recognized Joe Spencer immediately. She had been sure she had seen him in Booth Bay Harbor; she hadn't been imagining things, now she knew for sure—it was Joe.

Within the next few moments, Natalie Pickford Andrews completely lost her mind. She had always been in a poor state of mind, but now she no longer knew the difference between right and wrong or what was true and real.

"Joe darling, you've come for me and our baby. I always knew you would. Look, Joe, look at our beautiful baby girl. Our Melanie Anne." Looking down at the beautiful sleeping baby boy, Natalie said again, "Joe, we are a family now, look at our beautiful baby, isn't she just gorgeous? She looks like me, don't you think?"

Joe approached Natalie, and very cautiously asked, "Where did you get this baby, Natalie? " He touched her shoulder, and when she did not flinch, he asked her again, "Natalie, whose baby do you have?"

"It's my baby, Joe, our baby. We always wanted another baby, remember, Joe? You've always wanted me, haven't you Joe, and for us to have another baby, remember Joe? You always wanted our baby back, didn't you Joe?" She continued to look down at the baby with love and admiration, and Joe was immediately convinced that Natalie truly believed the child was hers.

From the way Natalie was acting, Joe presumed she had taken this baby from a new mother in the hospital. How, he had no clue. He knew for sure he needed to get some help, but wasn't sure how, or whom to call, and most of all he had no idea how to get this baby away from her without harming it.

"Natalie," he said calmly, "May I hold our baby?"

Natalie looked up at him with a confused look on her face. "No, this is my baby girl. You can't have her!"

"I don't want to keep her, Natalie," Joe said calmly "I just want to hold her a little, after all she is my baby too, right?"

Natalie smiled, nodded her head, and gently lifted the child out of the baby carrier. She started to hand him to Joe, re-wrapping him in his blankets, and as he did so the baby began to cry.

"Now look what you've done!" she screamed. 'You made her cry. I am her mother, I need to take her and feed her, and change her diaper, and then go home with her. She and I need to go home!"

Not real sure of what to do next, but knowing he needed to get help for both Natalie and the child, and get this newborn back into a warm hospital room and to its mother, he said to Natalie; "Natalie, do you realize that the baby you have is not Melanie Anne, but it is a little boy? I think you are going home with the wrong baby. We should go back into the hospital and make sure you get the right baby, our baby."

"No, no, no!" she screamed. "This is our baby, and no one is going to ever take her away from me again." She began moving towards her car, and, as she took the keys from her pocket and approached her car, Joe noticed three men and a woman approaching. His first impression was that they were police and that Natalie had been found out. He moved closer to Natalie and to the gray Chrysler and softly put his arm around her and asked if he could please hold the child while she put her bags in the car, and then he would hand the baby to her. Reluctantly, Natalie agreed. She handed Joe the baby, placed the keys in the lock and unlocked the car. She threw her bags over the seat, got into the driver's seat, started the vehicle, and reached out for the child. As she reached out for the baby, Joe stepped back and, began running towards the far end of the parking garage. As he did so, two police officers and the FBI agents approached Natalie's car. She saw them coming, locked the doors, started the engine, put the car in reverse, slamming into a green Volvo but not doing enough damage to stall her get-away. She rammed another car getting out of the parking garage, stormed the security guard gate and drove out into the morning traffic. The police officers ran back to their patrol cars, one of the FBI agents radioed the other agents in the hospital, told them the situation, that a strange man had the Kestwick baby, to get to the garage immediately and she too headed out of the parking garage in her black SUV. The fourth officer followed Joe Spencer with the baby.

Natalie only had a few minutes head start. There was only one main highway out of the area, and, although no one was certain as to her destination, they headed north, sirens blaring. The police officers called in to their supervisor, asked to have a helicopter put in the air immediately, gave him the coordinates, asked for backup, and then gave him the most important information of all. The Kestwick baby was, as far as they knew, safe.

CHAPTER THIRTY-ONE

Joe Spencer pushed the up button on the elevator and, just as the police officer following him reached the elevator, the doors opened. Two men who identified themselves as FBI agents and nursing supervisor Colleen Parker were waiting in the elevator. The agents exited the elevator, followed by nurse Parker, and they asked Joe to stand back and to hand the baby to Colleen. They asked him his name and for some form of identification.

Joe gently handed the baby who was now crying loudly to nurse Parker. He reached into his back pants pocket for his wallet, all while the agents held firmly to their encased weapons. Colleen turned, entered the elevator and, trying to soothe the crying baby, pushed the button for the sixth floor.

"Mr. Spencer?" one of the agents asked, looking at his driver's license, "May we ask why you are in the hospital, and how it was that you were in the parking garage with this child in your possession?"

Joe took several minutes to explain that he had been at the Maine Medical Center to give blood, and that he had run into Natalie strictly by chance. He further explained that he had known her many years ago. He further explained their relationship, the child they had given up, and Natalie's current state of mind.

"I haven't seen her in over twenty years," he told the agents, "This is truly all a coincidence. I had nothing to do with this kidnapping, if that's what this is? I saw Natalie this week in Booth Bay Harbor, or at least I was pretty sure it was her, and just now saw her again. Really, this is all a coincidence."

A few minutes later, Richard McLeary came onto the scene, and he asked that Joe and the agents join him in a conference room on the first floor. Once in the conference room, Joe was interrogated for over an hour. Joe could not believe the intensity of their questions or the situation that was unfolding. He had no idea what problems Natalie had encountered over the years or what triggered the kidnapping she had just tried to pull off. At the end of the interrogation, the agents were certain of Joe's story, and they released him. As Joe stood up and began to leave the room, he told the agents he had a friend whose daughter had just given birth, and if they were finished with him, he would like to go see her. The agents shook his hand, thanked him and said they might be in touch later on. In passing, McLeary asked Joe who is friend might be, and when Joe told them it was Jonas Waverly's daughter Sarah Kestwick, the stunned agents asked Joe to please shut the door and sit back down. They now had several more questions to ask him.

For another few minutes Joe explained his relationship with Sarah Kestwick, that he was her birth father but that, neither she nor her husband had any idea of his true identity.

"She and Ben consider me an uncle of sorts," he explained to those in the room. "Sarah has no idea who her real mother or father are, and that is the way it has to stay, a secret. Please," he asked, almost begging everyone in the room, "this has to stay a secret. Only her adopted father knows the real truth, and that is why he called me to donate blood. Sarah was in serious danger after delivery, needed blood, and I was the only one who was a match. No one else knows, or must ever know the truth."

McLeary assured him all would be kept quiet and for him not to worry, and he could leave and go see Sarah. He thanked Joe for his time, said they would remain in touch and Joe left the conference room. McLeary, his agents and the police officer remained for a few minutes. During that time, McLeary received two telephone calls, made a few comments to the others in the room and swiftly left the area for his vehicle.

While Joe was being interrogated further and informed of the situation unfolding, four Portland patrol cars and three FBI agents in three separate SUVs had been chasing Natalie through the streets of Portland and onto I-95. Luckily, it was mid-morning and the streets and highway was not overly crowded. Every time the officers and agents figured they had her cornered in town, she would escape down an alleyway or drive the wrong way down a one-way street. The helicopter pilot kept all those on the ground abreast of her northward direction, but it wasn't until two hours after the Kestwick baby's abduction that the chase ended.

Natalie weaved in and out of the cars and trucks on I-95, causing several vehicles to either take to the shoulder of the highway or crash. How she drove this far without seriously hurting or killing any other drivers was a miracle in itself. Throughout the entire chase, she laughed aloud, like an evil, possessed woman. She thought of seeing Joe again and she laughed, she thought of Melanie Anne and she laughed. She was so mentally out of control she had no idea where she was or what she was doing, but she constantly laughed an evil, cantankerous laugh.

Suddenly, after she had been on the highway for over an hour with seven vehicles chasing her, she turned off the interstate as if drawn to a new destination. She began to see visions of the baby, her baby, reaching out and calling to her. She saw the baby's reflection in the front windshield of her car and she heard it calling to her from the baby car carrier in the seat next to her. As she looked towards the car's passenger side window, she saw the baby's face seemingly rising out of the ocean's rough waters, her hands reaching out to Natalie. The ironic part was that Natalie wasn't even close to the ocean's white-capped waters.

"I'm coming, Melanie Anne," she screamed at the vision in the car's passenger window. "I'm coming baby, mama is coming to get you!"

As she approached the road leading to Bath, she came dangerously close to cutting off a pickup with three teenagers inside, causing the driver to spin out. They honked the horn, said a few choice words to her which went unheard, and she continued on in a world of her own. She turned right at the next corner without stopping for a red light, sped through Bath, and onto the road leading to Booth Bay Harbor.

The police officers and FBI agents continued their pursuit. They had radioed ahead to each town Natalie sped through and asked the police to close off their main streets, to try and keep vehicles out of her way, but to not try to stop the driver in the gray Chrysler. She ran red lights, swerved and missed several more cars, jumped a curb at an intersection, and somehow made it through each town without seriously injuring anyone.

Completely out of control now, her mind strictly on her child, she erratically drove through the streets of Booth Bay Harbor. She drove to the northeast side of this quaint, ocean harbor town where Ben and Sarah lived and turned onto Catamaran Street. The quiet neighborhood was lined with small historic houses where a few children played in their front yards. She pressed her foot down harder onto the gas pedal, and, as she approached the block where the Kestwick home stood overlooking the sea, she slammed the Chrysler into and through the guardrail plunging eighty-five feet onto the jagged rocks below.

Screaming Melanie Anne's name, the gray Chrysler bounced on and off of the jagged rocks; broken glass and bent pieces of steel flew through the air and fell into the thrashing sea below. The noise of the crash sent hundreds of perched seagulls fluttering and squawking into the blue skies, seemingly scolding Natalie as she and the car sunk into a deep watery grave.

Bloodied and broken and still screaming her baby's name, Natalie held onto the broken steering wheel as water began to pour into the vehicle from the shattered driver's window. As the vehicle filled up with dark, dirty water, she saw her baby's face, her hands out stretched and a voice from the deep calling, "mama, mama."

"I'm coming, Melanie Anne. Mama's coming baby," she called to the vision, blood pouring from her mouth, "Mama's coming! I'll be right there. Mama's coming!"

*   *   *   *   *

Seven officers and FBI agents had pulled up to the edge of the cliffs, stopped their vehicles, got out and walked swiftly to the edge overlooking the beautiful deep blue waters of the bay. They looked up at the helicopter circling above them and silently watched as what was left of the gray Chrysler, sank into the sea. Two agents quickly went to their vehicles, where they retrieved their cameras and the roll of yellow police caution tape. They quickly roped off the area, took a few photos and called in the accident. Two other officers left the scene, immediately driving their patrol cars to each end of Catamaran Street blocking off the street. One of the agents called McLeary, gave him a lowdown on the situation, while the other agents called into the Coast Guard for a Search and Rescue Team and for a lead detective from the Booth Bay Harbor Police Department to get to the scene as soon as possible. Within minutes, Lieutenant Tom Casey called back, informed the agents that an SAR team was on the way and that he would be on the scene as soon as possible. As an after thought, he asked about the Kestwick baby.

"The baby is fine, we think," the agent told Tom, "Natalie kidnapped him but got no further than the hospital's parking garage when our agents took control. As far as I know, the mother has no idea about the abduction." The agent continued, "I suggest Lt. Casey, that you make no comments to the press, or anyone for that matter, until you speak with Agent McLeary about the kidnapping, or this case in general."

Tom understood completely and told the agent so. He hung up the telephone and headed for his vehicle. As he unlocked the door, he breathed in the salty air, said a short prayer of thanks, looked up and as he headed toward the accident site, wondered how Ben Kestwick was holding up. He would call him the minute he got the go-ahead to do so.

CHAPTER THIRTY-TWO

Nurse Colleen Parker had taken the Kestwick baby from Joe Spencer and gone directly to the sixth floor nursery. There, another nurse and the doctor on staff had checked him over thoroughly. There were no signs of injuries anywhere on his little body, and other than being hungry and maybe a little agitated, he was fine. Colleen once again reminded everyone in the nursery that this incident was over, that no one was to speak of it again, and, the mother was never to know anything about her child being taken by a kidnapper. She informed them that the continuance of their employment was on the line, and that the FBI might request to speak with them again within the next twenty-four hours. Everyone agreed with their supervisor's request and, after the baby was bathed, re-diapered and fed enough to settle him down, she returned him to Sarah. The entire abduction, getting the baby back, checking him over by a doctor and returning him to his mother had taken a total of thirty-five minutes.

Sarah, still sitting in the overstuffed chair, grinned when she saw Colleen walk into the room with her son. "Is he okay?" she asked anxiously. "Did they do more tests?"

Colleen handed her the precious bundle, said the tests all went fine, that they had fed him just a little bit of formula in the nursery, and asked, if she would like to try nursing him again? "I think he's still hungry," Colleen said, helping Sarah adjust herself and the baby to nurse. "I think if you let him suckle for about five minutes, he'll be satisfied, and five minutes will help your milk come in stronger too."

The baby did suckle, and although Sarah mentioned it was a little uncomfortable, she was so glad to be able to nurse her son that the pain didn't matter. The nurse started to leave the room, said she would check on the both of them in a few minutes, and Sarah thanked her for her help. Sarah seemed to relax and, while the baby nursed, she gently ran her finger across his forehead, across his rosy cheeks, uncovered his little body and played with his toes and fingers, counting them as she did so. "I love you, little one," she repeated over and over. "You sleep now, and have sweet dreams of your daddy." Sarah talked to her beautiful sleeping son, told him what his daddy looked like, how he always laughed when he talked, that he loved to fish, that he had a boat, and when he was older his daddy would take him for a boat ride. "Tomorrow or the next day your daddy should be here to take us home," Sarah continued, "and then we will give you a name. I think we should name you Samuel, not Seth like we first thought, but Samuel. God talked to Samuel in the Bible story, and God has talked with me, and I have talked with God the entire time I have been carrying you and, during the last few hours when I was bringing you into the world."

Then, so no one else would here her speaking, she whispered to her son, "God will talk to Lieutenant Casey, or maybe Ron at the Port Authority, and the people keeping your daddy safe and God will tell them when to bring your daddy back to us." She chuckled to herself, then laughed a little harder, thinking God was certainly involved in her husband's last few days, but she knew she would be getting a phone call from an earthly friend, perhaps Tom or Ron, and not a direct call from God. She kissed her son again, chuckled a little more, and then said aloud, "Yes, I think we should name you Samuel, little one, Samuel Martin Kestwick, after the prophet, and after your grandpa Martin. I think your daddy will be happy with that name too."

Still smiling at herself and her son, Sarah took her sleeping baby from her breast, laid him over her shoulder, tried to burp him, and smiled. "Sleep now little Samuel," she said softly, "Sleep now and dream of your daddy." Sarah laid her head back, and, while rubbing the back of her precious child began to sing. "Jesus loves me, this I know, for the Bible tells me so..." She continued singing, and when she got to the third verse of the song, she realized she had not heard anyone come into her room, but, feeling a presence opened her eyes and saw Joe Spencer standing in their room. He was smiling, tears filling his eyes, holding a bouquet of blue and pink carnations in one hand and a large, blue helium filled balloon in the other.

"Uncle Joe!" she said, "What a great surprise! Mom and daddy must have called you." Moving Samuel from her shoulder to her lap and adjusting his blankets, she said to Joe, "Look at our beautiful little one. His name is Samuel." Continuing she said sweetly, "Samuel, meet your Uncle Joe."

Joe Spencer could barely speak. He was so overcome with emotion from not only seeing Sarah and her new son, but from the day's happenings: the call from Jonas for blood, seeing Natalie, handing over the baby to Colleen, the interrogation, and now just being here with his Sarah and his new grandson.

"Oh, Sarah, he is beautiful. I think he looks like Ben." Then realizing what he had just said, he got down on his knees, took her free hand in his and said, "Sarah, I am so sorry about Ben, has there been any word?"

"Not yet, Uncle Joe, but soon," Sarah said smiling and squeezing Joe's hand. " I know in my heart that Ben will be home soon. God has promised me, and I believe that with all my heart. Ben will be home soon to see me and his brand new son."

Joe stayed with Sarah for a little more than an hour and was about to take his leave when Pastor Terry knocked on the door, entered the room followed by Mary Anne, Jonas and Martin. They had stopped in for just a minute and then were going to leave to get something to eat.

"Martin acknowledged Joe Spencer, than said to Sarah, "I'm back for a little while Sarah, and then I will say goodbye," Martin said, "I needed to see my grandson one more time, too, but then I'm going to head up to Booth Bay and check in with the Coast Guard and Ron at the Port Authority. There should be some word about Ben and Jeremy by now, although no one has called, but if it's okay, and you and the baby are doing okay I'll head home."

Sarah assured her father-in-law that she and the baby were fine, told them all that, with Ben's approval she wanted to name the baby Samuel. She shared her reasons for the name, asked Jonas if it was okay to give her and Ben's firstborn son his grandfather Kestwick's name. When Jonas said fine, but he wanted the second grandson named after him, they all laughed. The Pastor and the family including Uncle Joe, then put their hands on Samuel's little head and, each said a blessing over the child. Martin said he always knew it was going to be a boy, and thanked God for a little boy and, asked for guidance in helping his grandson grow. Sarah's parents each said their own personal blessing, even Uncle Joe asked a special blessing on this miracle child. Sarah ended with her own blessing for her new son with the request that her husband return to his family and to his home soon. The words Sarah whispered to her God were with the truest belief that her prayers would be answered quickly. Pastor Terry ended the blessing and prayer requests with his own pastoral prayer of thanksgiving, and requests for Ben's safe return.

There were tears and hugs, more tears and more hugs, and finally Mary Anne took little Samuel, laid him in his bassinette, and asked Sarah if she wished to return to bed.

"I'm good for a few more minutes, mom," she said, heaving a big sigh. "This has been such a beautiful, memorable time, will you all do this with me again when Ben returns?" Everyone looked at one another quizzically, wondering how Sarah could muster such faith all the time? They assured Sarah that, of course, it would be appropriate to have Samuel's daddy be a part of the naming and blessing of his son. In their individual hearts, they all prayed that Ben would indeed be found safe and sound, and this entire ordeal would be over with soon. After all, Sarah had delivered a beautiful baby boy; he was healthy; she was now improving after the blood transfusions and surely God would answer the rest of their prayers as well. Jonas looked over to his friend Joe, made eye contact with him, and, silently the two men made a pact. If Joe did not want Sarah to know who he was, then that was okay with Jonas. If Joe did want her to know, then Jonas could live with that too. Time alone would tell. For right now, all was right with Sarah and Samuel, and with God's help, all would be right with Ben and Jeremy soon.

CHAPTER THIRTY-THREE

For over three hours, the SAR divers looked for Natalie's body. They searched in over twenty feet of dark murky water, in and around the sunken Chrysler, or what was left of it, but there was not even a trace of a body. The Coast Guard Search and Rescue Team called off the search about 6:00 p.m. figuring that Natalie's body had been washed out to sea. A large crane had pulled her car out of the bay earlier in the afternoon and, finding the trunk of the car intact and still locked, the officers opened it with a crow bar. They found waterlogged suitcases filled with food, baby formula, bottles of water and soda, women's and baby's clothing and one suitcase filled with thousands of dollars in one hundred dollar bills. The agents photographed all of the evidence, bagged it up and sent it to the FBI Crime Lab in Boston. A crew of investigators went over Natalie's car thoroughly and, the SAR boat crew and three divers searched for and found several pieces and parts of the car floating on over two miles of ocean. All evidence, including the car, was taken by flatbed truck to Boston.

While the police from Portland, Booth Bay Harbor and several FBI agents remained on the scene; Richard McLeary was finishing up the investigation at the Maine Medical Center. He had placed a call and spoken to Tom Casey suggesting that he call Ben Kestwick and at least tell him his wife and child were safe and that Natalie Pickford Andrews was missing and presumed drowned.

"Don't give Kestwick any of the details, Tom," he asked politely. "I'll meet with him later on this week and discuss at least some of the details with him, but for now he doesn't need to know everything. I'll let him decide how much he wants to tell his wife. "Also, Tom," he continued, "the press are going to be all over this in the next few hours. Let Ben know that all he should tell the press if they corner him is that he was involved with a secret FBI investigation, and he's been requested to say no more. The FBI will handle the press."

McLeary continued by telling Tom they needed to keep as much information as possible away from Sarah Kestwick, due to her birth mother being the prime suspect. "Let's handle this case from now on just like we have been, very carefully, Tom, we don't want to add any more distress to this already distressed family. Tom agreed, said he would be discretionary with the Kestwick family and thanked him for everything that had been done so far. McLeary said he would call Agent Sorenson, let him know that it was safe to let Ben Kestwick come back to Booth Bay Harbor with his boat, and that he had already called the Port Authority in Booth Bay to let Ron know that Ben would be coming into port late that afternoon. McLeary told him to call later in the afternoon and he would keep him abreast of the situation.

Tom did not ask about Ben's crewman Jeremy, and the agent did not mention Jeremy's release.

Tom immediately dialed Agent Sorenson's number, but the line was busy. He presumed McLeary had beaten him to the call. He waited a few more minutes, put in a second call, and this time Sorenson answered.

"Tom Casey here," he said to the agent, "Have you heard from Agent McLeary?" The agent said he had just received a call and Ben Kestwick was waiting to talk with Tom.

Tom informed Ben that the case was as good as closed. Sarah and the baby were safe, they were both doing very well, and that Ben was cleared to leave Nova Scotia, get on his boat and head for home. Without giving Ben a detailed account, he informed him of Natalie's presumed death and Ben could not thank Tom enough. He was so grateful, so thankful, and yes, very anxious to get back to the mainland and get to Portland to see Sarah.

"Sorenson will give you the low-down Ben," he said, "Take a deep breath, take your time, and just know that this situation is over;

you were a big part of it's success, and now your lives can return to normal."

Ben thanked him again, hung up and handed Sorenson the telephone, grabbed his dirty clothes and asked Sorenson if he was free to leave?

"I'll go with you to the docks, Ben," he said, "and see you off." Chuckling, but also needing to be serious, he said, "Our boats won't be following you this time, Ben. You're a free man and you'll be on your own. I'm sending one of our agents with you, however, just so you have company and in case you need any help with anything." Ben smiled, as the agent shook Ben's outstretched hand. Sorenson wished him the best of luck thanked him for his cooperation and opened the hotel room door for him; the agent followed him outside.

"Where's Jeremy?" Ben asked on the way to the SUV. "Do we need to pick him up, or will he be at the docks?"

Agent Sorenson looking Ben in the face said, "I'm sorry Ben, really sorry, but it seems that the FBI has found Jeremy to be involved in another situation, and they are keeping him here in Nova Scotia until they get some answers."

Shocked, Ben looked at the agent and asked "Jeremy? Jeremy is in trouble with the FBI? What could he possibly be involved in? He's been a loyal employee of mine for years." Sorenson informed him that he had no details, but that for now Ben was headed back to the harbor on his own. The FBI would be in touch with him about Jeremy and the entire last two day's operations.

Sorenson drove Ben to the docks where they checked over the SARAH JEANNE, filled her up with fuel, bottled water, snacks and more flares. Sorenson told him his weapons were back on board and he was free to head home. Ben started up the boat, said hello to the agent accompanying him, Agent Carlson, and they headed out of the Yarmouth Harbor.

The trip across the bay took a little over ninety minutes. During that time Ben had used the radio to call the Port Authority, informed Ron that he was on his way in and would he please call the hospital and have someone inform Sarah about his release. "Make sure there is a nurse or a pastor or her parents with her when she gets the news Ron," he asked, his voice breaking. "I 'm sure she was told earlier that, I was safe, but I don't want to scare her."

Ben docked a few feet down from his office, noticing that the Kestwick Boat House was dark. He tied up the boat, ran the two blocks to the Port Authority and walked in surprising everyone in the office except for Ron. Ron stood up, gave him a big bear hug, and Ben quickly asked if he could use his telephone. Ben pulled out a slip of paper from his wallet, checked the number and dialed the Maine Medical Center's main number. Shaking now but thinking ahead, he asked for Sarah Kestwick's room number when the operator answered, then asked the operator for the nurse's station on the maternity floor, and would she ring that number first. He knew if he called Sarah directly, he might just scare her to death when she heard his voice. Had he known how calm and collected Sarah had been throughout his whole ordeal, he may have dialed her room directly.

"Sixth floor nurse's station, Colleen Parker," came the sweet voice on the telephone.

"Ms. Parker?" he said his voice breaking. "This is Ben Kestwick, I am Sarah's husband."

"Mr. Kestwick! What a wonderful surprise. Are you okay?"

"I am, thank you," he said. "Could you please go into Sarah's room, tell her I'm, fine, and I'll be calling her immediately. I don't want to scare her. Is she doing okay? Is my son okay?"

After the initial shock of hearing Ben's voice, Colleen assured Ben that everything was fine. She would go into Sarah's room immediately, and for him to stay on the line. She would then transfer his call onto Sarah's extension.

Colleen pushed the hold button on the station's telephone and it flashed red as she left her desk. She walked into Sarah's room, softly closed the door and went to the side of her bed. Samuel was sleeping peacefully in her arms, evidently satisfied from the second feeding of his mother's milk. "Sarah," Colleen whispered softly, "Are you asleep?"

Opening her eyes, Sarah looked up at the nurse, said no, she was just resting, and, looking down at her sleeping child, asked if something was wrong? Colleen responded that everything was fine, and there was a telephone call for her. "Sarah, let me hold Samuel for a moment," she said, gently taking the baby from her arms. Knowing that the baby was secure in her arms and that Sarah would not harm or scare him when she heard the news, she informed her that her husband was safe, and that he was on the telephone asking for her.

"Oh my God! Oh my God!" Sarah said almost screaming. "Ben, is okay, where is he? Is he here in Portland? Is he here in the hospital? Where is he Colleen? Where is he calling from?"

Colleen, tears filling her eyes, told Sarah he was on the telephone at her desk, she was not sure where he was calling from, but she would put the call through immediately. "I'm going to put Samuel in his bed, and then I'll put the call through. Do you want me to come back in and stay with you?" She asked, a huge smile on her face.

Sarah, breathing hard now, told the nurse that she was fine; she could handle talking with her husband and please put the call through right away. She asked if Colleen would check to see if her parents were in the visitor's room and tell them the news too, but to give her a few minutes on the telephone with Ben first.

Tears streamed down Sarah's face, matching the tears streaming down Colleen Parker's face as the nurse placed Samuel back into the bassinette, placed the hospital telephone on the bed beside Sarah, and walked out the door.

There were no words to describe how Sarah felt when she heard Ben's voice. She cried for several minutes, as did Ben, before they could speak any words to each other. He told her how much he loved her, that he was so anxious to see their son, and that he was at the Authority with Ron. He would be in Portland within two hours, and he couldn't wait to see her and tell her all about his last few days. He asked if she was up to calling her parents or were they still at the hospital, and did she know where his father was? She told him, that her parents were still in Portland and that her father had left earlier to go back to Booth Bay Harbor. He was most likely at the boathouse or at home. The two friends, lovers, life-long partners and now parents of beautiful little Samuel talked for another fifteen minutes before Ben suggested they hang up so he could be on his way to Portland. They cried again and, when little Samuel started to cry, Ben asked if that was his son crying? Sarah said yes, it was, and together the three of them cried again.

Ben hung up the telephone, thanked Ron for all his help, told him he would be back later on and they would talk more, and headed out the door. He walked the docks to his office, noticed his father's vehicle now parked in the lot next to the docks and walked in the front door.

Martin Kestwick had seen the SARAH JEANNE tied up at the docks and knew that either Ben or Jeremy or an SAR officer had returned the boat. He had not had a chance to leave the offices and walk to the Port Authority before Ben entered the front door. Father and son hugged and cried, talked for just a few minutes, and Ben shared with his father that he would tell him all about the last few days later, but now he wanted to get to Sarah and his son. Martin agreed, asked if he wanted him to ride along and, when Ben said, no, that he would like to go on his own, Martin, realizing his son needed time alone, agreed. Ben gave his father another hug, left the offices and headed for his car, still parked in the parking lot just where he had left it on Tuesday morning.

Ben drove carefully out of the Bay area and onto I-95 towards Portland. He arrived at the medical center, parked out front, let the young valet park his car, took the parking ticket and ran into the hospital. He pushed the elevator button but decided it might be quicker to take the stairs and taking two stairs at a time, he made it to the sixth floor in record time. Once outside of Sarah's door, he stopped, ran his fingers through his long blond hair, took a deep breath and opened the door. Sarah was sitting up in bed, Samuel nursing at her breast. She looked up at him, her loving eyes never leaving his face. Ben slowly closed the door behind him and went to her side. He carefully sat down on the edge of the bed, gently kissed her on the forehead then on the lips, and then looked for the first time at his firstborn son. He touched his soft cheeks, caressed his soft, tiny fingers, all the while tears filling his eyes.

"He's beautiful Sarah," Ben said, softly touching her hair, "he's absolutely beautiful."

Sarah touched her husband's sun-tanned face, smiled, and then, looking down at their son, said to Ben. "Ben, God talked to me the entire time you were missing, and I in turn talked with Him. He held me in His arms for the entire time you were gone; He kept me strong; He never failed me and He never failed you. He told me we would have a strong, healthy child; He kept my faith strong, and He did give us a strong, healthy baby boy. I never doubted His love for us or that He would bring you back to us." Sarah continued and, looking directly into her husbands face she said, "Darling, because of God's closeness to me, and His keeping you safe and giving us this beautiful child, I have named him Samuel instead of Seth. I hope that 's okay with you. I talked with my dad and your father, and they all agreed with my decision. I have named him Samuel Martin Kestwick."

With those words, Ben kissed his beautiful wife, softly at first, and then long and hard. He then kissed Samuel on the forehead one more time and lay down beside the both of them. He took Sarah's free hand in his and they both closed their eyes. No words were necessary, and no words could ever describe their feelings of this moment. The Kestwicks were now a family, and nothing; nothing would ever keep them apart again.

CHAPTER THIRTY-FOUR

Ben spent Thursday night in Sarah's hospital room. He ate an evening meal with her, slept in the large overstuffed chair in her room and learned how to change his first dirty diaper. He left the room for only a few minutes to buy Sarah a dozen roses from the hospital's gift shop, along with a blue "baby boy" balloon and a loving, caring congratulations card for the "Love of his Life". Sarah thanked him, but this was not about flowers or cards or balloons, It was a time for thanksgiving and joy, and a time to thank God. She was just so thankful and jubilant that her husband had been returned to her and their son. She and Ben talked for hours, and when she tired, he would watch her peacefully sleeping from the big over-stuffed chair. When she nursed Samuel, he would ask how it felt, did it tickle, did it hurt and they would laugh together and kiss their beautiful son. Ben would lean over Sarah, kiss her on the cheek, the neck, the lips, make her laugh pause from their silliness and, once again, they would take a moment, hold hands and thank God for everything in their lives.

Ben waited until Friday morning after Sarah had slept peacefully throughout the night to tell her about his ordeal. She, of course, woke up twice to nurse the baby but the little one would fall fast asleep after a new diaper and a full tummy. Sarah, too, got much needed rest and felt much better in the morning.

Ben thought over and over to himself just how much he would tell Sarah about the last three days. She, did not know about the botched kidnapping of their son, and he really did not want her to ever know about it, at least not until much later in their lives. The hospital administration, in close relationship with the FBI, promised the name of the abducted child or it's family would never be released to the press, and this helped Ben in giving information to Sarah. He chose instead to tell her about the FBI, about Carl Andrews being caught in the act of setting explosives on their boat, and that it all had to do with drug dealings in and out of Canada and Nova Scotia. He told her that the FBI had set it all up in order to catch Natalie, who was one of the biggest drug dealers in the area and also a child abductor.

Sarah was shocked when she realized Natalie had been in their home several times, but Ben made it all sound like she had been after him and the SARAH JEANNE and it had nothing at all to do with Sarah or their son. He did tell her the truth about Jacqueline Chipley, about her kidnapping, her escape from Natalie, and that she was back with her parents in Portland. Ben told her Natalie had crashed her car into the Bay after a police chase and was presumed drowned. Ben never mentioned a word about Natalie being her birth mother and swore to himself that he never would. Finally, he told his beautiful wife that he had never wanted to be a part of this FBI investigation, but that he had no choice. The agents, in order to capture Natalie and Carl, needed him out of the area, away from Booth Bay Harbor and presumed lost at sea. They had promised him the end result would be positive, but at the cost of Sarah being put through pure hell.

"I know that you knew I was safe, somewhere," Ben said, "but this entire ordeal must have been so stressful for you. I am so sorry, Sarah."

He apologized to her over and over again for putting her through the past few days and for her being alone when Samuel was born. Sarah, in turn, assured her loving husband that she thought him to be a hero, and that with God's help, her parents and his father being with her, she had been just fine. "But," she said, "don't you ever to this to me again!" They laughed together, and Ben assured her she would meet the FBI agent in charge, and she could give him the same orders.

As Sarah's health improved, and after one more blood test, Dr. Foster told her on Friday afternoon she needed no more transfusions and she would most likely be discharged on Saturday.

"You are a very fortunate young lady, Sarah," he told her. "Your husband is safely back, your health is much improved, and you have a beautiful, healthy little boy." Looking at Ben, her grinning husband, Dr. Foster shook his hand, wished them all the best, and said he would check on her in the morning before her release.

Meanwhile in Nova Scotia, Carl Andrews had been informed of his wife's probable drowning. At first, he took it like the macho man he thought he was, then realizing his meal ticket and his sexual partner were gone, he broke down and cried like a baby. He also spilled his guts. He informed the two detectives on the case that he and Natalie had been dealing drugs for years, ever since they met in prison. He gave them names of dealers, buyers and other contacts in Maine, Nova Scotia and in Canada. He told them how they got the drugs in and out of the country, and then dropped a bombshell when he informed the detectives that a man named Jeremiah Brookings was one of the names at the top of the drug ring.

Jeremiah Brookings was a familiar name, but the two detectives could not quite put a face to the name. When they mentioned the name to Captain Lewis, he knew right away, but he contacted Richard McLeary to make sure. McLeary, knowing that Ben Kestwick's crewman was Jeremy Brookings was sure the two men were one and the same. McLeary had suspected Jeremy was more than a lobster fisherman months before, but had said nothing. When he had taken him aside in Nova Scotia he knew for sure. He was not forthcoming at first on any questions the FBI had asked him, but he became very nervous during the second interrogation. Now, with Carl Andrews' confessions, there was enough evidence to link Jeremy to nighttime activities in the Booth Bay and Brunswick areas of Maine. He had not admitted or confessed to any of the charges, so they had kept him under tight surveillance in Yarmouth. After Carl Andrews' confessions, they approached Jeremy again, told him the FBI and DEA had proof of his illegal drug activities, found enough evidence to keep him in custody, and he too gave up more names. He also admitted that he had helped Carl Andrews get onto the SARAH JEANNE and had left the scene before the FBI caught Carl trying to set the explosive device. McLeary now had the names he needed to close down the drug ring in this part of the country.

When Ben found out, he was devastated. Jeremy had been his right-hand man for all these years, very good at his job, and Ben could not believe it. It did, however, answer a lot of questions about where Jeremy lived, where he went at night, and what he did on his days off. Jeremiah (Jeremy) Brookings had lived two different life styles for almost twenty years, portraying himself as a lobster fisherman while in Booth Bay Harbor, and, as a man of means when living his other life in Nova Scotia. The ironic thing was, Jeremy admitted that he loved the lobster fishing business. He loved the work, the sea, and he loved Ben and Martin Kestwick. He also loved the money his dealers brought in and, loved his second life style. He always had money with which to buy booze, gamble and live the high life. Now that part of his life was over, in fact both of his life styles were now over. His years of deception had finally caught up with him.

Because he gave up names of Canadian dealers and cooperated with the DEA and the FBI, Jeremiah Brookings was found guilty of drug dealings, ordered to return much of the money, but sentenced to only five years in the state prison. Ben and Sarah never saw Jeremy Brookings again.

*　*　*　*　*

Joe Spencer left the Portland area in the early after noon. He had popped in one more time to see Sarah and the baby, was incredibly surprised to see Ben back, and said his goodbyes to Martin and the Waverly's. He promised he would see them all soon. He told Jonas he would be back to work on Monday but that he had requested both Thursday and Friday off from the Mill. His plan, now that Sarah was doing so well, was to stay in Booth Bay Harbor until Sunday. He would get up early on Saturday, finalize the sale of the building in the mini-mall with the realtor, hire a construction company and go shopping. He planned to purchase what was needed to re-decorate the building into a music studio; paint, curtains, dishes, coffee pot, wall hangings and more. He could do all of this on Saturday, and return to Millinocket on Sunday. He planned to call the Ball Music Company, set a tentative date to have the piano delivered, and hoped to have the grand opening for Sarah's Music Studio prior to the Christmas holidays.

He smiled to himself as he left the hospital, realizing how happy Sarah would be with his gift, or at least he hoped she would be happy with it. He still wasn't too sure.

One thing Joe Spencer was sure of, however, was that he would never tell Sarah the truth, that he was her biological father. After his lengthy talk with Jonas Waverly, he realized that telling Sarah the truth might hurt her more than anything in the world, and her mother, Mary Anne, as well. He and the Waverlys had become the best of friends over the years, and he would continue to do what he had always done, be her Uncle Joe and love Sarah from a distance.

On Friday afternoon just a few miles from the Maine Medical Center, a party was being held at the home of John and Sandra Chipley a welcome home party for Jacqueline. The last twenty-four hours at home had been the most incredible hours a little girl could ever spend. She had eaten her favorite foods, slept in her own bed and played with her own dolls, including a beautiful new Barbie. Jacqueline was healthy, happy, and, even the deep bruise on her face had begun to fade. She had received so many hugs and kisses from her parents, grandparents and friends, she had finally asked them to please stop. She laughed and played with her old friends and met new friends. She met many, many of the friends her parents had made over the past months after her abduction—all the people who helped form and join the prayer vigils, the ladies from the Wednesday afternoon coffee, work and prayer time. She saw Agent McLeary and Agent Benson again, although they only stopped for a few minutes. During those few minutes, however, Agent McLeary made a telephone call, and when Sarah Kestwick answered the call, he told her there was a very special young lady on the telephone for her.

"Hello," Jacqueline said softly. "Who is this?"

"Jacqueline, it's Sarah Kestwick." She said smiling. "I want you to know that Ben and I have a beautiful little baby boy, his name is Samuel, and sometime I hope you can come to see him."

She continued speaking with Jacqueline for a few more minutes, promised they would get together sometime and yes she knew about her being kidnapped. Sarah told her how thrilled she was to know she was safe and back at home.

"I hope you will continue to take piano lessons, Jacqueline," she said encouraging her. "I know it's a long way for your parents to drive you to the harbor, but I have a friend in Portland who gives lessons too, I'll call you later on with her number. Maybe she can teach you from now on."

Sarah told Jacqueline goodbye and asked if she could speak with Agent McLeary again. Jacqueline handed the telephone back to the agent and thanked him.

"Ben told me you told him all about little Jacqueline," she said to McLeary "I always thought her mother was a little strange, but wow, I never thought of her as a kidnapper. I'm so glad Jacqueline is safe and back with her parents. She's a sweet little girl." In addition, she thanked McLeary again for all the agency had done for Ben, bringing him back safely, and she hoped they could meet again sometime under different circumstances.

"I'm not sure I agree with your type of investigation Mr. McLeary," she commented, "But if it helped you catch a kidnapper and a drug dealer, I guess I can forgive you!"

Agent McLeary chuckled, apologized to Sarah and thanked her all at the same time, assuring her he would be in touch with Ben a few more times to clear up some unfinished FBI paperwork, and, yes, he would like to see her again too.

"Give that baby boy a big kiss for me, Sarah," McLeary said in closing. "And you all take care."

McLeary and Benson took their leave, thanked the Chipleys for their hospitality, and McLeary said he would be in touch over the next few days. He reminded them again of what a fabulous daughter they had, how brave she was, and that they should be very proud of her. As the two agents left the house and got into the SUV, McLeary picked up his telephone, dialed Tom Casey's number and, when there was no answer, left him an in-depth message.

In Booth Bay Harbor, the sun was shining brightly Saturday morning, with not a cloud in sight. Lieutenant Tom Casey had just been to the Breakfast Hut, where he had feasted on one of the best steak and egg breakfasts in all of Maine. Loren had sat with him while he ate, re-filled his coffee cup at least four times, and, when Tom felt the timing was just perfect, he told Jill's mother that he would like to have her permission to marry her daughter.

"I hope you don't feel this is too soon, Loren," he said somewhat shyly, "but I love Jill more than anything or anyone in the entire universe. I want to marry her spend the rest of my life with her, have babies with her, and be her husband, lover and friend forever." Realizing he was going a little overboard trying to impress his future mother-in-law, he slowed his words down, apologized to her for being so mouthy, and she laughed, not at him, but with him.

"You're a wonderful young man, Tom Casey," she said, still chuckling. "If Jill will have you, well, what else can I say but yes, I give you my approval to marry her."

Tom jumped up from the table, knocked over a glass of water, attempting to shake Loren's hand, then, with reddened face, somewhat embarrassed, gave her a hug.

"Thank you, Loren," he said, smiling. "Thank you, mom!"

Joe Spencer, after a good night's sleep at the Inn, his stomach growling, walked the short distance to get another memorable breakfast at the Breakfast Hut. He walked into the Hut just as a Coast Guard Lieutenant was standing up, spilling a glass of water and hugging an older, attractive woman who sat at his table. At second glance, he seemed to recall this woman owned the Hut, but he didn't recognize the Lieutenant. He had seen the beautiful lady the last time he ate breakfast here. He smiled, walked over to where the two of them were still hugging, and bravely asked if she was a lady in distress and could he save her? Somewhat embarrassed, Tom turned around, Loren stood up, and she playfully said, "This young Lieutenant wants to marry my daughter and I said, yes, it was okay with me…and didn't I just see you in here a few days ago?"

Joe introduced himself, said he was a friend of Ben and Sarah Kestwick, and did they know they were now the proud parents of a bouncing baby boy? He continued to tell them that Ben was safe, Tom smiled to himself knowing the whole secret story, and Joe added, he was starving and could he please order breakfast?

Tom, still red in the face, asked him to join him and Loren. Joe sat down; Loren called to one of her waitresses to bring the coffee pot and to take this man's order, as he looked like he was undernourished. The two of them watched Joe eat his breakfast and, before any of them realized it, the Hut's anchor shaped clock struck ten o'clock.

Tom excused himself to get back to the task at hand; the accident on Catamaran Street. Curious, Joe asked about the accident, and when Tom shared the story of a police chase from Portland to Booth Bay Harbor, the crash, and a woman who had possibly drowned, Loren noticed a most puzzling and sad look on Joe's face. Tom asked if he was okay, and Loren then asked the same. "I'm fine," Joe said calmly, "Just seems sad, you know, if a woman died and all. Do they know if she was from the area?"

Tom said no, she was from Brunswick. "She was a confirmed drug dealer, and possible kidnapper," and, knowing some things in the Guard were to be kept confidential, said no more, and headed for the door.

Joe, too, said goodbye and as he got up to take his leave, smiled at Loren and asked if she would like to have dinner with him that evening? She said she thought that would be nice, and what time could she pick him up? Joe chuckled and said he would pick her up at six.

At 5:30 p.m. Friday night, the telephone rang at the Portland Coast Guard offices. The secretary, almost out of the offices for the evening, turned and thought about not answering it but changed her mind and picked it up.

"Portland Coast Guard," she said cordially. "May I help you?"

"This is Search and Rescue #4578," came the voice on the other end. "We have just had a call from the mainland, somewhere around Bar Harbor. A body has washed up close to Seal Cove. The couple that found it called the police up there, and they in turn requested the Coast Guard come by immediately. We are fairly close by, so we are headed up there now." He continued to speak with the secretary, told her he had little information but that the body was believed to be that of a woman. "Can you locate Lt. Casey for us?" He continued. "I know he is working on that kidnapping and accident case in Portland and Booth Bay; this body just may be that missing suspect."

The secretary at the Guard offices assured the SAR rescue team officer that she would call Casey immediately and have him call the SAR team. "I think he's still in Booth Bay Harbor," she added. "I'll get on it right away."

Lieutenant Tom Casey, on his way to the Catamaran Street accident got the call. He in turn called Agent McLeary immediately. McLeary said he had also gotten a call, and they agreed to both head up to Seal Cove.

Casey called one of the agents still on the scene and told him to tell the officers and agents still on the scene that, per McLeary, to finish up their investigation, file their reports and call it a day. Their boss, Agent McLeary, would be checking in with all of them as soon as possible. Casey after explaining the situation turned around and headed for Seal Cove.

There was no fast way to get to the site. He drove the coast highway to Bucksport and then down Highway 3 to Seal Cove. The body was not found exactly at Seal Cove, but close enough off the roadway to where it had been spotted quite readily. He followed the line of flashing lights along the coast, slowed down, showed his badge to the officer at the entrance to the area, parked his vehicle, got out and walked to where the body lay, covered in plastic. He showed his badge again, noticed three FBI agents he had met earlier in the week, and asked if the agents were sure it was Natalie Pickford Andrews.

"The body was found down their floating in the rocks." The officer informed Tom. "The body is pretty badly broken up and large fish have gotten to it already, but we're sure it's a woman. She has long blond hair, is partially clothed, and, well, Lieutenant, let's have you take a look."

The SAR officer pulled back the plastic and uncovered the body. "We brought the body up here sir," he continued. "It was tough getting it out from those rocks down there, but we figured it was better to get it up on land than leave it in the water. We've roped off the entire area, and the coroner is on his way."

Tom Casey had never met Natalie, but from the information he had received from the FBI and DEA, he knew her to be a slight, attractive woman, with long blond hair, a light complexion, and Carl Andrews had mentioned earlier to an investigative officer that she had this cute, sexy little mole on the inside of her left thigh.

As they slowly pulled the plastic covering off the woman's body, her long hair was matted and tangled and there were large gashes and teeth marks on her face. Her left arm and hand were missing at the elbow, most likely from a large fish attack and there were severe bruises on her right leg. There was very little flesh left on her left leg, but on the upper inside of her thigh there appeared to be a mole. The thing that caught his attention immediately, however, was that gripped tightly in her right hand was a part of a doll—a life-like baby doll dressed in torn and stained pink clothing.

Tom backed away from the body and took a deep breath. He told the officer to recover the body just as Agent McLeary walked up beside him.

"Took me a bit longer than I planned, to get here," he told Lieutenant Casey, and taking a quick glance at the body, asked Tom, "do you think it's Natalie?"

Tom, knowing there would be an autopsy, and, that the FBI would need to get photos of Natalie from her husband Carl, for further proof, said he wasn't certain, but in his gut he knew it was her.

"We'll need more proof," he told McLeary," but, yes, I think it's Natalie."

Before completing the investigation and releasing the body to the coroner, Agent McLeary took a few more photos, both of the body and the area where it was located and he and Lieutenant Casey talked a little longer, even sharing their thoughts on what a traumatic death this must have been for Natalie—if indeed this was her.

The two FBI agents who had been working on this case for the last three days came up from the rocky ledge below, and also took a quick glance at Natalie's face, Somewhat taken aback, they asked McLeary if they were needed for anything else? He said, no that they could leave, and he would talk with them later.

McLeary told them and the other officers to allow the coroner to come through the crime scene tape, to let him do his job—to bring the body back to Portland to the county morgue for further testing.

As the officers and agents including Lieutenant Casey and Agent McLeary walked back to their vehicles there was one thing they all agreed on and one thing they would always remember—the dead but open, evil-looking eyes and the seemingly frozen, sneering look on Natalie Pickford Andrews' bruised and battered face. In death as in life, Natalie was seemingly angry, evil and in pain—maybe now she would finally find peace.

This case was closed.

A PINCH OF DRY MUSTARD: EPILOGUE

The Sarah Jeanne Kestwick Music Studio opened as Joe Spencer had planned, on Christmas Eve Day. Joe with help from his new best friend, Loren, had put up a beautiful, freshly cut Christmas tree, adorned it with music notes and a variety of musical ornaments. Throughout the day, piano music played softly in the background and, when the beautiful antique Baldwin piano was undraped Sarah could barely control her emotions.

Sarah was at times speechless and couldn't hug and thank Joe enough. She marveled at the work her Uncle Joe had accomplished in such a short time and was in tears during most of the opening. Most of her students and their parents, including the Chipleys, were present, as were many friends and acquaintances from both Millinocket and Booth Bay Harbor. Everyone brought gifts or cards to the opening and Sarah remarked that she felt like a princess. She could not thank her Uncle Joe and her family and friends enough for being there. She was however, the most thankful for her husband Ben being back from the sea, and she shared her enthusiasm and thankfulness with everyone present.

Tom Casey was there with his beautiful lady, Jill, sporting a gorgeous two-carat diamond on her left hand. Jill told all of her and Tom's friends that when she had returned from her last cruise on December 18th, Tom had met her coming off the cruise line, flowers and wine in hand. After an evening of wine, dinner and lovemaking at Tom's apartment, he had proposed, and when she said yes, he had slipped the ring on her finger. No wedding date had been set, but Tom assured everyone at the party that it would be soon.

The mayor of Booth Bay Harbor had cut the blue and yellow ribbons opening the new studio at 3:37 p.m. in the afternoon. Sarah and Ben wanted a time to always remember, a symbol of sorts of the time when Samuel was born and, although Samuel was born in the a.m. they cut the ribbons at the same time only in the p.m.

Barbara Roose Cramer

It was noted that when the mayor was not cutting ribbons, he was holding and playing with the center of attraction, little Samuel Martin Kestwick. The two-month old little boy smiled and cooed at the mayor, and everyone else who held him.

Mary Anne Waverly and several of her friends from Millinocket had prepared and served plate after plate of Lobster Elegante and fresh homemade bread, and, as people asked for the recipe, she gave it to them but also encouraged them to purchase a copy of the cookbook at the local book store. "The reason this dish is so tasty," she would say, "is due in part to the "pinch of dry mustard" that is added to the recipe. She also told them that all the profits of Jenny Kestwick's cookbook went to the local children's charity, and that it was a very good cause!"

At the end of the opening, and by the time the event was coming to a close, eight students had signed up for piano lessons, and Sarah was sure she would have to hire an assistant teacher to help her teach. As people entered and exited the new studio, they marveled at the etchings on the beautiful glass windowpane above. It read, "MUSIC IS GOOD FOR THE SOUL", and right below the etchings, "Give Thanks to the Lord for He is Good, and His Love Endures Forever."

ABOUT THE AUTHOR

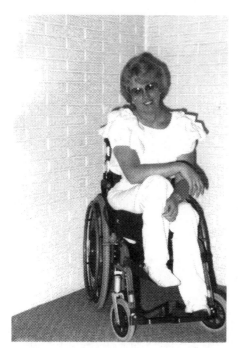

Barbara Roose Cramer has lived in Colorado fifty-eight of the past sixty-six years. She is married to Bill, her husband of forty-five years, has three sons and seven grandchildren. She is a paraplegic due to polio in 1951, a paralympic gold medalist and a retired high school bookkeeper. She writes for magazines and newsletters focusing on articles on the disabled and has several pieces of poetry and one autobiography in print. This is her first attempt at fiction.

LOBSTER ELEGANTE

½ CUP CHOPPED ONION
1 CUP DICED SHRIMP
1 MEDIUM CLOVE GARLIC - MINCED
½ DRAINED CUP TOMATOES
1 TBSP. BUTTER OR MARGARINE
1 CAN (10 1/2 OZ) CONDENSED CREAM OF MUSHROOM SOUP
I/2 CUP WATER
2 TBSP. CHABLIS OR OTHER DRY WHITE WINE
2 CUPS COOKED NOODLES
2 COOKED LOBSTER TAILS, SHELLED AND CUT IN HALF LENGTHWISE
3 TBSP. CHOPPED PARSLEY
1/8 TSP. MARJORAM
"A PINCH OF DRY MUSTARD"

COOK ONION WITH GARLIC IN BUTTER UNTIL TENDER. IN 1 ½ QUART CASSEROLE, PLACE SOUP, GRADUALLY STIR IN WATER. MIX ALL INGREDIENTS EXCEPT LOBSTER AND BUTTER. ARRANGE LOBSTER ON TOP, BRUSH WITH BUTTER. BAKE AT 350F FOR 30 MINUTES. 4 SERVINGS